UNDERSTANDING CORPORATE CREDIT

The book aims to cover, comprehensively but briefly, all the major and many minor aspects which make for better understanding of the risk of lending to private-enterprise companies. It goes into considerable detail on some aspects; however, its aim is not to provide a checklist, but rather to explain the way in which the different aspects of a company's business and finances link together to make it a strong or weak credit; to help bankers to think constructively about the implications of such things as capital intensity, fixed costs, cash flow, risk, competition, price sensitivity; and how they affect the need for, or availability of, liquidity, high or low leverage, high or low margin on sales, return on assets, equity, etc.

The book uses a building-block approach. The first section (after an introduction) discusses in some detail the individual items in the balance sheet and profit and loss statement, what they are and their implications. The second section describes various ways in which these come together into concepts such as leverage, liquidity, cash flow; looks at reconciliations, ratio analysis and the use of forecasts. The third section looks at non-financial aspects of the company; the product and production process, competition, management, labour relations, marketing, service and other aspects. The fourth section shows how to strike a balance and looks at risks and at asset-based companies. The fifth section discusses presentation, why it is important, some basic principles and an outline format.

T. H. Donaldson is Vice-President and European Credit Officer of the Morgan Guaranty Trust Company of New York, London. He was educated at Eton, the University of Cincinnati and Trinity College, Cambridge. In 1958 he joined the Empire Trust Company of New York. He was Assistant Secretary when he left in 1962 to join W. E.Hutton & Co., members of the New York Stock Exchange, as Securities Analyst.

In 1963 he joined the Morgan Guaranty Trust Company of New York and was transferred to London. Mr Donaldson was appointed Vice-President in 1971 and Credit Officer in 1974. He was responsible for drafting the written evidence given by the American Bankers Association in London to the Diamond Commission for their report on dividend control, and was heavily involved in the preparation and presentation of ABAL evidence to the Wilson Committee.

An Associate of the Institute of Bankers since 1966, he came first in England in the examination and won the Beckett Memorial Prize and the Hyde, Walker and Gwyther prizes. He is now a Fellow of the Institute of Bankers.

His first book, *Lending in International Commercial Banking*, was published in Macmillan's *International Banking Series* in 1979. His second book, *The Medium-Term Loan Market* (with J. A. Donaldson), was published by Macmillan in 1982. He has had articles published in *Euromoney* and in the *Institute of Bankers Journal*, and has given talks to the Foreign Credit Interchange Bureau and the Institute of Credit Managers. He has lectured on banking to a management course for Barclays Bank Ltd and a post-qualification course for the Institute of Chartered Accountants. He is the son of Lord Donaldson and Frances Donaldson.

UNDERSTANDING CORPORATE CREDIT

The Lending Banker's Viewpoint

T. H. DONALDSON, FIB, MICM

M

MACMILLAN PUBLISHERS
LONDON

First published 1983 by
MACMILLAN PUBLISHERS LTD
(Journals Division)
and distributed by
Globe Book Services Ltd
Houndmills, Basingstoke
Hampshire RG21 2XS, England

ISBN 0 333 34686 6

Printed in Great Britain by
The Pitman Press
Bath

Contents

List of Tables

1 Introduction

Analytical approaches

Banks take two broad approaches to analysing the credit of a company and the risk of losing money by lending to it. These have been named elsewhere as "going concern analysis" and "liquidation analysis" or occasionally "gone concern analysis". Broadly speaking, the difference between them is that going concern analysis assumes that a company continues to operate and tries to assess how it will service its debt. Liquidation of assets, except in the normal course of business, is thus not considered a primary source of repayment. Liquidation analysis pays more attention to the value of the assets, adjusted to allow for losses due to forced realisation; if they exceed the liabilities with a reasonable margin, this is satisfactory evidence that the loan can be paid. Although both types of analysis can lead to either secured or unsecured lending, the liquidation approach tends to emphasise security more than the going concern approach.

The ways in which banks analyse credit and reach their decisions are not as simplistically different as the above suggests. Going concern analysis certainly considers asset values in liquidation as a second way out if the primary analysis is proved wrong. In addition, the quality of the assets is important to the going concern analyst even if his interest is different to that of a liquidation analyst. It would be a gross distortion, moreover, to suggest that banks which use the liquidation approach do not analyse profitability, cash flow and other factors discussed in this book at all. Nevertheless, there is a broad difference of approach; any American banker who has discussed a problem loan with a British clearing banker will recognise the description in the first paragraph.

This book is about going concern analysis, the most important feature of which is the attempt to foresee the future. Thus although the analyst works mainly with historical information, the purpose is to draw conclusions about the future of the company; how will it meet its liabilities while remaining viable and profitable? Too often, however, analysts appear to overlook this point and discuss past history as if it were an end in itself, rather than a means to judge the future. The question is not "what has the company done?" or even "what has the company done recently?" Rather it should be "what conclusions do the historical information and the present situation of the company suggest about its future?" This leads on to two supplementary questions: "what resources will the borrower have to meet its commitments?" and "what commitments will it have to meet?" The analysis will only be complete if it provides satisfactory answers to both of these questions.

For most companies, future resources are largely dependent on the generation of cash flow, the makeup of which will be discussed in detail later in the book. In essence, however, it is net profit after taxes plus any non-cash items, of which depreciation is the most common, which have been deducted before reaching net profit. It is a sometimes imperfect but nevertheless useful measure of the cash which the company generates from its normal operations and which is the prime source of its ability to meet its debts; to invest in new or modernised fixed assets; to finance normal growth in working and permanent capital; to pay dividends and provide a cushion for emergencies. Cash flow may not directly finance all of this in every year, but the availability of other sources will depend, in the long run, on the ability of cash flow to service them. Depending on the country concerned, the company may have access to the equity markets, to institutional or public long-term debt markets (domestic or international) and to various forms of subsidised government debt, as well as to bank debt. With the possible exception of subsidised government debt, the funds will only be forthcoming if the market is convinced that they can be serviced; if the market is convinced but is wrong, failure to service debt will be as disastrous as the failure to raise it, sometimes more so, even though the pain may be delayed.

Nevertheless many bankers focus on the "refinancing ability" of the borrower, on the argument that borrowers rarely reduce their debt and that lenders should merely satisfy themselves that their borrowers have ready access to other sources of finance. This can be extended into a theory that banks are, and should be, "permanent" lenders. The word "permanent" is ill-defined and "indefinite" would probably be more accurate. The theory seems to be that, since sound borrowers need not repay their debt, therefore as long as the borrower is sound the bank can lend permanently. Only if the borrower starts to become unsound should the bank worry about repayment, hence the need for "refinancing ability". This book is not primarily concerned with this theory but it influences the way in which some bankers make decisions. It may be valid to assume that some lenders will repay others, but the whole market cannot repay itself; thus, the more permanent the borrowing the greater the importance of going concern analysis. Since the market as a whole cannot repay itself, individual banks have two choices if they are to avoid bad debts. They can be more alert than the market, see the problem first and be repaid by another lender which will then be left to sort out the problem. Or they can use their early identification of potential problems to insist that the company deal with them while it still can. Either way requires an accurate assessment of future trends some way ahead.

The analysis of the need for funds focuses mainly although not wholly on the balance sheet. With the exception of cash itself, and possibly of net worth, each item on the balance sheet represents at different times either a source of cash or a use of cash. Therefore the analysis must consider not just the nature of the assets and liabilities, but also what they imply about future needs for, and availability of, cash. For example, trade receivables represent the various costs, including the profit margin, which have gone into generating sales. Until collection, therefore, they involve a use of cash but on collection they become a source. Bank borrowing, on the other hand, is a direct source of cash and trade payables represent the cash value of assets received but not paid for. Thus, until paid both are sources of cash but when paid they use it. Therefore analysis of the balance sheet must consider the likely future changes in them and other assets and liabilities which will either absorb or release cash.

Other sources of repayment

This leads on to the recognition that although cash flow is the major source from which companies repay medium- and longer-term, and at least some short-term, debt it is not the only source of debt service even when business is running normally. There are several types of lending where the main repayment comes from unforced realisation of assets or long-term borrowing against them. An example of the first is a commodity company, which finances each transaction or group of transactions on a self-liquidating basis, with the profit on each covering only the interest on the borrowing not the principal. The second example uses assets with such a long working life that repayment is rarely possible over the short life of a bank loan. Property or shipping companies are examples where such long-term assets generate enough cash to pay debt only in the long-term but are sometimes financed on an interim basis first. Bank finance is then repaid in most cases either by sale of the capital asset or by long-term debt based on the capital value, which in turn derives from the cash flow. There is thus a sense in which these situations are cash flow lending but the cash flow is that of a specific asset, the capital value of which is often crucial.

Banks, leasing and finance companies combine some of the elements of the first two types, as do insurance companies. The last example covers companies where the level of business fluctuates. In a seasonal business like a toy company, or a construction company which builds up inventory to meet individual large contracts, there will normally be an underlying capital requirement which can and should be serviced from cash flow. There will also be a seasonal or cyclical requirement for short-term borrowing; this will build up as the assets accumulate and will then be reduced as Christmas passes or the contract is completed, and the receivables are collected in the normal course of business.

All these cases require the analysis of asset reduction as a normal part of the business rather than in liquidation.

The structure of the book

To understand a company's credit it is necessary to relate a wide range of factors to each other. There is no one factor, no one ratio, no one easy pointer which shows whether a particular company is sound. The analyst must balance the financial figures, the nature of the company's business, government interference, economic and competitive conditions and often many other items against each other. Nevertheless to form a coherent whole he must first understand the significance of each of the parts and the way in which they combine together. For this reason the book follows a pattern: it discusses first, in Part One, the individual parts: in Chapters 2 and 3 balance sheet items and in Chapter 4 the profit and loss statement. Chapter 5 discusses the use of forecasts and projections; these cover both balance sheet and profit and loss but will also require a number of assumptions about the business.

Part Two takes the various assembled components and discusses building blocks. Chapter 6, for instance, shows how concepts such as liquidity or leverage combine various specific aspects of the balance sheet, earnings and cash flow to broaden the overall picture being built up. Chapter 7 discusses reconciliations, an analytical tool which helps to assess the impact of various changes on the continuing viability of the company. Chapter 8 talks about ratio analysis which can be valuable when well used but also rather dangerous if badly used.

Part Three discusses the way in which the nature of the company's business affects its financial figures and the risk of lending to it. Chapter 9 looks at factors which are inherent to the company and Chapter 10 at external factors and those which are affected by the quality of management.

Part Four discusses how the analyst should strike a balance between the various financial, business, managerial and other factors in order to reach a sound judgement. Chapter 11 specifically discusses the trade-offs between various features of the balance sheet which may require or provide strength. Chapter 12 discusses asset-based lending and the need to recognise those companies to which the normal cash flow approach does not apply. Arising out of this it also discusses the question of security and the situations in which security can be either a help or a trap. Chapter 13 recognises that the bank very often does not have all the information it needs and that what information it has is often misleadingly presented or unreliable. It discusses various ways in which this may be true and their implications. And Chapter 14 emphasises the need in the whole of the analysis to focus on the risks and the ways in which they can arise.

Part Five looks at presentation. Chapter 15 first discusses the purpose of a presentation and the various approaches to it which can be taken. It also stresses that presentation can have real implications for the substance of the decision and can be a guide, even though sometimes a faulty one, to how well the presenter understands the credit. It then looks at the form a presentation might take and suggests some general principles which help to make it as clear as possible to the reader.

One point which should be made in relation to all of the earlier chapters arises from Chapter 12. This book is not about accounting, nor about ensuring that the information being analysed is accurate, but in its nature it cannot ignore either. It identifies some cases where limitations of, or questions about, the information are important. The underlying assumption, however, is that the analyst has investigated the accounting and is satisfied that he understands the presentation of the figures; to the extent that he does not he should at least have identified the area of uncertainty and its importance. The book does not underestimate the importance of this investigation nor of the accounting factors; these can change the apparent meaning of the figures dramatically. However, the purpose of accounting techniques is to make the figures as accurate as possible, while this book tries to make the significance of the underlying factors clear. Moreover, there are many books on accounting but few on credit judgement.

The book will use mainly American terminology, but will identify the English equivalent when the difference is significant.

Part I
The Details

2 The Balance Sheet– Current

A balance sheet represents the position at one particular moment. Some aspects can change more quickly and easily than others and the analyst must consider how the varying rates of change can interact with each other. The balance sheet, even more than the profit and loss statement, is a form of shorthand which presents in monetary form assets which in most cases are not money at all. The figures are merely more or less credible estimates of the amount for which the assets can be sold or of the cost to replace them. The actual money value can differ widely for many reasons, but the difference between a forced sale and one in the normal course of business is probably the most important, so that the view of a going concern analyst is very different to that of a liquidation analyst. This chapter and the next look at the individual items which appear on the balance sheet, broken down into five main categories which in turn are further subdivided. The categories are: current assets; current liabilities; non-current assets; non-current liabilities; and net worth.

Current assets

Current assets are normally defined as cash and those assets which turn into cash in the normal course of the company's business within one year from the balance sheet date. There is some disagreement between accountants and bankers as to whether the one-year period is more important than "in the normal course of business" and also exactly what is "the normal course of business", but it usually only affects minor items. It is sometimes important where a company has a very long manufacturing or cash conversion cycle, so that receivables are paid after more than one year or inventory is held for a prolonged period (as with maturing whisky).

Following the American presentation of the balance sheet current assets are usually listed in the order in which they can be expected to turn into cash. The first of these is:

Cash and near cash. Although cash seems a simple concept there are several points an analyst should check. For instance the cash may be restricted and so not available to meet all of the company's obligations. There are several types of restriction; some companies make deposits with the authorities to meet legal requirements, or with trade associations or other bodies such as commodity clearing houses to support margin or other requirements. Or there may be some form of pledge on the cash, so that one creditor or group of creditors has a claim which is preferred over other creditors. The most common restriction, but also sometimes the hardest to discover, arises from exchange control or other limitations on subsidiaries. These may either prevent funds being remitted to the parent company at all, or permit remittance only in a way, such as dividends, which is subject to withholding tax. Thus although the cash is available to meet the liabilities of the local subsidiary it is not freely available to the group as a whole. Even where the subsidiary is in the same country as the parent local laws do not always permit funds held in one subsidiary to be freely used to meet group obligations, although the most serious restraints arise from crossing borders.

Near cash should only include short-term money market instruments or short-term fixed deposits with banks which can with certainty be turned into cash at short notice. It should exclude investments which while marketable are held for longer-term strategic reasons and speculative investments, longer-term deposits or investments where sale may involve a substantial loss.

Published balance sheets and even management balance sheets do not always distinguish between the various categories of investment. Often the banker knows enough to accept the figure (under whatever caption) without further work. But he should be aware of the possible need for investigation.

The free cash balance must suffice for the company's minimum needs. Sometimes companies hold large cash balances temporarily or semi-permanently because they are throwing off more cash from operations than the immediate opportunities for investment. Some hold more than they really need from excess caution or inertia. But there are two main reasons why companies may actually need cash balances.

Most companies have a different pattern of receipts and payments. Some have a steady flow of small payments out and a more intermittent flow of larger receipts; some the reverse and others a mixture. Whatever the pattern, companies must be able to pay their debts as they come due. In some countries the need for cash can be met by holding unused overdraft facilities, against which a cheque or other payment order can be drawn as easily as against a credit balance. However in countries where overdrafts are either illegal, as in the United States, or unusual a larger cash balance may have to be maintained for this purpose.

Companies also accumulate cash to meet large individual payments outside the normal course of day-to-day business. These may be taxes, loan amortisation, capital commitments or a wide range of other possibilities, but whatever they are the company must be able to meet them.

Trade receivables, or in English terminology trade debtors, are usually referred to as "receivables" or "debtors". They are the amounts due to the company for goods or services sold, and are thus the essential means by which most companies generate cash flow. Although a few companies such as retailers sell largely for cash, most sell on credit. Thus the quality and liquidity of a company's receivables are vital to its financial health and can also be a useful pointer to its financial management.

Receivables can be shown gross or net. Most companies have at least some credit losses on their receivables and many carry a reserve against potential bad debts. Few, outside the United States, publish the size of such a reserve although rather more show it in management figures. The reserve can be deducted from the receivables which are then carried net (normal practice in Anglo-Saxon accounting) or it can be shown as a current liability (usually as part of a larger reserve), and the receivables shown gross. The size of the reserve gives an idea as to whether the receivables are conservatively stated or whether their value is somewhat overstated; a rapid increase in the reserve may be a warning that what should be the company's second most liquid asset is deteriorating. The primary indicator of the quality of receivables is the turnover rate, "days sales" or collection period (also discussed in Chapter 8). It measures the average speed with which the receivables turn into cash and is a useful pointer to the need for liquidity to carry the receivables arising from a given volume of sales. This is an absolute factor which is not affected by the nature of the business; receivables which turn over in 90 days require more liquidity than those which turn over in 45 days (or conversely the latter are more liquid than the former), whatever the reason for the difference.

The rate of turnover of receivables also helps the assessment of their quality and that of financial controls, but only after allowing for differing conditions. Industries with a long manufacturing cycle tend to give longer credit than retailers. The practice in some countries is for much faster collection than in others; exports, because of the longer shipment period, exchange controls and other factors, tend to take longer to collect than domestic sales. For all these reasons a banker can only judge the quality of receivables and financial controls when he has some knowledge of the pattern of sales.

Moreover, there may be other explanations than credit for an apparent reduction in the quality of receivables. The company may be giving longer trade credit to compensate for higher prices, lower quality or some other weakness. If so, lengthening the trade credit will be no more than a temporary palliative which may however give the bank some advance warning of potentially serious future problems. Or the change may result from a higher level of exports, a change in the product mix, or any one of a number of factors which have no automatic adverse implications.

The concentration of receivables, as well as their average turnover, is important but cannot be assessed directly from the balance sheet. For larger or more secretive companies, the banker may have to rely on inferences. For instance some automotive components manufacturers are known to sell mainly to the original equipment market and thus have a relatively small number of large customers whose quality is well known. If they also sell to the replacement market directly or through wholesalers they are likely to have a much greater spread of customers; while it will be harder to assess their quality individually, each one is likely to account for only a small part of the total credit, reducing the importance if any one fails. A major company with several divisions selling different types of product through different outlets will have more diversity of risk but may also need tighter controls.

Where possible, and particularly with smaller or weaker borrowers, the banker should try to obtain more information than is normally available in published balance sheets or even sometimes in management accounts. He may be able to confirm his impressions as to the concentration and quality of the customers in discussion with the borrower. Even where discussion provides only general information with no figures it has some value; where the banker can get statistical support the value increases. All companies should have, for internal management reasons, both a detailed listing and some form of summary of their receivables by age and amount. A summary breakdown between receivables not yet due and those past due by periods from 30 to 90 or 120 days is the minimum management should have, and is of great value to the banker. It might also show the percentage of past dues from the largest individual customers or some other indication of the extent to which any problems are concentrated or widespread. With smaller companies where the list will be relatively short, the banker may be able to see complete accounts name by name, with up-to-date details of the amount owed, when due and the recent record of payments. In a few cases the banker may even wish to analyse his borrower's larger customers but this would be unusual.

The information on receivables can be used to draw three types of conclusion. The first is the quality of the assets concerned. The turnover, when related to the type of business and perhaps to the country in which it operates, gives a pointer as to whether, on average, receivables are being collected promptly and in full, or whether there are delays which add to the cost of carrying them and raise questions as to whether they will ever be paid in full. As an average, turnover may conceal individual slow or doubtful payers, but if these are significant or increase rapidly the average will be affected. The detailed information makes the general deduction more reliable.

The second conclusion relates to the concentration of risk, both the credit risk of a large bad debt and to the marketing risk. At worst the two may combine and the company not only suffer a large bad debt but lose a substantial percentage of sales and profits as well.

However, they can happen separately and a company which is

too dependent on a few customers may be unable to survive the loss of even one or two to the competition or because the customer decides to make the product itself. Either way the risk is that a large and unexpected drop in sales volume damages or even destroys the borrower's ability to cover its overhead costs; in an extreme case a previously profitable company can be forced into liquidation.

The third conclusion relates to the quality and cost of credit controls. Poor or deteriorating turnover suggests inadequate credit controls and possibly wider problems with financial controls generally. But there is a cost to good credit controls; on the one hand a heavy concentration of business requires deeper analysis of each customer, since the impact of an individual loss can be so great. On the other hand a wide spread of small customers reduces the risk of any individual loss but makes it harder to follow the overall quality of the portfolio. Only more detailed and costly systems will ensure that there is no general deterioration in quality; it is important to the bank to know that this is done effectively but at a reasonable cost.

Other receivables. There are two forms of receivable which appear only occasionally but which should be considered separately when they do appear. Leasing companies will be discussed among the asset-based companies in Chapter 12, but there are some other companies which lease rather than sell some of the equipment they produce. (IBM and Xerox are well-known examples.) Payment may be due over any period from under one to occasionally as long as ten years. It is important to understand the accounting and in particular how much of the value of the lease is shown as a receivable, since this can distort the receivable turnover.

Intercompany receivables normally appear either in the balance sheet of a subsidiary, in which case the amounts may be due from the parent or from fellow subsidiaries in the same group; or in unconsolidated figures of the parent. The old-fashioned view was that they were of lesser quality than normal trade receivables and sometimes even excluded from current assets. This was partly on the grounds that they were not truly arm's length transactions and partly on the grounds, relating back to the liquidation approach, that it was unlikely that the subsidiary would be liquidated at a loss unless the parent was in difficulties too, in which case intercompany receivables would be worth less than claims on the assets of independent third parties. The modern view recognises that while a parent may distort intercompany payments to obtain tax, interest or currency advantages this is not automatic; many companies export through fellow subsidiaries to take advantage of their distribution networks, local knowledge and so on. It is absurd if the balance sheet of a company is considered weaker because it uses strong associated companies to improve its sales, so that receivables are from strong affiliates which pay promptly without the need for detailed controls, rather than from weak distributors which need constant policing. In brief, intercompany receivables should be examined carefully but only assessed as lower quality if the facts justify such downgrading.

Inventory. The English terminology for this American word is stocks, i.e. the stock of goods and materials in all stages of production which a company must hold prior to making the sale. For a distributor, whether retail or wholesale, inventory will normally consist of finished goods only. For a manufacturer it will consist of some combination of raw materials, components, work in process and finished goods. The exact breakdown will depend on the nature of the company's business and should be reviewed in that light.

Unfortunately, however, many companies give a single figure for inventory without any breakdown, sometimes even in their management accounts. In some countries even this figure will be distorted by hidden reserves for tax or other purposes. A turnover calculation, similar to that performed for receivables, should ideally compare inventory with the cost of goods sold (i.e. the material and other costs directly incurred in producing the final product) rather than with sales; the latter include the cost of administration and selling and also the profit margin which are not directly connected to inventory. In practice, however, companies often give no breakdown of cost of goods sold, so that the comparison has to be with sales. This has the advantage of putting it on a comparable basis with both receivables and payables and simplifies some of the net working investment calculations discussed in Chapter 6.

Conclusions similar to those about receivables can be drawn from inventory turnover. Again, the speed of turnover must be related to the nature of the business when assessing the quality of the asset and of management controls, but is more absolute when judging liquidity. The faster the inventory turns into receivables the faster it will start the process of turning from receivables into cash, regardless of what causes the speed. On the other hand perishable goods in a supermarket should turn over very much faster than the inventory of a manufacturer of large and complicated machinery. Nevertheless, within the constraints of the particular process, the speed at which inventory turns over and the trend to faster or slower turnover are important pointers to the quality of the assets and the management controls.

To probe beyond the single figure for inventory the banker can rely to some extent on his knowledge of the company to ask the right questions and get a more or less detailed feel. For instance, if the company manufactures wholly or mainly against specific orders, there should be less risk of inventory proving unsaleable or only saleable at a reduced price or after a prolonged delay. On the other hand, if firm orders are cancelled there is a risk that the product will not be adaptable to other uses and will have to be sold as scrap. In each case the degree of risk depends on the nature of the business and the stage which has been reached in the manufacturing process. Some components may be usable in several different products but once combined the end product may only be saleable for the original purpose. The risk of cancelled orders can be assessed against the nature of the business, the quality of the borrower's production, pricing, the strength of competition and the quality of the customers.

At the other extreme companies which sell through the wholesale and retail trade always need a pipeline of finished goods. Lack of control risks making the pipeline too large or failing to recognise that certain items are not selling well and thus inventory is building up in a near worthless product. The figures rarely specifically reveal this type of information; at best they suggest that something is wrong which the banker should investigate.

There is often a delicate balance between too much finished goods inventory and too little. Too much inventory may be a sign of inadequate marketing or inadequate controls, or a change in the pattern of demand to which the borrower has been slow to adjust; too little may mean lost sales. Again, the company has to weigh the advantages of possible additional sales and competitive strength against the disadvantages of carrying costs and loss of flexibility. Among the factors are the impact on leverage of higher borrowing, the interest cost and the operating margin earned on the additional sales.

With only one figure for inventory the banker may have to ask, or guess, whether an increase results from growth in only one part, such as finished goods, or whether it is a more general increase. A breakdown enables him to watch the trend between the components and to make sure that the relationship between them and with sales remains appropriate.

There is one crucial difference, however, between the relationship of inventory to sales and that of receivables. The increase in sales can only occur after inventory has been built up while the increase in receivables reflects sales already achieved. Thus the judgement as to whether an increase in inventory is justified requires a view as to whether the expectation of increased sales is realistic; the judgement on receivables requires knowledge of whether sales have already increased.

The risks of carrying excess inventory in whatever form can be summed up as follows:

(i) Inflexibility and an inability to sell to a different customer or for a different purpose than the originally intended one.
(ii) Obsolescence, or actual deterioration in the case of perishable or semi-perishable goods.
(iii) Inability to adapt to a falling or changing market.
(iv) Possibility that failure to control costs means that the inventory can only be sold below book value, with the implication that management is failing to recognise this.
(v) The cost, in terms of high leverage and interest, of carrying it.

Naturally any two or more of these factors can combine; for instance, few products become obsolescent overnight. More often, management fails to notice gradual changes in competing products or a gradual decline in the customer industry and its controls do not show the resulting increase in inventory in time.

Other current assets. Normally cash, receivables and inventory are the only substantial current assets for a manufacturing company. There are some other items which accountants consider current, such as pre-paid insurance premiums. These are sometimes included in receivables and sometimes shown separately; in the latter case, bankers normally feel they are not receivables in the normal course of business and treat them as non-current.

There are also some companies which have specialised forms of current assets; for instance, some companies place deposits or make advance payments on goods they are using or ordering. Apart from specialised items of this sort there are no generally acceptable other current assets. Instead, commonsense must be used in each case to decide whether the asset concerned is likely to turn into cash within a year in the normal course of a company's business. If it is not it should normally be excluded from current assets and from concepts which use current assets. Usually the amounts involved are small and their treatment makes little difference, but where they are significant (more than, say, 10% of current assets or 5% of total assets) then careful attention should be paid to the nature of the asset and the question as to whether it is genuinely current or not. The approach should not be one of niggling accounting techniques, but an assessment of the contribution the asset actually makes.

Current liabilities

Current liabilities include all liabilities which are either actually due in one year, or which, as with an overdraft, can be called back "on demand" or at a stated notice of less than one year. The qualification about "normal course of business" made in considering current assets does not apply; if the amount is payable in less than one year, for whatever reason, the company must demonstrate ability to pay it.

Short-term bank debt is probably the most volatile item, along with cash on the balance sheet; together, they are the swing items through which the net changes in the balance sheet flow. Genuinely short-term debt finances differences of up to a year in the timing of receipts and payments, both trade and capital items, i.e. it finances temporary needs with a short-term source of repayment. Short-term debt is often treated as that which finances working capital (basically receivables and inventory); however, where the financing requirement is continuing rather than temporary, the debt is medium-term in nature whatever the form, although in some cases it has a self-renewing feature similar to that of trade payables, discussed below.

To decide whether nominally short-term borrowing is accurately so described the banker must look at its purpose, the pattern of usage and the extent to which it is unused at least part of the time. A company needs to have a margin of unused facilities to allow for short-term fluctuations and unexpected eventualities. Where there is a seasonal or other predictable pattern it may be acceptable for the facilities to be fully used at the peak, but there should be some period each year when they are not. Facilities which are consistently fully used suggest that they are short-term in form only; this in turn may mean that the company is not generating sufficient cash to allow normal fluctuations in its borrowing which can be a pointer to emerging problems; however, the banker should recognise that a growing company may need larger facilities and that the right answer to full usage may be an increase to avoid strangling the business. Usage of the enlarged facilities should then fluctuate even though at a higher level; otherwise the explanation may be, at best, that the company has outgrown its ability to retain earnings and needs an injection of capital. At worst, continuous usage can point to inadequate cash flow or other problems.

Short-term bank debt takes varying forms depending on the country concerned. In many countries the overdraft is common; in some, advances for periods from demand to 90 or 180 days; in many, various forms of bill of exchange or analogous financing for domestic as well as export trade, sometimes including government subsidised finance. The precise form is not relevant to the credit unless it differs in some way from the normal expectation in that market, in which case the reasons for the difference should be investigated. The banker should also be familiar with the various forms of security possible in each market and how they arise; if other banks are secured this puts an unsecured lender at a disadvantage which it should only accept consciously, after careful consideration, not through ignorance.

Discounted bills. There are a number of different forms of discounted bills but there is also a question as to how they should be considered. The normal accounting practice is to take both the asset represented by the bill and the liability to the bank off the balance sheet. More advanced countries will footnote it as a contingent liability. However there is an argument that both sides should be reinstated in the balance sheet since elimination distorts the receivable turnover and the liability of the company to meet the bank debt. The borrower is only contingently liable on a discounted bill, but it is arguable that this is no different in principle from pledging the receivable to secure a bank loan, with the proceeds of the receivable seen as the first source of repayment although the borrower retains a direct obligation. Following this analogy, some bankers even go so far as to consider discounted bills as being secured debt which they try to prohibit or regard as an unfavourable factor in analysing the balance sheet. (Of course, where the bill is without recourse to the drawer, he has no liability, and elimination is clearly correct. The analogy then is with granting a discount for early payment.)

The precise accounting treatment is of secondary importance to banks. They need to understand whether the company is obtaining cheap finance with a mechanism which is normal in the market in which it operates; or whether it is using unusual methods because normal types of finance are unavailable to it. The former carries no adverse implications and the balance sheet treatment becomes one of choice. The calculation of receivable turnover can be made either way with the proper mental adjustments to compare it with situations where there are no bills discounted. An unusual use of bills, or at least a change in the pattern which suggests that use of bills may be the result of some form of problem requires close investigation.

Current portion of long-term debt. This is not always broken out separately from other current debt, but has rather different implications since unlike normal current debt it must be paid on a specific date and is not self-renewing. Furthermore it is likely to recur annually and can provide a first warning of a debt servicing problem, depending on its size in relation to the borrower's liquidity and cash flow. If the amount is manageable then, by reducing total debt, payment should improve the company's leverage. If, however, the amount is excessive in relation to liquidity and cash flow then its existence can suggest that total debt is too large or that the maturity profile of debt is out of balance. The first is more serious, but both can be dangerous.

Trade payables. In English terminology these are trade creditors; "trade" is often omitted in both cases. They are the amounts due to suppliers for raw materials, components, transportation costs, electricity or other power costs and so on. They should be directly related to the volume of business the company is doing. A payable turnover calculation, similar to that for receivables and inventory, has a three-fold value. It indicates whether the borrower is taking advantage of any discounts for prompt payment which can be more than the interest on borrowing. Secondly, it indicates the extent to which payables are financing receivables and inventory on a self-renewing basis. (This is discussed further in the section on net working investment in Chapter 6.) And the third point is the opposite of the first; it may show a danger that the company is paying its suppliers too slowly, so that they may withhold supply or take legal action; or at least suggest how close the company is to such a danger.

Trade payables vary in importance as a source of finance but most manufacturing companies and many others have some. They are normally self-renewing, since as long as a company continues in business it will wish to buy new supplies on credit as it pays for the old ones. They also have the advantage that they are usually interest free, although sometimes interest is charged on trade payables after a specified period. However, one company's payables are other companies' receivables, so that a generally slower payment will be matched by a similar slowing of receivables; the overall burden on industry of financing trade will not change, therefore. Bankers should watch trade payables more carefully than they usually do, as slow payment is a warning sign of potential liquidity problems, which in turn may warn of weak cash flow, poor sales, slow inventory turnover or other problems. Thus a slowdown should be investigated unless it reflects a build up of inventory anticipating an increase in sales.

Intercompany payables. Intercompany payables are the other side of intercompany receivables. They can be used by parent companies to finance their subsidiaries without the commitment (or sometimes the government approvals) which would be involved in formal loans, or in an injection of equity. Equally, they can result from goods delivered and payment on the normal terms. Some companies use "leads and lags" (speeding up or slowing down payment) to protect themselves against currency risks, to concentrate borrowing in low-interest countries or profits where they attract least taxation. Then intercompany payables can no longer be relied on as a form of finance, since the parent may demand payment for reasons unrelated to the company's current trading; the resulting rise in bank debt will increase the interest burden significantly and in extreme cases can threaten the viability of the subsidiary. The bank, either directly or through its local branch, should be aware of the intentions and the strength of the parent, particularly to avoid any chance that it is in trouble and is using intercompany payables and receivables to generate cash for itself. An adverse movement in intercompany items can be the first warning that the parent is using illegitimate means to syphon cash out of the subsidiary. A bank which is lending only to the subsidiary, without a parent guarantee, must guard against this; to do so it must be able to tell the difference between leading and lagging for legitimate profit reasons, and a weak parent milking a strong subsidiary.

Dividends. A company normally declares a final dividend at its annual general meeting; in some countries it may also declare interim dividends at other times of the year. In most countries once a dividend has been declared it is a legal debt and shareholders rank as unsecured creditors. Usually it must be paid within a stated fairly short time, so that its presence on the balance sheet means that money must be found within a month or two, from cash or unused bank facilities. Even without a legal requirement, a company normally declares a dividend intending to pay it promptly, although there are some countries (Spain for example) where it need not be paid for several years; in these cases the bank may be able to prevent payment if it feels that the situation is so serious that the declaration should never have been made. However, this is unusual; and for normal analytical purposes a dividend can be considered as a current liability which will have to be paid within a month or two, i.e. a specific outflow of cash.

Taxes payable. There are three types of tax payable. One is tax which the company has collected on behalf of the government; withholding tax from salaries or VAT or sales tax on products sold for instance. The company is obliged to pay these sums to the government, usually quarterly but again this will vary by country and by the exact nature of the tax. The second type includes a variety of taxes on assets or on capital, usually payable annually and having no relationship to profitability or to volume of business, but only to the particular assets or capital taxed. The third and usually by far the most important is a tax on income or net profit, although its name varies from country to country. It may be payable on an estimate made in advance, as in the United States; or up to a year or eighteen months in arrears in some other countries. Thus, some knowledge of the nature of the tax, and of the tax laws of the particular country, is needed to judge how soon the tax is likely to be payable and therefore the impact on the need for cash; generally, unless the amounts are large or the cash situation unusually critical it is sound to assume that it will be a cash drain within a few months.

Liability provisions. Current liability provisions are common in certain countries, almost unknown in others. Anglo-Saxon accounting deducts from the assets many items that appear under liability reserves in, say, Continental Europe. Depending on the company and the country concerned, these items may be a reserve for bad debts, for obsolescence or possibly for tax on inventory and in a few countries for depreciation of fixed assets. Occasionally there will be provisions for depletion of mineral assets or amortisation of intangible assets such as patents and copyrights. Other liability provisions may be added for special purposes;

where the figure is sizeable the banker should investigate and assess their importance. Occasionally, he may adjust the asset side of the balance sheet if he prefers the Anglo-Saxon accounting approach.

Liability provisions are rarely a direct cash drain, but rather a warning that the cash value of some of the assets may be overstated. However, occasionally a provision for tax or some other actual payment will be included under liability provisions rather than under taxes payable or other current liabilities. This may be because the exact amount payable is being disputed but the company expects that an amount will be due, and often knows the date by which it must be paid. This type of reserve is rather different from the deduction from an asset but is sometimes included under the same balance sheet heading.

Advances and deposits. This is a rather specialised item but when it appears is often important. It most commonly appears on the balance sheet of a construction or heavy engineering company. Payment on account may be made at the time of contract or in stages as the project is completed or delivered. In either case it represents payment for goods or services not yet received. However, completed contract accounting may mean that payments shown as an advance actually represent inventory delivered and paid for, but not billed. A true advance reduces the need for bank debt and if it is large enough may eliminate bank debt altogether and even provide a substantial cash surplus which can generate a significant investment income.

However, advances are sometimes too easily treated as if they were not a true liability at all, on the grounds that as long as the company delivers the advance will not need to be repaid. This is only true if all contracts are completed on time and otherwise in accordance with their terms; otherwise advances may well have to be repaid in cash. Moreover, the advance is used to meet the payables generated by purchasing and processing inventory, which would normally generate cash via receivables. Thus in a sense the sale is used to pay off the advance rather than generate a receivable which in turn becomes cash. This will affect the calculation of receivable turnover.

At any given moment the amount of inventory that has been paid for but not billed, compared to the amount which is genuinely owned by the company, depends on the accounting. The completed contract method means that sales are only billed and profits taken when the contract is complete, so that during the life of the contract even work which has been accepted by the customer shows as inventory, and any payment as advances. Under other forms of accounting the same items would show as sales, with no asset on the books; these factors will affect whether there is a genuine payment in advance, or a mere accounting mirage.

The impact of advances on the company's balance sheet, liquidity and profitability are discussed further in Parts Three and Four.

Other current liabilities. There are a number of miscellaneous items which crop up with more or less frequency as a current liability. In most cases they are small and will not affect the overall assessment of the company's business but where they are large their impact on the company's balance sheet and on its cash flow, liquidity and other factors should be considered.

3 The Balance Sheet–Non-Current

Non-current assets

Non-current, or slow, assets include all assets which are not shown as current.

Fixed assets. Fixed assets are the land, building and machinery and tools used to manufacture the product, distribute it, research it and administer the company. They thus include land, office blocks as well as factories, typewriters and computers as well as machine tools, salesmen's cars as well as lorries and so on. Fixed assets are usually represented on the balance sheet by a single figure; sometimes gross, more often net of depreciation.

The single figure, even if it is net, is of very little value without some idea of the breakdown between the types of fixed assets. The analyst needs to be able to assess the "true" value, the remaining useful life, the flexibility and other aspects affecting quality, and the likely cost of replacing the assets.

The relationship between the balance sheet figure and approximate real value depends on whether the fixed assets are shown and depreciated at the original cost or after being revalued. Accounting principles (including inflation accounting) vary from requiring full value on current or replacement cost to a historic cost valuation. For a company with plants in different countries, exchange rates can be an additional complication.

The "true" value is normally a factor of the original cost and the remaining useful life, but inflation means that this is rarely the figure shown on the balance sheet. Land never wears out and many buildings last decades, even centuries, so that inflation ensures that their money value rises, sometimes to a large multiple of the original cost. Comparison of companies in countries where the land and buildings are shown at a nominal value with others where they are shown at something approximating the true value is obviously difficult. This is less important where there is no question of selling or replacing these assets, since then they provide a store of hidden net worth but do not affect cash flow. However, the undervaluation distorts the calculations of profitability and return discussed in Chapters 4, 6 and 11.

The distortions caused by inflation are more serious for items with a shorter life which wear out or become obsolete in between two and perhaps twenty years (see Chapter 13). Here it is enough to say that without at least an approximate idea of the breakdown of fixed assets between long and short life, and the cost of replacing those assets which wear out, the analysis becomes less reliable.

The flexibility of the fixed assets is also important; can they be replaced gradually or must they be replaced in very large lumps? Can they be used to produce a range of products or are they very specialised? How modern are they, how efficient and labour saving, how liable to technical obsolescence and so on?

Assets which the company has produced itself and is leasing to a third party as an alternative to sales are sometimes included in fixed assets. The analyst needs to know what proportion of the total are in this category and as much as possible about the terms on which they are leased; how long is the lease, how easily can it be broken, how likely is to be renewed at maturity? And he must consider the credit of the lessee companies since their failure might leave his borrower with equipment which was producing no income. If new technology makes the leased equipment obsolete or uncompetitive, will the lease expire before payments have covered the basic cost of the equipment, plus interest?

Long-term receivables. These appear infrequently, usually on the balance sheets of companies selling very heavy equipment or complete plants on deferred terms, such as construction companies. Where this is standard practice in the particular business, the normal receivable turnover calculation may be less significant than usual in assessing quality, but the overall need for greater liquidity to carry slow receivables is unchanged.

However, the reason for the presence of long-term receivables must be understood; if unrelated to the nature of the business, it may be a sign that the company is having to behave abnormally to obtain sales. Alternatively the item may not be a trade receivable at all but may arise from the sale of surplus fixed assets or investments; in that case it can be treated as a sound if non-current asset and a future source of cash. Long-term receivables are sometimes lease receivables, with a different accounting treatment than when they are shown as fixed assets. However, most of the other considerations are the same.

It is difficult to avoid discussing accounting in talking about fixed assets or long-term receivables. However, these are items where accounting treatment can distort rather than clarify, and the analyst must identify the underlying reality which is essential to the impact on the credit.

Investments. Investments fall into two main categories. On unconsolidated figures they may be holdings in subsidiaries (and may include loans to subsidiaries as well as shares, or the loans may be shown separately). These represent an essential part of the company's business so that the larger the investments are the more important it is to know about the subsidiaries they represent. The ideal, in the absence of full consolidated figures, is to get figures on the subsidiaries and perform a rough consolidation. Where this is not possible the banker should still seek as much information as possible on the nature of the subsidiary's business, the structure of their balance sheets and their profitability so that he can adjust his view of the parent accordingly.

Subsidiaries need not be wholly owned, and investments may represent holdings of only a few percent. The questions then are whether the business is related to that of the parent, whether the parent influences management of the affiliate, and particularly whether it is morally or legally liable to support it or pay some of its debts if it runs into problems. If any or all of the answers are positive and the amounts significant the affiliate should be investigated.

The other type of investment is held purely as a financial asset, with no connection to the investor's business and no ability or wish by the investor to interfere with the management. Provided this last point is clear to outside parties there should be no risk that the investor will have to rescue the investment if it runs into trouble, so that the banker may not need to investigate it in detail. Even here, he will wish to know whether the price at which it is carried in the balance sheet is reasonable and whether it could be readily realised to provide cash in an emergency.

Both types of investment may affect the profit and loss statement in ways discussed in Chapter 4.

Intercompany loans. As with intercompany receivables and payables, intercompany loans normally only appear in non-consolidated figures. Where they are large enough to be important then information as to the viability of the borrower is necessary to judge the quality of the asset. This may be covered under investments if the intercompany loans are to the same companies. In both cases attention should be paid to exchange control or other regulations which might limit payments from foreign subsidiaries and reduce the value of the asset by this loss of flexibility.

Intangible assets. Intangible assets either have a value which is theoretical and impossible to quantify or one which by definition ceases to exist in liquidation, or both. Common examples of intangibles are goodwill, patents and various types of capitalised expense.

Goodwill arises when one company buys another and pays more for the shares than book value. The theory is that the book value of shares represents the true net value of the assets which have been purchased; thus anything in excess represents the current value of a future stream of earnings the purchaser expects to obtain from the assets which is above the normal return on the price paid. This may result from better management or the ability to use the assets more intensively (for instance by putting more products through an underused distribution network) or some other factor. In practice, since assets are often undervalued on balance sheets, the goodwill may merely represent the difference between the book value of the assets and their market value. In some cases acquirors will revalue the assets to a more realistic level and write off the goodwill against that revaluation. In some countries, such as the United States, this type of revaluation is frowned upon and the goodwill figure often remains on the balance sheet for many years. Since it represents the value of expected future earnings it should be written down over a period as those earnings are realised, but this is not always done.

Patents, trade names and similar protections of products are other common types of intangible. Again it is difficult to put a value on these and they are often carried at one unit of currency but they can also be carried at the cost of developing the patents or at some estimate of future earning power. Again, if the company went into liquidation it would cease to sell the product and there would be no future earning power (although patent rights may have a sale value of their own).

The third most common intangible is capitalised costs. One of these is interest; some companies such as property companies, which are involved in projects lasting several years, have a choice as to how to treat interest on borrowing prior to completion. They may charge it against current earnings like any other cost; this is generally considered conservative. Or they may say that interest is a cost which contributes to the value of the asset and should be amortised from the earnings of the completed project. A similar approach can be taken with research and development costs of developing a new high technology product, most or all of which are incurred before any sales can be obtained. Once the product is developed and successful it may generate income for as long as twenty years. The argument is that to charge this cost in the year incurred against earnings of products to which it is unrelated and then not to charge it against the new product which it made possible is to distort the true earnings pattern of the company. Alternatively it is argued that the patents, engineering drawings or other features which result from the R & D, and which will generate income over the next twenty years, are themselves an asset. On either argument, the appropriate part of the R & D is not charged against earnings in the year in which it is incurred, but is shown on the balance sheet as an asset and then amortised over the life of the product developed.

While there are some sound accounting arguments, this treatment is dangerous for two reasons. It distorts what is actually happening to the cash position of the company. Interest has to be paid and the R & D costs met when they occur and capitalising them makes the apparent position better than the real position. There are cases on record of companies paying dividends and in other ways acting imprudently because they did not appreciate this distinction. Nor does management always recognise that the need to capitalise may be a sign of inadequate financing. A company which cannot meet the interest or R & D cost of a project from current earnings probably needs an unusually strong capital base to justify the risk of such a large project, but may not face up to this need if it is able to report better earnings than a conservative approach justifies.

Moreover, while the theory is clear the practice often is not. If the project is unsuccessful it may not generate enough earnings to amortise the capitalised item. Worse, companies which are having difficulties sometimes change their accounting practice; by capitalising items which were previously, or on a prudent basis should be, expensed they seek to conceal the difficulties. This is particularly dangerous in countries with lax accounting or disclosure rules so that the nature of, and case for, the change is not clear to an outsider.

Banks used to deduct all intangibles from net worth in considering various measures of balance sheet strength. This is based on the liquidation approach; the intangibles represent future earning power and a company which goes into liquidation by definition will not realise that earning power, making the intangibles worthless. Nowadays, however, some analysts look more closely at the exact nature of the intangible and try to estimate its real earning power and value. This fits more closely with a going concern basis but carries the danger that the analyst's estimate of earnings is excessive and the intangibles less valuable than thought. (Of course, this danger applies to most tangible assets too.) Certainly where intangibles are large the banker should pay very close attention to their nature, to the earnings expected from them and to the company's practice in amortising them. Closest attention should be paid where there may have been a change in practice or the reason for creating the intangible may be to show a better position than actually exists.

Other non-current assets. There are a number of other items which appear occasionally but none sufficiently frequently to justify individual discussion. The banker should, if an item is important, make sure that he knows what it is and understands its significance and value.

Non-current liabilities

All liabilities, and some reserves, which are excluded from current liabilities come under this heading.

Term debt. All borrowings with a remaining life of more than one year from the date of the balance sheet are term debt whatever the nature of the lender. Term debt is a crucial part of the structure of the balance sheet and the calculation of such concepts as leverage. But other factors should be considered as well. The first is the maturity profile; a £10 million loan is long-term debt whether it is payable in one amount eighteen months or twenty-five years from now or over twenty years in small instalments. Debt with a well-spread amortisation pattern is obviously more favourable than debt with either a bullet maturity (i.e. payable in one amount at maturity) or a small number of large amortisations.

There is no reason why term debt should consist of only one borrowing. A company may borrow from a number of different types of lender with varying amortisation patterns. The total amounts coming due in the next few years and, further ahead, the amount due in any one year must not be excessive in view of the company's size, cash flow and refinancing ability.

Interest fixed at a low rate is favourable; even interest fixed at a fairly high level at least gives certainty as to the amount due each year. Floating interest gives no such certainty; the basis on which it floats (over LIBOR, prime rate, base rate or the local equivalent) will affect the likelihood of a sharp increase in interest cost and its possible impact. High inflation causes interest rates to become more volatile even in countries where they are traditionally low and stable; combined with the tendency of monetarist policies to cause high real interest this has made floating rate borrowing both harder to avoid and more dangerous. As a result, the mix of interest rates payable on term debt and the extent to which interest floats can have important implications for the company's future ability to service its debt without undue strain. This is particularly important if interest is being capitalised; if the project is not going to start earning for two or three years and interest rates are 20 or 25% per annum, as they are in some countries, the extent by which earnings are overstated, and the level of profitability needed to justify the project, can be dramatically affected.

Secured, senior, subordinated and convertible debt. Bankers must also consider the relative seniority of different types of debt, term or otherwise. Broadly speaking, although there are minor variations in different countries, debt can be secured on specific assets, or on all assets, in which case it ranks ahead of other debt which is not secured; this will be discussed in more detail in Chapter 11. Or it may be senior but unsecured; in most cases this means that in a liquidation it ranks equally with all other unsecured obligations, such as trade payables, dividends etc. Even in the case of senior debt, however, the analyst needs to know the local practice; in Spain, for example, registered debt takes priority from the date on which it is registered.

Finally, there is subordinated debt, which by its terms cannot be paid in liquidation until either all other debt, or specified debts, have been paid in full. Subordination may apply even prior to liquidation and interest may only be payable on it if all interest on non-subordinated debt has been paid or some other criterion has been met. It is necessary to know the exact terms of the subordination to see how the debt ranks, as well as to understand the legal situation in the country concerned. Subordination is an American practice which has spread to other countries, but not all of them have legal systems which properly recognise the concept; it may be difficult to enforce a subordination in countries which either do not recognise it or have no specific provision for it in their law. Until somebody sets a precedent, the courts' reaction can be difficult to judge.

A complete and clearly enforceable subordination at least in theory strengthens the balance sheet for other creditors, and it used to be considered almost as good as equity. In many cases it still is, particularly where the subordinated lender is a parent or affiliated company which for tax or other reasons prefers subordinated debt to an outright equity injection. However, experience in the United States has shown that subordinated lenders are often so concerned about their inferior position that they threaten to put an ailing company into liquidation well before the senior lenders consider it necessary or desirable. The banks then have to choose between allowing a salvageable company to sink or bailing out the subordinated lenders to prevent them sinking it. As a result, subordination is less favourably regarded than it used to be.

Any form of debt can carry with it the right to be converted into another type of security. Usually conversion is into ordinary or common stock, but sometimes it is into special non-voting or preferred shares, described later in the chapter. From the banker's viewpoint, the conversion right is only of value if exercised (at which point debt is reduced and equity increased, with a double impact on the balance sheet structure); or if the conversion right has allowed the borrower to obtain more favourable terms (lower interest is the most common). However, if the terms of the conversion (i.e. the notional price put on the shares in deciding how many the lender will receive when he converts) are favourable, the banker may make some allowance for probable future conversion.

Deferred taxation. There are two main causes of deferred taxation, one where the tax does not become due for more than a year after the balance sheet date and the more important where items are treated differently for tax and normal reporting purposes. The most common examples are investment allowances or accelerated depreciation, deductible for tax purposes although they would not normally be charged against profits for other purposes. The company thus pays less tax in the current year, but the depreciation has been used and will therefore not be available to reduce future years' taxable profits. The company will thus pay more tax in those years than would otherwise be the case; the government has not eliminated the payment of tax altogether, merely deferred it.

The importance of deferred taxation depends on how it arose, and when (and if) it will be payable. In the United Kingdom investment allowances were so generous that for many years companies investing at all actively were able to defer taxes almost indefinitely; a special inventory allowance introduced in the mid-1970s was only subject to call-back if inventory values declined over a relatively short period of time. The United Kingdom accountancy bodies therefore decided to treat deferred taxation as equity rather than a liability unless tax is likely to be paid. In looking at the balance sheets of companies in other countries comparable situations may exist.

Pension reserves. Pension reserves are common items on balance sheets in certain countries such as Germany, but unknown in others. They arise when the future liability to pay pensions has been recognised but not funded off the balance sheet in a separate trust fund or insurance scheme; there are thus no assets wholly separate from those of the company set aside for the pensioners as there are with a trust fund.

Pension reserves give rise to two main questions. Is the reserve sufficient, or even more than sufficient, for the likely future needs? And how imminent are those needs? Companies rarely publish sufficient information to provide a complete answer to either question; but a banker should be able to judge whether there is a potential problem which needs to be investigated further.

Part of the answer depends on the structure of the workforce. A relatively newly established company with a young workforce will wait a long time before many workers start to draw on the pension reserves. At this extreme they can be considered as non-interest-bearing long-term debt, almost as good as equity. (Even where, as in Germany, companies are required to accrue interest on pension reserves, this in turn becomes part of the reserve.) At the other extreme an old, well-established company, a good employer whose people stay with it, is probably already paying out substantial pensions and can expect to pay out more as the relatively elderly workforce retires. Between the extremes are companies in cyclical businesses or which hire and fire freely so that only a relatively small proportion of their workforce is likely ever to qualify for a full pension. If such a company is compelled to provide for pensions the provision may be substantially greater than is necessary and a concealed form of equity.

Another approach is to look at the profit and loss statement; this should show either pensions actually paid or the amount set aside from earnings for addition to the pension reserve. Where both are available a comparison, particularly if it can be done over several years to establish the trend, should help to indicate whether the pension reserves are building up or declining and, if the latter, how rapidly. A net figure can be taken from the balance sheet, but this is less informative than the two separate items.

All this is necessary to avoid the danger of assuming too easily that pension reserves are almost equity. The purpose of establishing a pension reserve should be to use it, so that at some time pension reserves should actually reduce, creating a net cash outflow rather than a form of concealed equity or interest-free debt. Pensions are a relatively recent development in many countries, with the level of provision for future pensions still outgrowing the amounts actually paid, so that this has not been a frequent problem yet. But statistics show an increasingly elderly population in most advanced countries, so that it is likely that in future more companies will find the pension payments a heavy burden unless they are adequately funded.

Finally, pension reserves appear on a balance sheet where the liability has not been funded separately, so that there are no specific assets set aside to service the pension payments. Thus when pensions are paid, they are a direct drain on cash and must be served directly from earnings and cash flow. A company which has not allowed for this may find itself in serious financial difficulties; even one which has a substantial pension reserve on its balance sheet may find that turning this bookkeeping item into actual payments to the pensioners is considerably more painful than expected.

It remains true, of course, that it is possible to overstate pension reserves, particularly where there is a tax benefit from doing so; this then understates the company's profits and creates a form of hidden reserve or equity.

The absence of pension reserves can mean that the liability is funded off balance sheet (in which case inflation may cause it to be underfunded and a large catch-up payment may be required); or the company may pay no pensions and have no liability; or there may be a liability for which no provision of any sort has been made. Not all countries permit this last position; where they do it can be extremely damaging. Analysts should not therefore assume that because there is no visible pension provision there is no liability.

Liability reserves. Although liability reserves may include deductions from assets, as discussed under current liability provisions, the concept is of a reserve against an expected future liability, the amount or timing, or both, of which are uncertain. One example could be a disputed tax bill where it was clear that something would have to be paid. Another would be a litigation which, if lost, could involve payment of damages, expenses etc., but where the result and/or the likely amount of any damages is uncertain. There are too many possibilities to discuss them all, but the point is that a liability reserve is either expected to be used or at least carries a concrete possibility, outside the control of the company, of a loss or of becoming a liability which will have to be met.

Minority interests. Minority interests arise only in consolidated figures. The whole of the assets, liabilities, net worth and earnings of a subsidiary are consolidated even where the parent owns less than all the shares and is only entitled to a pro rata share. The item "minority interests" on the balance sheet reflects the interest of the outside shareholders in the net worth of the subsidiary. Usually it is a small part of the total balance sheet but occasionally it is more substantial; even more occasionally the subsidiary concerned is more important than the size of minority interest suggests; the vagaries of valuation may mean that the subsidiary's balance sheet value does not truly reflect its importance to the parent.

A minority interest is probably most important in liquidation but can also reduce freedom of the parent's management to use its resources freely; this can be important if the partly-owned subsidiary is generating cash and other subsidiaries are net users. Outside shareholders may also limit the subsidiary's ability to guarantee borrowings of the parent or other members of the group, and generally make the use of its assets less flexible. Conversely if the subsidiary is losing money, the consolidated figures may overstate the parent's share of the loss. On the other hand, the parent may have to choose between rescuing a weak partly-owned subsidiary although it will not obtain the whole benefit; or declining to rescue unless other shareholders share the cost. Letting a subsidiary fail may mean missing an opportunity or have adverse affects on the market's perception of the parent's credit.

However, in practice these considerations are rarely important; a minority interest is not a liability in the sense that the parent company actually has to pay anything.

Other. There are other possible long-term liabilities which can appear and which must be assessed individually, but none of them are sufficiently common to justify comment.

Net worth

Net worth is the difference between the total assets of the company and its total liabilities; put another way it is the residual value of the assets which belongs to the shareholders after all liabilities have been met. On a going concern basis this may be hard to assess accurately since there is no intention of selling most of the assets to pay the creditors, who should rather be serviced from cash flow. However, the existence of a form of financing which ranks behind all creditors and which can only (subject to certain qualifications mentioned below) be paid away when all the liabilities have been met is an important protection to the creditors. Moreover, net worth has no mandatory cost of servicing; thus assets it finances can help to support the payment of interest on assets financed with debt. This makes it more likely that the company will survive the start-up period before earnings begin to flow and during recessionary periods. If the overall return on assets is lower than the rate of interest being charged on borrowings (as has been the case for industry generally in a number of countries in the late 1970s and early 1980s) financing solely by borrowing would lead to inevitable losses and, if continued, bankruptcy. Adequate net worth is necessary to protect against that as well as other dangers.

The question of what is adequate and what changes the view of adequacy will be discussed in Parts Two and Three. This section describes the various components of net worth and their significance.

Equity capital or share capital is the amount of money (usually in cash but occasionally in the form of machinery or other assets) contributed originally and through any subsequent issues of shares by the shareholders to meet the initial financing requirement and to keep a sound proportion of equity to total liabilities. Share capital broadly falls into two types although the details differ by country. Ordinary shares in the United Kingdom or common stock in the United States and their equivalent elsewhere usually carry voting rights in the management of a company; in some cases they may include non-voting shares or shares with different levels of voting rights. Nevertheless they are the purest form of capital, the last item to be repaid in liquidation and earning their return in the form of dividends, declared at the discretion of the board of directors out of actual earnings for the current or previous years. Accounting conventions in different countries vary as to what may be treated as earnings for this purpose (extraordinary profits are available in some countries and not in others and the definition of extraordinary varies) and of course the overall accounting standards by which earnings are calculated are important. Nevertheless the prime point is that common stock carries no mandatory financing requirement; dividends can be cut or eliminated altogether if the company's earnings (or losses) and/or financial condition require it. Admittedly directors are often reluctant to cut dividends, because to do so is seen as a damaging admission of failure, but they can and in some cases banks can compel them to.

The second type of equity share is generally known as preference shares in the United Kingdom and preferred stock in the United States. The "preference" relates only to the position vis-à-vis ordinary shares; a stated level of dividend must be paid on the preference shares before any can be paid on the ordinary, and in liquidation preference shareholders must be paid in full before the ordinary shareholders receive anything. The entitlement to the preference dividend may be cumulative (i.e. amounts not paid in one year are carried forward and the accumulated total must be paid before any ordinary dividends) or it may be non-cumulative, in which case if it is missed in one year it is gone for ever. Usually the preference dividend is fixed but occasionally there may be a minimum amount after which preference shareholders share any dividends that are paid to the ordinary shareholders. They usually carry votes only if the preference dividend is in arrears or on proposals which would change their rights. Preference shares are sometimes convertible into common shares.

Since preference shares rank behind all liabilities they are full equity to the bank lender. However, it is harder for the directors to cut a preferred than an ordinary dividend, and doing so may impair the company's ability to raise new capital, and sometimes even the market's view of its creditworthiness. Even in a recovery situation, the existence of a backlog of cumulative preferred dividends may make equity very difficult to raise when it is most needed. Nevertheless dividends can be cut and as with ordinary dividends they can only be paid out of retained earnings.

Treasury stock. In the United States and in some other countries (including recently but on a restricted basis the United Kingdom) companies may buy their own shares. Occasionally these are shown as an asset in which case they should be treated as intangible or better still the balance sheet should be adjusted to the more normal treatment which is to show them as a deduction from the shares in issue. However, they can be sold again in the United States and some other countries without the normal formalities of a share issue, so that they can represent a potential reserve of capital. Nevertheless since they have been purchased for cash the existence of treasury stock should cause bankers to look at the company's financial structure and the surplus liquidity required to justify such a purchase.

Capital reserves. The broad definition of capital reserves covers those types of reserve which cannot be used to pay dividends. They can arise in a number of ways and the precise definition is a matter for the company law of each country and should be checked where the capital reserves are large.

One common way in which they arise is the issue of shares at a price above the par or nominal value. If a British company issues one million shares with a par value of £1 each but at a price of £2 each the accounts will show £1,000,000 of ordinary shares and £1,000,000 of capital reserve. In some countries capital reserves also include profits on sale or revaluation of capital assets or investments or other individual items. Accounting or disclosure rules in many countries do not require definition of the amount or exact nature of capital reserves and they may all be lumped together under one heading. Nevertheless, the broad distinction is that capital reserves should not be available to justify the payment of a dividend.

Retained earnings or earnings reserves. Net profit, as defined in the company law of each country, can be distributed as dividends, converted to capital or allocated to a particular reserve. Anything left over is added to retained earnings each year and is normally freely available to be paid as dividends in subsequent years. Retained earnings are often included under the same heading as, and are then indistinguishable from:

Equity reserves. Some countries more than others require reserves to be established against designated contingencies. To qualify as equity reserves the contingency should be a general one, with no specific reason to expect it to occur, in contrast to the liability reserve discussed above, where there is good reason to suppose that it will occur. For example, a consumer products company might establish a general reserve against the possibility of product liability suits; it would be an acknowledgement that no such company can guarantee freedom from them. On the other hand, if a specific suit were already under way or clearly threatened a liability reserve would be appropriate.

Legal reserves. There are a variety of types of reserve required by the law of various countries; they may be a specific portion of net worth or earnings, or to meet specific requirements in relation, say, to inventory. They are too numerous and too specific to discuss in this book, but the analyst should be aware of their existence. Where they occur their legal basis decides the extent to which they must be used for a particular purpose, and therefore perhaps are potentially unavailable to general creditors in liquidation.

Tax-free or tax-reduced reserves. Many countries require specific reserves for tax purposes or to obtain favourable tax treatment. Again, the analyst should be aware of their existence or at least of the law about them in countries which permit them. He should also be aware of their impact on other parts of the balance sheet (as they may arise from a write down of assets against earnings) and the conditions under which tax may be payable if the borrower reverses the process which initially created the reserve.

Contingent liabilities

These do not normally appear on the balance sheet itself but rather in one or more notes. In countries where the accounting requirements are not very strict some contingent liabilities may not be disclosed at all and this can be a worrying factor if they are believed to exist but their size and importance is not known.

They arise when the borrower would only be liable if one or more adverse events happen; rather than, as with a direct liability, being obligated whatever happens. Two common examples arise out of the discounting of trade bills (the acceptor of the bill is primarily liable but the supplier remains liable if the acceptor fails) and guarantees. The guarantor is liable only if the primary borrower fails to pay or defaults in some agreed way. Guarantees of the debts of subsidiaries are, of course, eliminated in consolidated statements.

There are many other types of contingent liability, about which there are two main questions. The first: "how likely is it that this contingent liability will become a direct liability?" And the second: "how important would it be if my borrower had to meet the whole of his contingent liabilities?" If the answer to both of these questions is "not very", then the analyst can pass on; if, however, a combination of answers suggests that the borrower might have to make a payment which would harm it, then this must be carefully factored into the analysis.

4 The Profit and Loss Statement

The profit and loss statement, unlike the balance sheet, covers the operations of a company over a period of time; the revenues generated, the expenses incurred, and the net result.

Published figures usually cover a year, and many companies show nothing more frequent to their creditors or shareholders. All companies should - and most companies do - prepare more frequent figures for their own use; most monthly, some only quarterly. These management figures can be very useful to a banker if seen regularly.

Sales

Sales are often referred to as turnover in British terminology; they show the amount the company has invoiced its customers for goods delivered or services performed. The sales figure is usually thought of as fairly straightforward, but there are some unusual situations and a number of points to be checked. For instance, some companies operate as agents for a commission and then the analyst needs to know whether "sales" refer to the total amounts sold or only to the commission. Other companies' products, such as tobacco, are subject to excise or other taxes, which the company collects and passes on to the government. It can make a major difference if these taxes are wrongly included in reported sales.

Sales are normally booked when the invoice is issued to the customer, usually when the goods are delivered, and at that moment the underlying goods cease to be shown as inventory; instead a receivable appears which includes the cost of the inventory, plus the profit margin. However, construction companies and other companies which sell large projects delivered over a long time sometimes account in different ways. Some take into sales work done in the period, whether delivered or not, others only actual, if incomplete, deliveries; others solely projects which have been completed. The impact on reported sales can be very large where a single project is worth several hundreds of millions of dollars and the underlying work is spread over as long as two or three years.

Leaving aside these exceptions, however, and looking mainly at manufacturing and distribution companies, there are still several points to be checked. First, are sales shown gross or net? There are two types of deduction which may be made from the invoices and they can either be shown by reducing the sales figure or as an expense. In most cases they are small and the treatment will make very little difference to the overall picture. However, occasionally they can be rather larger, with adverse implications. In practice, few companies outside the United States publish this information and the analyst may not be able to find the answers. Nevertheless, if he has any reason to think they might be significant he should certainly investigate further.

Discounts provide one type of deduction, most often for prompt payment (see Chapter 2 under trade payables). Where they are less than the cost of financing the receivable for the period covered, they are an intelligent form of financing with no adverse implications. Sometimes a discount larger than the interest saved is common in a particular industry, and although it is then arguably a form of reduction in sales, nevertheless there is no reason for concern. If, however, a company gives a larger discount than its competitors this represents a hidden price cut which reduces sales rather than being an expense and raises the question as to why it is necessary.

Discounts may also be given for volume of sales or for a firm contract which allows the seller to plan his production; either should help to reduce costs. Provided the discount is in line with the saving this is perfectly normal. But if discounts represent the use of customers' muscle to obtain a concealed price cut this can suggest a threat to profits.

The other type of deduction from sales results from the return of goods because they are faulty or for other reasons. Clearly this is a reduction in the true sales figure and not an expense; modest returns are standard in many industries but abnormal returns can conceal a weakness in manufacturing, in quality or in market position. The invoicing of sales to customers who do not want the goods or are unable to pay for them can sometimes be fraudulent.

In most cases the analyst will have to assume that the sales figure is a true figure. However, he should be alert for evidence of concealed deductions and ready to investigate further, particularly if the figures are unaudited.

Whether any of these items are used to reduce sales or shown as an expense also affects the margins, returns and ratios discussed in later chapters, many of which are calculated as a percentage of sales. If the sales figure is inaccurate, particularly if the inaccuracy is not consistent from year to year, the ratios and conclusions drawn from them become unreliable and sometimes misleading.

Finally, exchange rates can affect the reported sales figure if sales are billed in more than one currency. If sales are made by foreign subsidiaries, with expenses in the same currency, the distortion may not be important. But a company which bills large exports in foreign currencies may show a sales figure differing from the amount of domestic currency it actually receives, with the difference depending on how it handles the translation.

Cost of goods sold and gross profit

Cost of goods sold (CGS) covers those expenses which are directly related to production, such as raw materials, direct labour, power in any form to produce the goods and transport for raw materials to the factory and finished goods to the customer. They also include depreciation of fixed assets used in production, as well as maintenance costs and property taxes.

CGS expenses are thus directly necessary to produce; the gross profit is the amount left after they have been met, which is therefore available to meet all other expenses. It must be sufficient to cover all other types of cost, including the servicing of capital, and still leave a reasonable net profit and cash flow. The required level of gross profit depends on the type of product and the amount of marketing and other costs which have to be covered; if it is inadequate or declining, other expenses may not be covered and the company will be in danger of making a loss.

The make-up of CGS, how well it is controlled and what

scope there is for saving are therefore important. Usually, general knowledge of the industry and of companies in similar industries will tell the banker approximately what to expect and what pointers to look for which suggest a weakness. For instance, if he knows that an expensive raw material is used, and wastage rates are critical he can try to find out his borrower's comparison with the industry average. Even where this level of detail is not available such knowledge may help to ask the right questions if a decline in gross profit or an unfavourable comparison with competitors suggests that something is wrong.

Selling general and administrative expenses

Costs which arise from marketing the product and in the general running of the business are usually given under one heading. They include such things as advertising; other indirect marketing costs; salesmen's salaries, commissions, cars etc.; senior management salaries and all the office and administrative costs, such as wages, rents, depreciation, taxes and maintenance of administrative fixed assets; accounting and the collection of receivables. With the possible exception of some selling costs they do not relate closely to the volume of production and may even move counter-cyclically. For instance, in a depression some companies spend more on marketing to maintain the volume of sales than in a strong economy. Certainly in a recession they may need to spend more on credit controls and trying to collect bad debts.

Research and development costs

The importance or even the existence of R & D costs varies from company to company and depends on the technological level of the product concerned. Some companies spend 5 or 10% of their sales on R & D, others spend a much smaller amount on development only. Very often the amount is not broken out separately, but in companies in a high technology area or one where the technology is changing or threatening to change fast it may well be important to assess the quality as well as the quantity of the R & D. Unfortunately the amount spent only tells the quantity and gives no help in judging the quality. Where exploration suggests that the R & D is of doubtful quality, this can be a serious warning sign.

Operating profit

Deducting all the above expenses leaves an operating profit, the figure that the company has made from its operations before allowing for the financing costs (or profits) or unusual items. The distinction is important because the latter reflect the way in which the company is financed, the former the success of its day-to-day operations. While operating profits must be sufficient to cover the cost of finance, they are mainly an indication of the efficiency with which management runs the company's basic business. The level of operating profit and its trend, as well as the specific factors which affect the likely future levels and trends, are of key importance.

Financial expenses and income

The way in which the company is financed can create a cost or sometimes an additional profit. It is vital that operating profit should cover financial expenses with a margin to allow for fluctuations beyond management's control. The better the financial structure, and the lower these financial expenses, the more flexibility management has to absorb temporary fluctuations in operating profit or use the operating profit to finance expansion. More detail is often available on the breakdown of financial items than the higher levels.

Interest expense. For most companies interest is the most important financial cost. Often only a single figure is given in published balance sheets, but sometimes a breakdown is given between bank and non-bank, or interest on short-term, medium- and long-term debt, or fixed and floating rates of interest. Even where this information is not specifically given it may be possible to calculate it roughly from the breakdown of the various types of debt on the balance sheet or in the notes.

The importance is that interest is for most companies largely or wholly a fixed cost in the sense discussed in

Chapter 9; it does not vary with the volume of business. Only the relatively small proportion (for most companies) which is directly tied to fluctuations in net working investment (see Chapter 6) is a variable cost which reduces automatically as sales decline. However, interest can be variable in the different sense that the rate fluctuates. Indeed, the combination of tight monetary policies and high inflation, seen in many countries in the early 1980s, often reduces the volume of business and operating profit at the same time as it dramatically increases interest costs.

Interest expense may be excessive if the financial structure is wrong for the particular company, or if the company is not earning the return which is normal for its business and which is a major factor justifying a particular financial structure. Where interest appears excessive the analyst must assess whether the reason is an unsound capital structure or a poor operating profit, inadequate to service even normal interest. Also whether it is likely to be temporary or a continuing or even accelerating problem. Although the end result of a continuing failure to cover interest adequately is the same whatever the reason, the chances of reversing the situation and the methods used to do so are very different. If the problem is purely a financial one the right answer may be simply to raise equity and/or, when market conditions allow, to convert short-term floating rate debt to longer-term fixed rate debt. Inadequate operating profits on the other hand can be a temporary difficulty due to a cyclical decline which will be reversed when the economy recovers; or a decline in the overall industry conditions in which the company operates; or evidence of a deterioration in some aspects of the company's operation which makes it less competitive. Very often two or more factors are combined, so that the analyst must not allow the effects of a cyclical decline to mask the longer-term weakness.

For this reason, among others, it is particularly important to look at trends and to ensure that interest cover is no worse at the same stage of the current cycle than in previous cycles. Conversely the analyst should also look ahead to assess the factors which are likely to permit an improvement in profits as the cycle improves; and then monitor whether the improvement in the cycle is reflected in the actual interest cover.

It is not of course enough for a company just to cover interest with no margin. Depending on the nature of the business a larger or smaller proportion of interest will be a fixed cost. The higher the fixed cost, the higher the margin of safety that is required to ensure against loss if business turns down. But interest must also be covered with a margin large enough to meet other financial or extraordinary costs and to provide profit for reinvestment and expansion as well as for dividends to the shareholders.

Interest income. Some companies show an interest income as well as, or rather than, an interest expense; occasionally the income is substantial. Some companies report a figure which nets the two, but a breakdown is desirable since lack of it may distort the understanding of interest cover. It can be argued that the net interest is the significant figure, since interest income as well as interest expense results from the company's financial structure and therefore reduces the amount of expense that needs to be covered from operations.

However, the better argument is that interest always has to be paid but that interest income may arise from any number of sources which may be temporary or accidental. Thus in any year and, more importantly, over a period the analysis should focus on the company's continuing ability to generate funds from operations to service debt, interest as well as principal. It is certainly true that some companies balance weakness in operating income with strength in investment income, and there are cases where the two are directly connected. For instance a company which invests large advance payments at a high rate of interest may feel able to take a lower operating margin on the relevant contracts because of the investment income they generate. This may well be sound business in some cases, but even so it is important for the analyst to understand what is happening, to be able to track the level of the operating margin and the extent to which it covers interest and to assess the net impact on interest expense and income of a change in rates. If a company concedes lower operating margins in expectation of high income from advances, a sharp drop in rates may be damaging. Put another way, some erosion in operating margins may be acceptable in return for advances, but its extent needs to be carefully watched. The risks related to advances will be discussed in more detail in Chapter 9.

Sometimes interest is collected on receivables. In a few industries this is normal practice, and may go some way to offsetting the adverse affects of slow receivable turnover. Outside these limited cases, however, it is rare and suggests some unusual circumstance, possibly weak customers, which should be investigated further.

Investment income. There are two possible sources for investment income; first, surplus cash invested in a medium which produces a return other than interest. Provided the investment is appropriate for such a use the investment income can be treated in much the same way as interest income.

The alternative source is long-term investment in subsidiaries, affiliated companies or, less often, independent companies or property. This investment income may be purely dividends or may include royalties, management fees and even interest on loans to subsidiaries or affiliates. (This may alternatively be included in interest income.)

The questions about this type of investment income are first, how large a proportion is it of operating profit and of net profit before taxes? If it is small some of the following questions are of minor significance but the larger it is the more important they become.

The next question is how reliable is the income? The answer depends on its nature. The flow of dividends (at least without risk of damage to the subsidiary) depends on stable or growing earnings from the subsidiaries and their ability to reinvest sufficient earnings which are not used to pay the dividend. If there are outside shareholders, or if the bank's customer is itself a minority shareholder, dividend policy may change for reasons of which it has no advance knowledge or control. Where the investment is fully controlled, is the parent setting the dividend policy in the best interests of the subsidiary, or is it milking the subsidiary to hide its own illiquidity, possibly killing the golden goose in the process? If the latter, do local accounting rules and corporation law restrict the subsidiary's ability to pay dividends before irreparable harm is done?

Much the same questions should be asked about interest on loans to affiliates or subsidiaries. Are the subsidiaries sound, are they able to pay the interest without undermining their financial viability and future ability to pay? Are they paying a market rate or are they being over or undercharged by the parent? If so, is there any chance that this treatment may be challenged by the tax or exchange control authorities in either country concerned?

Investment income may also take the form of royalties or management fees, although these are better shown separately. Royalties may be payable from third-party licensees; often it makes sense for a company to obtain a return on its R & D in this way rather than undergo the expense and risk of establishing a local manufacturing facility or trying to sell into a market over high tariff barriers. Patents and other agreements have a limited life and if the income is significant, then the remaining life of the patents and the extent to which the royalty income is concentrated on one or two key patents rather than well spread is important. Royalties can also be paid by a company's own subsidiaries and this type only shows in non-consolidated figures. Broadly the same questions arise as about dividends or interest. Is the subsidiary or affiliate getting value for the royalties or is this just a method of sucking income out of it? If the latter, is it liable to be challenged by the local tax authorities? Is it being used to mask the problems of the parent in a way which undermines the longer-term viability of the subsidiary and therefore its value as an investment? Where management fees are shown under financial income or investment income the same basic questions apply as to royalties.

Other income and expenses

There is no easy categorisation of what may appear under this heading and indeed some of the items which have been discussed under financial income or expenses may show as other income or expense in some statements. For instance a company that was paying rather than receiving royalties or management fees might show them as another expense.

Net profit before tax

It is important to measure the company's continuing ability to produce profits from all normal aspects of its business and financial structure. This should exclude extraordinary factors or actions which, while perfectly legitimate, are not usual for this particular company. Profit before tax and extraordinary items is usually the best measure of the overall combination of operating efficiency, financial structure and general management competence.

Tax

There are two broad categories of tax expense. The one which most correctly appears in this position is any form of tax on income. In the United States this is corporate income tax, in the United Kingdom it is corporation tax and most other countries have a rough equivalent even though the details may vary. The nominal level of tax required is rarely much above 50% and in some countries it is lower. In many countries the actual tax paid is much lower than the nominal tax rate; permitted deduction of investment allowances, accelerated depreciation, tax subsidies on inventory holdings and so on mean that the profit before tax shown by normal accounting is not necessarily the same as the profit on which the authorities actually levy tax. Tax laws are usually complicated and it is rarely possible for the banker to have a complete view of the difference between taxable income and reported income; it is desirable, however, to have at least a general idea in each country of the way in which the tax system works and of the factors which allow a company to report a lower income to the tax man than to shareholders or bankers. Often the difference will result from perfectly legitimate accounting treatment and gives no cause for concern. But without at least a general knowledge of what may affect this difference the banker cannot be sure whether the published figures or the taxable figures are more realistic. Indeed, in countries where tax accounting and published accounting are required to be the same, the company will go to great lengths to reduce the reported pre-tax profits in order to reduce the tax bill. The banker has no desire to see his customer pay more tax than is necessary since tax is not available to service his debt, but if he knows that the reported taxable income is inaccurate then he must try to get an idea of the true figure. Without it he has no indication as to whether profitability and cash flow enable the company to service its debt in the ways discussed later in the book and to remain viable.

The other form of tax is payable either on volume of business (such as a sales tax or a value added tax) or on property or capital. It is not a tax on income at all and should not be shown under the same heading, although it often is. Tax on volume should probably be considered (to the extent not recovered from the customer) as a deduction from sales rather than an expense of obtaining sales. The second is clearly an expense of doing business and should be charged against earnings at the appropriate level. For instance, a tax on real estate might be charged against cost of goods sold (if it relates to the factory) or selling, general and administrative costs (if it relates to office blocks). A tax on capital is more of a financial expense since it relates to the company's capital structure.

Ideally these types of tax should be shown under the appropriate expense headings and sometimes they are. Quite often, however, there is a single figure for tax with no details broken out and in these cases the banker is compelled to assume that it is all income tax, unless he has good reason to believe the contrary. Nevertheless, the distinction between tax which is payable regardless of profitability, and even regardless of volume of business, and tax which is payable only on profits earned is an important one. Usually other taxes are deductible expenses for income tax purposes; for a company paying income tax of around 50%, half of all such expenses are borne by the government. Income tax, however, is a direct reduction of profits after all expenses have been borne which is only payable if the company is profitable. Since the other forms of taxes are payable rather like interest regardless of profitability they are twice as expensive for a company which pays no income tax, since the government no longer pays half its expenses.

Net profit after tax

The profit which the company earns on its normal operations after paying tax but before taking account of extraordinary items and minority interests is also important. In a straightforward company this is the "bottom line" figure and is the best indication of overall efficiency (operating, financial and tax management) and of the ability to service liabilities and to give the shareholders a return on their investment and risk. If this return is satisfactory the shareholders, both present and potential, will probably be prepared if necessary to increase the investment; the lower the return (in relation to the particular type of business and risk) the greater the need for additional equity to reduce the cost of debt service and the harder it will be to raise that equity on acceptable terms.

Extraordinary items and minority interests

Extraordinary items and minority interests appear in only a few cases. They then represent an adjustment to net profit after tax to take account of a change in the amount being made available to the shareholders (or for reinvestment in the company) as a result of something separate from the company's business results.

Extraordinary items cover a wide range of possible events. When a manufacturing company sells an old factory or office building any profit is available for use in the business or, perhaps, distribution to the shareholders even though the company is not in the business of selling factories. The same is true in reverse if the property is sold at a loss or if the item sold is a piece of machinery or a subsidiary.

On the expense side there are a number of items which are sometimes treated as extraordinary; perhaps the most topical is severance or redundancy costs, when a company is cutting the size of its workforce in a recession. Profits or losses as a result of foreign exchange fluctuations are also sometimes treated as extraordinary items.

Each large extraordinary item requires careful analysis. Some companies adjust the treatment of extraordinary items as a more or less blatant method of smoothing the reported profit, so that the first thing to check is consistency of treatment. Does a company show losses on sale of fixed assets as extraordinary but profits on the sale of a subsidiary (most of whose assets were fixed) as normal? Does it show foreign exchange losses as extraordinary but gains as normal? And so on.

Even where treatment is consistent, the so-called extraordinary items may not be outside the particular company's normal business. One clue may be frequent recurrence. For instance, a company with substantial imports, exports and overseas subsidiaries is inevitably in the business of taking foreign exchange risks. It may argue that the profit on receivables and inventory is part of trading, whereas the loss of value of overseas investments is not, but even this distinction is doubtful if the investment is necessary for the company to carry on business in the country concerned. It is true that the swings in exchange rates in the last few years and the vagaries of different methods of accounting for them (particularly the unlamented FASB8) caused the swing in profitability sometimes to swamp the underlying progress, or otherwise. Nevertheless, if this is a true reflection of the impact of exchange fluctuations on the company's business, it should not be concealed. Similar comments apply to redundancy payments. The closure of one large factory may be an extraordinary item, since no company is in the business of going out of business. On the other hand a company may constantly adjust its business, laying off people here and expanding there; these adjustments are a genuine part of the normal cost of continuing to do business efficiently.

The treatment of extraordinary items is important in looking at trends. Genuinely extraordinary items should be excluded because they distort the trend and conclusions drawn from it, but fluctuations should not be eliminated merely to smoothe the trend; if there is no trend, or if profits fluctuate widely around the trend, this is important information. Smoothing by inconsistent use of extraordinary items can distort or conceal the trend.

Minority interest is the income equivalent of the balance sheet item of the same name and can thus only occur in consolidated or partly consolidated figures. It recognises that part of the profits which have been consolidated do not belong to the shareholders of the parent company; the parent receives its pro rata share of dividends from the subsidiary and dividends paid to outside shareholders are a cash drain on the consolidated balance sheet. A pro rata share of the subsidiary's retained earnings is added to the value of the minority interest on the balance sheet.

In most cases minority interests will be a small part of net profits after tax. However, if they are large or growing rapidly this suggests that a high proportion of the parent's reported profit does not belong to the parent, which therefore is not free to use it interchangeably in other parts of its business.

Different forms of presentation

So far the discussion has assumed a presentation of the figures following probably the most logical pattern, although certainly not the only possible one. In practice, few companies outside the United States give a detailed breakdown of their expenses and where they do may break them down differently. Sometimes particular items will appear in footnotes in order to meet local legal requirements. Most countries require companies to disclose depreciation and some, such as the United Kingdom, total wages as well.

One common approach is to lump the various types of expense together under broader categories rather than giving a detailed breakdown. The category cost of goods sold with no breakdown but leading to gross margin is one possibility; followed by selling, general and administrative, leading on to operating profit. Research and development may or may not be included in a general category.

Some countries go direct from sales to what in the United Kingdom is called trading profit and elsewhere might be called operating profit before depreciation, with no breakdown of the expenses. Another approach gives categories of expense regardless of the area in which they arise; for instance, one item for wages, salaries etc. which would include those directly involved in production and all the administrative, accounting, head office and management salaries. Similarly a single figure for depreciation is quite common with no indication how much relates to productive assets and how much to office blocks or salesmen's cars.

On the other hand one item may be broken out which other presentations include under wages and salaries, i.e. pension payments. There are two broad approaches to establishing a pension fund although there are many minor variations to meet local tax and other regulations. With a trusteed or insured pension fund the company pays an amount each year to the trustees or insurance company; this is invested to generate future pensions. The company has no title to the assets of the pension fund, but provided the payments it makes (which will normally be calculated by skilled actuaries) are sufficient to meet the expected pensions it will also have no further liability. Thus the payment to the trustees each year is a legitimate deduction from profits, but should also be an accurate reflection of the overall cost. Apart from this payment, the underlying assets and the actual payments to the pensioners are completely off the company's financial statements.

In Germany and some other countries a "self-funded" pension fund is common. Despite the name the contributions are rarely segregated or used to buy specific assets to provide future pensions. There may therefore be a liability item "pension reserves" or some similar title (severance reserves in Italy for instance) but no asset assigned to meet the liability. Or the pensions actually paid may be changed to expenses, but no allowance be made for future liabilities, which can be very dangerous if pensions grow when the company's earnings are declining.

Where the pension reserves are legitimately treated as near equity, transfers to them are a non-cash charge on the company and can be added back in calculating cash flow. However, it is dangerous to follow this course with insufficient consideration; as discussed in Chapter 3 the purpose of establishing a pension reserve is to meet a real, if future, liability. The same factors which can cause a pension reserve to be a liability rather than quasi-equity can make payments a real cash drain. The same applies to the net balance of payments into and out of a reserve.

Analysts in countries where all or most pensions are trusteed/insured normally have no reason to spend much time considering pensions, and in analysing a foreign company may miss the significance of the pension reserve - or of the lack of one when it is needed. Analysts in countries where pension reserves are common, on the other hand, often seem to take them for granted.

But AEG-Telefunken in Germany is only the largest of many companies in recent years where unfunded pension reserves have been a major factor in final failure. And unless bankers, and financial managers, face the fact that pension payments are a real liability, and provision for them a true charge on earnings, there will be many more.

Cash flow

Cash flow is an extremely important item that arises from

the profit and loss statement and is, or should be, related to profitability but with a different timing arising from the accrual nature of most accounts.

Accrual accounting measures profit at the time that the action which will generate the profit is taken, or completed, rather than when the cash is actually received. The same is true with expenses. Accrual accounting also distinguishes between capital items and revenue items in a way which differs from the cash inflows and outflows. For instance the purchase of fixed assets, which involves a cash outflow, is shown as a capital item which does not go through the profit and loss statement. On the other hand, depreciation is a revenue item reducing reported profits. It does not involve any outflow of cash but represents an allocation of the pro rata cost of the fixed assets to the year concerned (or alternatively a recognition that a portion of what would otherwise be profit is needed to replace the fixed assets used to produce it). For most companies depreciation is the largest non-cash item and the main and often the whole difference between net profit after taxes and cash flow. A similar distinction is made between borrowing and repayment of principal and the payment of interest.

The concept of cash flow therefore arises from the recognition that a company does not pay its bills with accounting profits but with cash; if accounting profits recognise profit before cash is received or expenses after they have been paid the cash profit is less than the accrual profits, and vice versa. In practice the difference is not as great as this since many items largely repeat themselves. For instance, profits are taken when sales are invoiced but the cash may not be received for anything from 10 to 200 days later. However, at the end of each year a company has some sales on which profits have been booked but cash not received, and during the year receives some cash from sales on which profit was booked in the previous year. Roughly the same applies to expenses. Therefore in a stable company there should not be any significant difference between cash and accrual profits from this source.

Variations in receivables, inventory or payables which are the main revenue items whose timing affects the difference between cash and accrual profits are not normally included in the calculation of cash flow. Rather, net changes are looked at as items that have to be financed from cash flow or which provide a supplement to it and will be discussed in Chapter 6 under the heading of net working investment.

The definition of cash flow therefore is net profit after taxes plus any non-cash charges which have been deducted from profits and minus any cash outflows of a revenue nature which have not been so deducted. In practice, for many companies this means that cash flow is net profit after taxes plus depreciation.

However, there are other possible adjustments. One is deferred tax which, as discussed in Chapter 3, has been charged against earnings but not actually paid. However, it is expected to be paid at some time in the future, when it will be a cash outflow to be deducted from cash flow. Many companies at one and the same time defer some tax from the current year but pay tax deferred from previous years. The adjustment to cash flow should then net these two items. Where the two flows are not available, simply add to cash flow any increase in the balance sheet figure, or deduct any decrease.

The same approach is applied to pension reserves, to any other form of equity or liability reserve where a transfer passes through the revenue account above the level of net profit before taxes (NBT), and to capitalised expenses.

The treatment of extraordinary items in cash flow depends on their nature. With non-cash items the easiest thing is to calculate net profit before allowing for them; otherwise an offsetting adjustment to cash flow is needed. Where a specific movement of cash occurs it may well make more sense to include it in the calculation of cash flow. This is particularly so when the item, even if unusual, has some relation to operations. The sale of fixed assets at a profit, for instance, brings in cash and suggests that perhaps the depreciation previously charged was too high. Redundancy costs use cash and suggest that previous labour expenses were too high. In both cases, the actual cash movement has some relationship to prior statements of profits. Profit or loss of an investment unrelated to operations, however, would more naturally fall outside the normal definition of cash flow.

An alternative approach is to calculate cash flow both before and after extraordinary items. Calculating it before allows the trend to be more clearly seen; calculating it after allows the analyst to see the affect on cash availability in the year in question. Both are useful because the point of calculating cash flow at all is to see how much cash is actually available as well as where it comes from. Later chapters will discuss the various ways in which cash flow can be used and the requirements for the appropriate levels of cover for those uses. But the first step is to find out what it is.

Dividends are a discretionary item and therefore cash flow is normally calculated before allowing for them. They are paid from cash flow, but are not an expense which reduces it. However, where it is difficult for a company to cut its dividends, particularly on preference shares or when a cut would mean hardship for members of the owning family, many banks calculate "net cash flow", i.e. cash flow minus dividends. Certainly if dividends are an important demand on cash flow, this raises the issue as to whether the dividend should be paid. Equally, if companies feel obliged to pay a dividend whether or not it is prudent to do so, some of the advantages of its discretionary nature are lost.

5 Budgets, Forecasts and Projections

Purpose and criteria

Chapter 1 argued the importance of looking to the future to understand a company's ability to service its debts and the weaknesses or risks which could prevent it doing so. For this reason budgets, forecasts and projections, which are the various forms of attempt to foresee the future, are extremely important, whether made by the company or independently by the bankers. They are also, however, by definition, only attempts since nobody can see the future with certainty; their fallibility means that they have to be treated with caution. There is a danger that since budgets and forecasts are normally expressed in figures the banker will allocate to them a precision which must be spurious, since figures only represent an underlying reality which cannot be foreseen precisely. There is an opposite danger that bankers will dismiss forecasts as an irrelevancy, because they can never be guaranteed and can only by chance be completely accurate.

This is a mistake; if a company does not try to foresee where it is going, and if the banker does not participate in this effort, it becomes much harder to tell when the company is going wrong. If the company, and its banker, do not know where it wants to go, they will not know when it is lost.

It may be helpful to distinguish between what is meant by a budget on the one hand, and a projection or forecast on the other. The budget is the detailed one-year target, broken down by division, and also by month or at most quarter. It covers sales, costs, profits and resulting balance sheet structure.

Beyond one year the words "projection" or "forecast" are used interchangeably to indicate a less rigorously tested estimate of the future. In particular they aim to identify difficulties which foresight may help to overcome.

The word budget also has a slightly different meaning,

although it relates back to the basic point. It refers to the time period and the areas which can be accurately foreseen and even controlled over the short term. For instance, the period for which it is possible to make a sales budget varies with the nature of the product, the ordering system and so on. One can budget fairly precisely for a product with a long manufacturing period requiring firm orders before it starts. The orders already received or so far on in negotiation that the company can be confident of obtaining most of them provide a firm basis. On the other hand, for a company selling products to retailers, with orders coming in weekly or monthly, the budget period is very short; a decline in demand will have an almost instantaneous impact on orders which in turn will be passed on to sales. Thus for this type of company any assessment of sales much beyond one month becomes a forecast or projection rather than a budget.

On the other hand fixed costs may be predictable over a long period for both companies. Interest on fixed rate borrowings certainly is; the amount of floating rate debt can be budgeted even if the exact level of interest payable cannot; so can depreciation, property taxes and maintenance costs on fixed assets. Basic labour costs are more or less fixed over the short to medium term, whatever the case in the longer term, although overtime may vary. There may be minimum notice periods, but even if there are not a company is unlikely to dismiss large parts of its labour force on the basis of what may be a temporary hiccough in demand, so that labour costs can be accurately budgeted in most companies for at least three or four months ahead and very often more. This is particularly true where the labour is highly skilled and, if laid off prematurely, might be difficult to replace when demand picked up.

On the other hand there are some variable costs which cannot be confidently budgeted even on a stated volume. For instance, companies for which the more volatile commodities (copper, lead, cocoa, coffee, sugar) represent a significant proportion of costs may not be able to budget for more than a very short period, unless they have fixed price contracts with producers or have hedged in the futures markets. If the commodity is both volatile and important it is sensible to do one of these.

Companies do not prepare a sales budget for one period and

a cost budget for a different period, nor should they. The point of the distinction is to draw attention to the difference between items which management can more or less control over a given time period and items which, while they need a serious effort to forecast them, are nevertheless beyond control either at once, or gradually more so with time. Management must then position itself as favourably as possible to take advantage of the expected and to be hurt as little as possible by the unexpected. Exchange rates, interest rates and the price of major raw materials or of power sources can all affect the prospects of a company's survival, but it can never control them and rarely predict them with confidence. Their importance varies between companies and sensitivity analysis (discussed later in the chapter) may help to identify which items are crucial and which merely marginal.

The assumptions

The value of forecasts or budgets depends on the assumptions used in their preparation. Only when these are realistic do the figures which result from them repay attention. Too often the assumptions are not stated and the analyst cannot be sure that the company has clearly thought through and tested them. For instance, a forecast of 10% growth in sales is of little help unless the expected rate of inflation is known. It could mean anything from quite respectable real growth to a significant decline. The validity of a given sales forecast can depend on whether it assumes a growth, decline or no change in market share; or put another way, what is the assumption about the market? To increase a company's sales by 10% in a market growing at 1% p.a. has very different implications than if the market is growing at 15%. Companies should be able to develop their own assumptions and some will disclose them to their bank; otherwise the bank may be able to develop its own from government statistics, publications of various research institutes, trade associations or even sometimes stockbrokers' reports.

But these are merely ways for an outsider to assess whether the sales budget forecast is prima facie reasonable. The most important point is to know how the company prepares its budgets. Are sales figures developed by making an underlying assumption and then a simple mathematical calculation?

Or are they based on a specific and careful assessment of the sales prospects for each product and from each customer or major group of customers? How committed to the budgets are the people who generate the sales? If the company's business allows it to take orders forward, the budgeting of sales can be that much more rigorous. But even where buying is largely off the shelf the sales force should be getting, and feeding back, information as to the acceptance and competitive standing of the product, its price competitiveness and so on. All of this can then be used to prepare budgets and forecasts, combined with economic and industry information from a company's own economics department and/or external sources.

The banker may have to extrapolate the development of controllable costs from the past and from general background information, particularly when he does not have any breakdown between costs. The company, however, can anticipate the specific effect of the various measures it takes to control or reduce costs. It should therefore assess the costs and the factors that might change them in detail before budgeting the profit margins, and actual profits, at various levels.

Assumptions also need to be made about the balance sheet. For instance, the turnover periods for receivables, inventory and payables will combine with the sales figure to produce specific balance sheet figures for each item. Here again the company should be able to base its budgets on actual experience with customers and on any changes it may be making in its controls or its invoicing or payment procedures. The banker does not usually have this detailed information but should know enough to judge whether the customer has it and is using it well. He can also check for inconsistencies in the company's assumptions. A company may, for instance, assume that it reaches its target of a 60-day receivable turnover when it has never before managed less than 75 days; unless it has introduced specific new procedures to achieve 60 days this is likely to be wishful thinking. As a result receivables will be approximately 25% higher than the budget assumes, which will affect bank borrowings (or cash). This increases the interest cost and reduces earnings, which in turn reduces net worth and makes yet more bank borrowing necessary. If receivables for this company are, say, 30-40% of total assets and particularly if interest rates are high this sort of facile optimism can throw the whole budget out. Furthermore, the pattern of higher borrowings leading to lower earnings which in turn require yet higher borrowings can have a cumulative effect over several years.

Where the company is in several lines of business with different underlying assumptions it can be even harder to judge the quality of the budgets; the figures conceal an average of different assumptions making it difficult for the outsider to tell what assumptions have been made and how realistic they are.

Scepticism not cynicism

So budgets and forecasts need a proper degree of scepticism. Budgets can and normally should be reasonably accurate, although even their inaccuracies will increase over time. Sometimes they will appear accurate because divergences in one direction will offset divergences in others. For instance, higher than predicted sales will initially create higher receivables and therefore higher borrowings and interest costs. An unpredicted drop in interest rates may offset the latter; or higher profit margins resulting from higher than budgeted sales may be wholly or partly offset by higher interest costs; very high profit margins may even, after an interval, reduce borrowings. The speed of receivable turnover will also be a factor here; the slower the receivable turnover the bigger the increase in margins needed to contain borrowings for a given increase in sales, and vice versa.

But to be sceptical of the details of budgets and even more of forecasts is not to doubt their value when carefully prepared. They show the path the company expects to take; they show the likely affects of that path on the balance sheet and profitability of the company and therefore the likely needs for borrowing or ability to repay debts.

They also give a benchmark for judging the quality of the management. This arises in two ways. Carefully prepared budgets, with assumptions tested and results credible in the light of past performance and of what is known about market conditions, competition, inflation rates and so on, provide a prima facie indication that management is on top of its job. Achievement of budgets also makes future budgets and forecasts more credible and further strengthens confidence. While forecasts can rarely be 100% accurate, achievement of the key items adds even more credibility. This applies to more than just financial management. The end product is usually converted into figures by the finance department, which sets some of the more general assumptions to be used, but the primary source of information on sales, costs, competition and market share comes from the marketing, production, purchasing and other management. If their combined input is sloppy then their reaction to developments is likely to be inadequate.

The way management uses budgets once they have been prepared is also an indication of its quality. The budget is a tool for monitoring the company's progress and that of the various units which contribute to it. Proper use of it helps to ensure that individual managers are performing appropriately and that the company itself is still on the right track with no need for major course corrections. Conversely if such a need develops, budgets can help the management to identify both the need, and the specific problem which causes it, early enough to take remedial action.

Conversely, however, a management which never reaches its budgets provides a warning. Its reaction to the failure can also be illuminating. If it merely changes the budget, this may mean the original budget was unrealistic - once; if this happens frequently, so that the budget is constantly being adjusted downwards to meet performance, the main problem is likely to be with top management.

The banker in reviewing budgets cannot expect to have as much detail as the management will have nor does he need it. He is not concerned with the quality of individual units but rather with the quality of the company as a whole; although a poor individual unit can undermine the company this is a management problem and the bank is mainly interested in the evidence that the problem is being successfully handled.

In lending to small companies, or to companies whose credit is suspect, a bank should ideally receive budgets with a monthly breakdown. It should then get monthly or quarterly figures, prepared on the same basis as the budgets, to compare results against expectations. This gives it the chance to discuss problems with, and if necessary put corrective pressure on, the management early rather than late.

Reviewing the company's budget and forecast

Against this background the banker should review budgets and forecasts given to him by the company. First he must assess the realism of the assumptions. The best way of course is to discuss them with the people who prepared the forecasts. However, this is not often possible and may well take more time than the results justify.

There are several ways in which the banker can generate some independent feel as to the soundness of the base or the questions he should ask if he has doubts. A critical review of the figures may suggest that they are simply an extrapolation of past performance, or assume some steady mathematical progress; this may look pretty on paper but be unlikely in the real world.

A harder but often more fruitful approach is to review the figures against the banker's knowledge of previous performance of the company and of the industry, the economic environment, the competitive position and so on. Is the company assuming a sales increase in a declining market? If so, is it realistic to believe that it can increase its market share to that extent? Is it assuming that it will pass on all cost increases in full, or do its selling price increases reflect the competitive position and the likely demand for the product? Are its assumptions about the cost of key raw materials unreasonable? Do they make insufficient allowance for market volatility? Do assumed improvements in working capital management, and therefore borrowing, conflict with the economic climate (i.e. the company may assume a faster collection of receivables, but if money is tight customers will try to conserve cash by paying more slowly; the reverse applies to payables)? Are the assumptions about items out of its control (interest rates, exchange rates, prices of key raw materials) conservative or does its forecast depend on favourable developments which are possible but not probable?

Similarly, are the projections internally consistent? If the company is already producing at close to its physical capacity, a projection which shows a steady real increase in sales with no new capital expenditure clearly lacks something. Similarly, an increase in sales exactly offset by a faster receivables and inventory turnover (so that the balance sheet does not change) requires explanation; how is this better control to be obtained?

Several individually minor inconsistencies can reinforce each other. For instance, a slightly low forecast for interest rates may alone be insignificant; so may a low allowance for capital expenditure (and therefore for borrowing to finance it); or a faster than historical receivable turnover. Combine the three, and their total impact may be surprising.

The banker also needs to check the company's assumptions and the priorities for using the cash flow it expects to generate. In the short run the ability to repay debt or finance other items will be affected by such things as equity issues, new borrowings, sale of fixed assets or investments; in the medium to longer run the main determinant of the company's ability to meet its commitments and maintain a sound balance sheet will be the cash flow and the way it is used. Without a reasonable idea of the company's priorities the banker cannot assess accurately the affect of a short fall in cash flow. Will this mean less capital expenditure, less R & D or smaller dividends? Will it inhibit the company's sales growth by making it too expensive to finance the higher working capital? Or will it reduce ability to meet debts as they come due, perhaps in particular the bank's own debt? This last question can be put another way. Does the company have a balance sheet which is liquid enough to ride out a temporary reduction in cash flow, by use of surplus cash or by additional borrowing, without cutting back on other necessities but also without unduly weakening its structure? Or is there a real danger that it will try to finance expansion or dividends at the risk of overstraining the balance sheet?

The banker, in other words, must not pay so much attention to how the forecasts have been prepared that he overlooks what they show. He hopes to see continuing sound profitability, ample liquidity, net worth growing in line with the growth of sales and assets, a credible capital expansion and R & D programme financed with only a reasonable amount of new debt and so on. To decide whether this hope is reasonable he applies the analytical techniques discussed in the rest of the book to the forecasts (both before and after any adjustments to make them more credible). If he finds that the company is likely to have difficulty servicing its debt, or to weaken significantly from an initially strong position, then clearly he must look into the problem closely.

It is important to look at the company's own forecasts first; if they need some adjustment it is likely that they are too optimistic rather than too pessimistic. Thus, if the company's own forecasts show a deteriorating picture, perhaps with breach of covenants in a loan agreement, the bank is in a strong position to press the company to react to its own warning. Where the company's forecasts show a sound position but the bank feels that they are too optimistic its position is less favourable. It should certainly discuss the forecasts with the company, explain why it thinks they are too optimistic and the implications it sees if the pessimistic view is correct. Sometimes a company accepts the bank's views and the two can work together to improve the situation. Sometimes the customer will convince the bank that the pessimistic interpretation is wrong, in which case the bank has a better understanding of the customer's business and greater confidence in its forecasts. But the middle position where neither convinces the other is probably the most frequent and certainly the most difficult.

The amount of debt maturing during the forecast period should always be carefully checked. Excessive bunching of maturities may mean that a larger amount is due in a short period than can easily be handled out of cash flow. Even where it is reasonable to expect that the company will be able to refinance from the same lender or another, severe bunching is dangerous. If the borrower's credit should deteriorate and make lenders reluctant to renew, the bunching will make this problem more serious; in addition, market conditions can be temporarily unfavourable, so that the borrower is either unable to refinance at all, or can only do so on very unfavourable terms, for reasons that do not directly reflect on its credit.

A second danger is that the maturing debt may be fixed rate debt at a level well below the current rates of interest. Thus even a straightforward refinancing may involve a large jump in interest costs which could weaken the interest cover and cash flow. If this coincided with a weakening in the company's operating profits for other reasons it could be particularly damaging.

Preparing the bank's forecasts

There are not many customers who freely provide their banks with forecasts and in most countries (except the United States) banks rarely insist on seeing them before lending. Reluctance to discuss forecasts arises from one or more of three reasons. First, the company may not have prepared them or may have little confidence in what it has prepared. Secondly it may have prepared them and feel that they show such a weak picture that it does not want the bank to see it; thirdly and most commonly companies hold a misguided view that forecasts are none of the bank's business.

The third reason is merely wrongheaded, but the first two are positively dangerous to the bank, a deterrent to lending, and a hindrance in deciding whether to be concerned about money already lent. Therefore some banks now produce their own forecasts, usually using computers to handle their purely mathematical side. This aspect does not need to be discussed in this book, except to point out that it is just that, mathematical. The figures that come out of the computer depend entirely on the figures that go into it, and on the assumptions which tell the computer what calculations to apply to them. If the original figures are wrong or if the assumptions are unrealistic, the forecasts will be useless. "Garbage in, garbage out" applies here as much as anywhere else.

The bank, then, has to make reasonable assumptions with little help from the customer. It does not have access to the order book or to the detailed information from the salesmen and marketing department which the company should have in preparing its own forecasts. On the other hand, the bank probably has an economics department, a financial analysis or investment research department which will provide macroeconomic or industry forecasts into which to fit the company's prospects. The analyst should also have some feel as to the company's competitive position, whether it is increasing market share, holding steady or losing; whether the reasons for the trend are likely to continue or there are factors which might reverse them. He then allows for the general rate of inflation in the country concerned (and in any relevant export markets) and for the trend of price increases in the product. All of this allows him to generate a forecast for changes in sales; perhaps a relatively straight line, or perhaps accelerating growth, a cyclical pattern or even a decline. This is a fairly simple procedure for a company with one major product or group of products; it is more complicated where the company is active in a number of products with different inflation rates, demand elasticities and so on, but the basic principle is the same. From the combination of all these factors, including some intelligent guesses, the analyst produces his assumption for the annual change in sales.

Given a detailed breakdown of costs a similar process can be followed in forecasting each major expense, adjusting for measures such as redundancies or reduction in waste (to mention only two), which the company is implementing but the full effect of which has not yet been felt. Often the bank will lack sufficient knowledge of the detail of costs to forecast the individual items and the analyst may have to make more general assumptions about the relationship of groups of costs to sales. He may, for instance, assume that total cost of goods sold remains the same percentage of sales as the average of the last three or four years; the gross profit will then change in line with the sales figure. Or he may be able to forecast that one cost (labour for instance) will grow faster than cost of goods sold as a whole. Since the starting level of wages is not known he has to estimate it and apply the fast growth rate to this, the slower to the other costs of goods sold. Similarly with selling, general and administrative costs, he may know that the company plans a substantial advertising programme for the main product; the assumptions will allow for this but keep other operating costs growing at the same rate as sales.

The computer program will forecast operating profit before depreciation using these assumptions, with the latest available actual figures as a starting point. There should be sufficient information on rates of depreciation and on the present and anticipated future capital assets to which they apply to make a specific forecast possible. This may be based on detailed depreciation rates for each type of asset, if known, or on an extrapolation of past depreciation as a percentage of gross fixed assets. Occasionally the reported depreciation figure is unrealistic, perhaps being used to smoothe an erratic profit figure; the analyst may then use his own estimate of a reasonable figure.

The computer program will provide a figure for operating profit after depreciation. The analyst can usually make his own specific forecasts of each cost more easily from here on - or at least provide the information for the computer. The most important one is usually interest, the forecast of which includes three components. Interest on fixed rate borrowing can be budgeted to continue at the same rate until maturity. Existing floating rate borrowing can be forecast to continue to float at the same margin over the same market rate (prime, LIBOR, base rate or whatever) but the computer program needs assumptions as to the level of the market rate. Or it may be reasonable to assume that the borrower will adjust his borrowings to give him the most favourable combined cost and an average interest rate can be assigned. The final factor is any changes in borrowing; the computer program will work these out from the various combinations of cash flow, net working investment, capital expenditure and so on which the various assumptions will create. Unless some of this borrowing is on a subsidised fixed rate basis, or unless there is a fixed rate market open at levels different from current floating rates, the analyst can assume a single interest rate for all new borrowing. The simplest assumption where the computer program forecasts lower borrowing is that specific maturities will be paid when due, otherwise short-term fluctuating interest rate facilities will be reduced first. Given these assumptions the computer program will then work out the interest cost.

If the borrower has large cash balances or any other source of financial income, earnings on them will depend on the rates of interest. The program should also be told whether to assume liquidation of some or all of the investments before an increase in borrowing.

With other income such as royalties, intelligent assumptions are better where possible. However, unless they are unusually large a simple extrapolation is acceptable.

The program produces a pre-tax profit figure, but then needs an assumption as to taxes to enable it to produce a figure after tax. Past history, and knowledge of the local tax laws in relation to the company's investment plans, growth in inventory and so on should enable the analyst to make a reasonable estimate of tax as a percentage of pre-tax profit.

Some assumptions may be needed about extraordinary items,

although if they are truly extraordinary they should be unforecastable. In practice, the bank will often know of plans to sell a factory or a subsidiary which is expected to produce a capital gain or loss. Or that the company expects to lay off people or close some plants, which will involve redundancy and closure costs which may be treated as extraordinary. Specific information should be included in the forecasts even if the figure is only approximate.

Finally there is the question of foreign exchange exposure. Whether to forecast this is a difficult decision which depends on the currencies concerned. A Spanish company accounting in pesetas but importing or exporting in deutschmarks is likely to show fairly consistent exchange profits or losses unless it has taken out forward cover, in which case the cost can be easily budgeted. Forecasting changes between two currencies of comparable strength is much harder. Unless the analyst knows the company's practice regarding forward cover or other forms of hedging, it may be safer to assume a fairly consistent loss from this source. If this is too pessimistic the company will be doing better than the bank expects; forecasting a loss at least highlights the risk.

Finally, the analyst needs to forecast a dividend which should match what is known of the company's policy. However, it may be necessary to make an assumption as to the percentage of net profit after tax, perhaps with a proviso that the dividend will only be reduced if the company makes a loss or if profits fall by more than a certain percentage, such as 50%. This allows for the reluctance of management to cut dividends even when in financial terms it is clearly right to do so.

In making the assumptions for the balance sheet there are relatively few items which can fluctuate substantially except as a result of other items in the forecast. Cash will be kept at a minimum if the company is borrowing short-term; otherwise, it becomes a residual item adjusting to the net effect of its various sources and uses. Receivables and inventory relate to sales through the turnover rate, about which an assumption must be made. The program will then produce the actual figure. If there are sizeable intercompany receivables their turnover must be assessed in the light of corporate policy. Other current assets are, or should usually be, small and can be assumed to be constant;

if there is a large item, then the assumption must fit the particular circumstance.

Payables can also be calculated on a turnover rate. The dividend and tax can be assumed fairly easily from what is known of dividend and tax policy. Advance payments, if any, must also be assessed; perhaps they will relate to sales or inventory, but if the order book can be forecast advances probably relate better to that. For many companies borrowings are the only remaining major item, and these have been discussed under interest. For a few, pension reserves or liability reserves may be large and volatile, in which case the assumptions must be considered carefully in the light of the particular facts; more often, they can be simply forecast as stable, or growing slowly.

Finally there is net worth. Normally the only changes to this that would need to be specifically assumed would be any expected equity issue or conversion of debt. Other changes would result from earnings, dividends and forecast extraordinary items not included in earnings.

Sensitivity analysis

A computer greatly widens the variety of sensitivity analyses which can be performed economically. Their purpose is to show how much difference changes in one or more assumptions would make to the forecasts. This helps to focus attention only on items that are genuinely important. Thus if the bank feels, for instance, that the company's projections of receivable turnover are too optimistic, it feeds modified assumptions into the program to see whether the result is significant; if so, it may be useful to point out the danger of an error to the company.

Where the bank makes its own forecasts and is not wholly confident about some of its assumptions, sensitivity testing can be very useful. In fact the bank may produce two or even three cases. The base case uses the assumptions which the bank thinks most likely, but an optimistic and a pessimistic case allow for errors in either direction.

It is sometimes useful to test a single assumption or combination of assumptions when one factor is unusually volatile. Thus a slowdown in receivable turnover or a high level of capital expenditure may be acceptable at forecast interest rates of 10% but look very different if rates rise to, say, 15%. Similarly, a given level of physical inventory may have a very different impact if the price of the main raw material increases sharply; doubly so if interest rates do likewise. And exchange rate assumptions can make a big difference to companies with large foreign currency borrowings unmatched by assets. A bank can usefully draw attention to the need to guard against this type of vulnerability.

In practice, even with a computer, the benefits of running numerous alternative sets of assumptions will rarely justify the effort. However, where the bank has doubts about the quality of the credit, this is an extremely valuable tool which should not be overlooked. Of course the point which was made about forecasts in general, that the computer's results are purely mathematical, applies equally to sensitivity analysis. This does not damage their value provided they are looked at with proper scepticism, because sensitivity analysis quantifies the result of changing the assumptions, it draws no conclusions as to which are more likely.

Sensitivity analysis can also be used to test the effect of possible actions by management. A pessimistic forecast, for instance, may assume that management continues to invest heavily and pay dividends even when sales and profits are slumping. This is often as unrealistic as management's assumption that there will be no slump. On the other hand, cancelling investments, closing down plants and laying off people may be a correct long-term response but can have significant short-term costs. A sensitivity analysis, therefore, which assesses the impact of a (perhaps belated) change in management attitudes, and the actions which might result from that change, can be helpful in selected cases.

Part II
The Building Blocks

6 Some Concepts

Some concepts are used in financial analysis, and in discussing balance sheets, profitability and so on, as a shorthand for particular combinations of factors. They can be considered as building blocks because they summarise the quality of several lesser aspects; in turn the analysis of the whole has to balance the quality of the various subsectors or concepts. It is necessary to understand the meaning of each individual item before combining them to understand the implications for the whole; it is equally necessary to understand the various building blocks.

Liquidity

Liquidity is the ability to meet current liabilities as they fall due, with a margin of safety to allow for unexpected fluctuations. These may arise because cash is not received when expected or because liabilities become more pressing than anticipated. Liquidity must be judged not only in terms of balance sheet liabilities but also of commitments, for capital expenditure for instance, which only appear on the balance sheet after a payment has been made but failure to meet which can lead directly to liquidation. Particularly if sales are growing fast, there should also be a margin to permit a growth in net working investment (see below) without significantly impairing ability to meet current liabilities.

The components of liquidity (or lack of it) are, first, the quality and nature of the current assets; secondly the size and due date of the current liabilities; thirdly the size and due date of any off balance sheet commitments; fourthly the adequacy or otherwise of cash flow to generate additional liquidity; and fifthly, sources of liquidity from special factors independent of operations.

The quality of current assets depends on three main factors. The first is the amount of unencumbered cash on the balance sheet. Clearly the more cash, the less the likelihood that the company will be even temporarily unable to pay its debts.

The second is the size and quality of receivables. As the item which turns most quickly into cash, this is the crucial item where the unencumbered cash balance is small. As outlined in Chapter 2 the speed of collection of receivables, a main indication of quality, varies with the nature of the business. Other indications can be obtained from whatever information is available on the quality of the underlying debtors and on whatever is known about bad debt experience. Occasionally a company may have export insurance for part or all of its receivables which will add to their quality. In brief, a fast-moving, high-quality receivable portfolio which is a relatively large portion of current assets is a useful contribution to liquidity.

The third main item is inventory and here again the considerations set out in Chapter 2 decide the quality of inventory. The main point is how fast it converts into receivables and receivables into cash. The two periods put together are sometimes known as the cash conversion period and the shorter this is the better the quality of the liquidity, for given amounts. Although other current assets sometimes affect liquidity, they are rarely significant.

The most important single liability is usually trade payables. A low figure turning over rapidly is a sign of liquidity because it means that the company is able to pay its suppliers promptly from its existing resources; because payables then represent a small claim on the proceeds of current assets; and because, in a pinch, the company could temporarily slow down payment to its suppliers and use the cash elsewhere without causing problems. (Trade payables are also discussed under net working investment.) Too large and slow-moving a trade payable item is a warning sign for the opposite reasons. At worst it may cause suppliers to become impatient and demand payment more quickly, creating a severe drain on what is probably already inadequate liquidity, or refuse to supply.

After trade payables the most important item is current bank debt, whether in the form of overdrafts, short-term advances, bills discounted, acceptances or something else. It will normally be renewed as necessary, and can be treated as self-renewing, providing it either substitutes for trade payables or is reasonable in relation to the size of the working capital requirement and its fluctuations. If nominally short-term debt becomes more than can be justified on this basis, liquidity is reduced quite seriously, since the bank's right to demand payment becomes much more likely to be exercised and damaging if it is.

The current portion of long-term debt has a different implication, since it is a payment which specifically has to be met during the year; if it is substantial, the exact timing is important since the company must build up cash availability to meet it. It may, of course, be paid from unused short-term borrowing facilities, but if this is more than a temporary source it reduces liquidity.

Other items with specific payment dates and not easily rolled over are current taxes and dividends. Advances, when they appear, are more like trade payables; as the company uses one advance to fulfil the contract which generated it, it signs new contracts and receives new advances. However, for a company dependent on advances a decline in orders has an adverse effect on liquidity, since it gets less new advances. Companies not so dependent might initially improve liquidity as orders dropped; receivables would be collected and used to meet payables while lower purchases would be generating less new payables.

In addition to rapid turnover of assets, a high cash flow is a source of liquidity which can be used to meet liabilities as they come due. A high cash flow usually indicates high profit margins and means, among other things, that the element of surplus cash in receivables is substantial. "Surplus cash" in this context is non-cash costs (such as depreciation) included in the sales price, plus the element of profit; put another way, it is the cash available for other purposes after the company has paid for the inventory and the cost of processing and marketing it. If sales are growing fast, or if costs of raw materials are rising faster than selling prices, this surplus may be needed to finance new sales and new receivables. Otherwise it can be used to pay maturing debt, meet dividends, finance part of capital expenditure and so on.

In addition to actual bank borrowing, unused short-term facilities or revolving medium-term facilities provide a source of liquidity; although if they are allocated to other specific purposes this may be very temporary.

A review of the individual items leads to a conclusion as to whether on balance the whole provides sufficient liquidity, with little possibility of the company failing to meet its obligations and sufficient surplus for unexpected fluctuations. There must be a reserve to protect against such things as a slowdown in inventory or receivable turnover, failure of a major customer, pressure from a major supplier to speed up payable turnover, a switch from outright sales into leasing, to mention only a few possible demands on liquidity.

With a seasonal or cyclical company, the precise stage of the cycle is important. A toy company just before Christmas will normally show short-term debt financing high receivables and inventory which, based on annual sales, are apparently turning over slowly. However, a few months later when the toys have been sold and the receivables collected, debt will be much reduced and liquidity will look much better. If, however, the company shows the same picture in March or April as in November/December, it will be alarming.

This type of seasonal or cyclical release of liquidity results from operations, although not from cash flow. Non-operating sources include such things as proceeds from sale of surplus fixed assets or of an interest in a subsidiary or proceeds of an equity or long-term debt issue. These are not regular items, but when the analyst knows of a definite inflow of this nature, he can adjust his view of liquidity accordingly.

Working capital or net current assets

Working capital is a narrower concept than liquidity; it is the difference between current assets and current liabilities. It can be expressed as a ratio (current assets ÷ current liabilities), and referred to as the current ratio (see Chapter 7). It is often used as a proxy for liquidity, but is in fact only one component of it. It measures the extent to which current assets are financed by current liabilities (bad for liquidity) or by long-term finance including net worth (provides liquidity).

A change in working capital in the same company at different times suggests a change in liquidity, but gives no indication whether there has been any movement in assets which might counteract or aggravate its effect. And the working capital figure says nothing about the quality of the current assets, the nature of the current liabilities or the other factors influencing liquidity so that a comparison of working capital in two different companies is of little value unless it sums up other factors pointing in the same direction. If the figures apply to wholly different companies (a supermarket chain compared to a heavy machinery manufacturer, for instance) a company with nil working capital may be more liquid than one with £5 million of working capital and a current ratio of 2-1. Thus working capital is very much a starting point in analysing liquidity; strictly it only tells about how current assets are being financed.

In the old days many bankers used a rule of thumb which, in the United States, said that current assets should be twice current liabilities. In other countries where the overdraft system was used this ratio might be different, but in any case modern practice recognises that working capital alone tells us too little to be a reliable indicator of liquidity.

Nevertheless, in stable situations working capital (or the ratio) provides a reasonable proxy for many of the factors involved in liquidity. Comparison of it in the same company at different times or similar companies at the same time has some value, but can be dangerous if the weaknesses are ignored. Thus, the tendency to treat it too easily as synonymous with liquidity, while wrong, is not often critical.

Net working investment

The amount needed to finance those assets (mainly receivables and inventory) which are generated by, and responsive to, the volume of business, minus the finance provided by liabilities which arise directly from the creation of the asset or are connected to it, is known as net working investment (NWI). There are two types of financing requirement a company must meet. The first is for everything needed to get it ready to operate (fixed assets, R & D and so on). The other is the requirement to take it from that stage to actually producing and selling. The latter is partly self-financed, but the portion which is not is NWI.

In many companies, the calculation of NWI is simply

receivables plus inventory minus trade payables. However, the definition can be both more detailed and more flexible than that. For instance, receivables may include unusual terms that do not relate to volume of business; this is particularly true of intercompany receivables, which may represent loans rather than trade items, or may be a means by which a company transfers interest cost to a low borrowing country, or profits to a low tax country, or hedges against currency risk. Much the same is true in reverse of intercompany payables. In all of these cases, finance is needed or provided for reasons that do not arise from the volume of business.

Some bankers argue that short-term bank debt is part of the NWI calculation. There is a case for including short-term debt which directly finances sales volume (perhaps particularly for including bills discounted) or which enables the borrower to obtain discounts on his trade payables; otherwise, however, bank debt is merely one way of financing NWI and unlike the main liabilities (payables and advances) used in the NWI calculation carries an interest cost.

Advances from customers clearly should be deducted because they arise from the nature of the business and will vary with the volume of orders taken. Similarly, unpaid sales taxes and VAT should figure in the calculation but income taxes should not, although the figures provided do not always permit this distinction. There are other items which are arguable, or which depend on the nature of the company, but most of them appear infrequently. The important point is the concept; does the item add to, or reduce, the amount of finance required for a given volume of business, past, present or anticipated? Does the requirement change with changes in volume (whether before, after or simultaneously)? If the answer is yes, it affects NWI.

NWI in a typical company results from the combined turnover of receivables, inventory and payables. The company which collects its receivables and turns its inventory over fast needs less financing; a company which pays its trade payables fast obtains less financing from that source. And vice versa in both cases. Similarly a company which receives large advance payments reduces its need for outside finance to carry the inventory while it is completing the contract. The net result is that a low NWI is usually an indicator of good liquidity or a lower need for liquidity (little need for extra finance to meet higher volume) and high NWI the reverse.

Where NWI is, as in many companies, a stable or increasing figure it needs permanent or long-term finance. Thus a high NWI indicates a high need for finance, and should normally be matched by a high working capital figure, to indicate that the finance has been provided on a long-term basis, i.e. in a way which does not reduce liquidity. Conversely a company with a low NWI can usually afford a low working capital, since the amount of current assets which need to be financed is small. It is usually although not always true that a low NWI indicates fast-moving, good-quality assets while a high one indicates slower movement, though not necessarily lower quality.

The difference between NWI and working capital therefore is that NWI indicates a need, or otherwise, for permanent finance; working capital indicates how that need has been met. A high NWI matched by a high working capital indicates that the need has been met by longer-term finance; a low NWI suggests little need for longer-term finance for this purpose and can safely be matched by a low working capital. However, a high NWI combined with a low working capital suggests that the need is being met by short-term finance instead of long and this may pose a threat to liquidity.

A company normally has a fairly stable NWI in relation to sales. Receivables change after sales have been generated, inventories and payables before, so that there may be some lags in NWI if there is a sudden change in the growth rate of sales. Nevertheless in general terms net working investment is a sound indicator of the likely change in finance required to carry a change in sales. As such it is a useful forecasting tool for changes in borrowing, interest costs and profits. It may make forecasting and analysis easier to think of it as a percentage of sales rather than a flat amount.

However, although normally stable, the relationship of NWI (or one or more of its components) to sales can change either as a result of management action or inaction, or because of a change in industry conditions. Sometimes changes in conditions can reinforce each other; in periods of tight money, receivables tend to turn over more slowly, but suppliers press for more rapid payment. This change in turn can affect borrowing, interest and profits; a sensitivity analysis can be a valuable predictive tool as to the impact of assumed changes either on a company's present financial condition and profitability or on its ability to finance an increased volume of sales (see examples at end of chapter).

To sum up, although both working capital and net working investment are often looked at as proxies for liquidity, this is probably the wrong approach. It is more accurate to say that NWI indicates the need for permanent finance to avoid illiquidity, working capital the extent to which it has been provided.

Leverage or gearing

Leverage (or gearing in English terminology) measures the extent to which the assets are financed with various forms of liability or net worth, i.e. the relationship between the shareholders' funds and those of outside creditors. Shareholders' funds require no mandatory servicing and they do not have to be repaid, so that the higher their proportion in any given balance sheet the lower the risk.

Leverage is normally measured in one of two ways. It can relate either borrowed money or total liabilities to net worth. Sometimes, however, the relationship is expressed differently. For instance, some British companies look at the share of debt in total capitalisation and express it as a percentage (see Chapter 8).

Although some bankers will argue quite strongly about whether total liabilities or total borrowed funds is the better measure of leverage, they usually give broadly comparable readings in which case it does not matter much which is used. Where the gap between them is unusually large or the readings diverge, however, it is important to look at both to assess why the difference arises, particularly where either trend is adverse. Without this dual assessment there is a danger that, for example, an apparently favourable trend in borrowed funds may mask the use of non-borrowed funds as a cosmetic substitute for borrowing. Even where this is not true, an increase in total liabilities eventually becomes dangerous, whatever their nature.

The main differences between borrowed funds and other forms of liabilities are that borrowings carry an interest cost which must be met and they must be repaid either at a fixed date or on short notice. However, even borrowed funds vary in nature in ways which affect the total amount which is acceptable. For instance both floating rate debt, with its risk that interest will escalate sharply, and short-term debt which may be called at the worst moment, tend to reduce the maximum amount of total borrowing that is sound. Long-term and/or fixed rate debt, other things being equal, permit higher leverage, subject to there being no adverse factors such as a bunching of maturities in the next two or three years; particularly important if the maturing debt is at a fixed interest rate lower than currently available. All of these points affect the real leverage of the company but may leave the mathematical shorthand unchanged.

Most non-borrowed liabilities have to be paid at some time, but they do not all represent the same strain on cash flow and therefore the same danger if cash flow should prove inadequate. Trade payables, as discussed earlier, are normally self-renewing or almost self-liquidating if volume declines, since receivables and inventory also decline, releasing cash. Various other items have been discussed in Chapters 2 and 3 and the probable timing of their payment affects the extent to which total liabilities represent a less burdensome form of leverage than total borrowed funds.

An acceptable level of leverage on either definition depends on a wide range of factors discussed in Chapter 11. Broadly speaking, however, it relates back to the company's need for protection against various risks, particularly fluctuations in earnings, which inhibit its ability to service debt. The greater the combination of these risks, the greater the need for equity to protect against them and the lower the leverage the company can support.

Although leverage is usually thought of as affecting only the balance sheet, some aspects also affect operations and are sometimes referred to as "operating leverage". For instance, two companies might have a similar balance sheet structure, and each have debt of £10 million, on which they pay 10% interest. But if one has sales of £10 million, the other £20 million, the first must earn 10% of sales to cover interest, the second 5%; the impact is even greater if the company needs to cover interest three or four times. From another point of view, operating leverage relates the asset side of the balance sheet, and costs arising from it, to sales. For instance, two companies might each have £10 million of fixed assets, with similar depreciation, property taxes, maintenance costs and so on; here again the impact of these fixed costs is much greater on the company with smaller sales than with larger; if the larger sales carry a comparable level of NWI to the smaller, they must therefore be turning over faster. The smaller sales therefore imply higher "operating leverage".

Interest cover

Interest cover relates earnings before interest and taxes but after all other normal expenses to the actual charge for interest in the period. It identifies the extent of capacity to pay interest and still have profits available to meet other requirements. It can also be looked at as a measure of the suitability of the financial structure in relation to profitability. If operating profit is low, interest-bearing debt should also be low; otherwise interest will erode profits below the safety margin and perhaps cause a loss.

Interest cover should normally be more than marginal. If interest is just barely covered, the company is making no profit, after servicing interest, with which to meet principal, build up net worth, increase the safety margin and the ability to service extra debt needed for expansion. If interest is covered several times (and a minimum of four or five times is desirable although many sound companies do less) the company is earning a return on its assets substantially larger than the mandatory financing costs and has a correspondingly greater freedom of choice as to how to dispose of its earnings.

The minimum acceptable interest cover is affected by the actual interest paid and by its makeup. If most of the debt is long-term fixed rate, then the margin can be smaller since the chance of a sharp upward fluctuation is limited, at least unless substantial new borrowing is expected. Even then if the new borrowing is expected to generate new earnings, any decline in interest cover should be temporary. With a large portion of floating rate debt the risk of a sharp upturn in rates increases the need for interest cover, particularly in a period of high or volatile inflation, or in a currency which is inherently weak; interest rates may be raised internationally as well as for purely domestic reasons. The danger of a low interest cover is greatest when rates seem low and more likely to go up than down. The lower they are the greater the risk in percentage terms, since a 5% movement in interest rates over six months has become almost common; a move from rates of 5% to 10% doubles the need for cover, while from 15 to 20% is only an increase of a third. The impact on interest cover is more dramatic the lower the starting cover; if interest is covered 1.5 times, an increase from 5 to 10% in rates pushes cover down to 0.75 and the company is losing money. If it was covered three times, the increase still leaves it covered 1.5 times, which may be manageable.

Finally, interest cover must be related to expected trends in borrowings. If a sharp increase is expected, a previously inadequate interest cover is very serious, although it may be partly offset if the borrowing finances constructive developments expected to generate substantial new earnings quickly; if the borrowing is to cover a loss or some special cost such as redundancy payments or factory closure which generates no new earnings (although it may in the long run save costs) the need for a high starting cover is that much greater. Conversely a low interest cover may be acceptable if it results from a temporary peak in borrowing with the source of a major reduction clearly known.

Cash flow

Although interest cover tells about the profits of the company in relation to a particular aspect of its capital structure, this information is of negative rather than positive value. A company which cannot cover its interest is in trouble; but one which covers its interest several times over may still have inadequate cash for other purposes. In particular, since interest is a pre-tax charge, interest cover says nothing about profit after tax.

A better tool for this purpose is the coverage by cash flow (as defined in Chapter 4) of various requirements. The two that are most commonly used analytically, and even occasionally in loan agreements, are cash flow to total liabilities (CF/TL) and cash flow to total borrowed funds (CF/TBF). Neither total liabilities nor total borrowings would normally be paid in a single year but it is important to know what contribution cash flow could make. Sometimes the phrase used is operating cash flow (OCF) to make it clear that it excludes extraordinary and other non-operating items.

The minimum safe coverage of total liabilities varies with the nature of the business and with national practices, both of which affect the proportion of total liabilities which are normally repaid from cash flow. Thus two otherwise similar companies, one in Germany and one in Italy, almost certainly have very different receivable and payable turnovers, both faster in Germany than in Italy. Higher payables may finance roughly the same proportion of higher receivables, so that net working investment in both companies is broadly comparable. However, payables will still represent a larger liability and reported cash flow cover in Italy will be lower although the true claim on cash flow will be about the same. Liabilities such as advances or pension reserves, as discussed in Chapter 3 and subject to the provisos in that chapter, are not always expected to be repaid from cash flow at all in some cases or for many years in others.

Nevertheless, after full allowance has been made for these factors there is a level below which cash flow should not fall in relation to total liabilities; a company must always retain the ability to apply some cash flow to liabilities in case of sudden change. Studies some years ago in the United States suggested that, for a normal manufacturing company with no special features, cash flow consistently below 15% of total liabilities was a bankruptcy warning. In other countries and for other types of business a ratio as low as 10% may be acceptable. The word consistently is also important. Most companies can afford one or even two years of cash flow below the sustainable minimum as long as the figure was at, and is expected to recover to, a healthy level.

Cash flow cover of total borrowed funds (TBF) will be higher because they are only a part of total liabilities. The level of coverage is also more important because a higher proportion, in some cases all, of TBF is expected to be repaid from cash flow. Cases where a large part of borrowing is paid from other sources must be identified, however; for instance the comments which were made in previous sections about figures prepared when seasonal borrowings are at a peak apply equally to cash flow cover. There are also many companies which use short-term debt to obtain larger trade discounts than the interest costs of the borrowing. This short-term debt is renewable in much the same ways as trade payables or at a pinch can be paid by lengthening payable turnover rather than making a demand on cash flow.

Not all nominally short-term debt can be treated as making no demands on cash flow, however; some companies borrow on a technically short-term but in practice continuing basis because their capital base is not high enough to finance their current assets, or sometimes because medium-term debt which might be more appropriate to their needs is not readily available. So that for this purpose, as for others, the analyst should distinguish between debt which is genuinely short-term and that which is short-term in form only.

Nevertheless, it is often useful to look at the coverage of medium-term debt separately since this always must either be paid from cash flow or be refinanced as it matures from sources which in turn require cash flow coverage. The level of coverage which is acceptable even then depends on the nature of the debt. Modest and wellspread maturities justify somewhat lower cover than if all the debt matures in a matter of two or three years or if the amortisation pattern is very uneven, with large requirements one or two years in the near future.

However, although a high coverage of TBF indicates that the debt could be paid down quite rapidly there are usually other demands on cash flow as well. The analyst should assess at least two other needs, for NWI and capital expenditure. NWI is predictable from forecasts of sales growth and of receivable, inventory and payable turnover. Increases in sales will require higher borrowing which will eventually distort both liquidity and leverage, unless enough of the NWI increase is financed from cash flow. Conversely, if there is a reasonable expectation that net working investment will decline then the analyst can be slightly more relaxed about coverage of other items; only slightly, however, because a continuing reduction is only possible if sales weaken.

The analyst can usually review capital expenditure over the last few years. In theory, if the company is relatively stable this capital expenditure need be no larger than depreciation. However, inflation and the fact that few companies value, and therefore depreciate, their fixed assets on a replacement basis means that a company which consistently spends no more than its depreciation rarely maintains the quality of its fixed assets. And of course a growing company will need to expand its fixed assets anyway.

There are two types of capital expenditure for the purpose of this discussion. One is the expenditure on relatively small individual items which can therefore be spread fairly evenly. For instance a company that has a hundred machine tools may in the normal course of events replace ten of them each year and can choose to reduce this to five or increase it to fifteen in a particular year with no major repercussions. Here it may be possible to finance all or most of the expenditure from cash flow directly.

Some types of capital expenditure, however, come in very large lumps. For instance, to build and equip a new factory which will add 50% to its capacity a company will concentrate expenditure in a period of perhaps two years but will eliminate the need for further such expansion for perhaps as much as five years thereafter; however, it may then have to replace fifteen machine tools a year instead of ten. In such a case, the expenditure is likely to be largely financed by debt initially. The analysis of cash flow therefore falls into two parts; will the present level suffice during the construction period, and will the extra cash flow generated by the expansion cover its debt service thereafter? Whatever the pattern of capital expenditure, cash flow must at least provide reasonable coverage of the debt or equity raised to finance it over the life of the assets concerned.

As well as looking at the coverage of liabilities, changes in NWI and capital expenditure individually, the analyst should consider them together. Cash flow must cover not only existing debts but the expected increase; a capital expansion programme which generates rapid growth in sales will be a disaster if cash flow cannot service the consequent increase in NWI.

Finally there is the question of dividends. Normally cash flow is looked at as money available and dividends as a use. In the legal sense this is undoubtedly correct; dividends are payable at the option of the board and in any case only out of earnings after tax (including retained earnings from previous years). In practice, however, many boards regard the dividend as almost sacrosanct; they will only reduce it, let alone eliminate it altogether, under enormous pressure. In dealing with such a company the analyst should probably look at net cash flow (i.e. after deduction of dividend payments) in relation to all the above items, as well as gross cash flow. If management will not cut the dividend early, the dividends it pays while pressure builds up may undermine the company's balance sheet.

Earnings returns

The concept of a return is that the use of resources or the creation of liabilities should be justified by a reward as great or greater than could be obtained by alternative uses. In the analytical sense the size of various types of return are used to measure how well the company uses its assets, its ability to service liabilities, or to give shareholders a profit which increases their likely interest in future investment.

Depending on the purpose for which the particular return is used it will be calculated in different ways. (Full details are given in Chapter 8, Ratio Analysis; only an outline description is given here.)

The most commonly used is return on assets (ROA), which measures earnings generated by the assets under management. It is a measure of the efficiency of the present use of the assets to allow comparison with alternative uses; it should not therefore be distorted by differences in the ways in which assets are financed, so that the return will be earned before financing costs or tax. Occasionally analysts calculate an operating return on assets (OROA) which involves eliminating financial income and purely financial assets. This can be a useful check on whether operating weaknesses are being covered up by financial income which relates to past successes, is temporary or unreliable in nature, or is in some way incidental to the main operations.

Return on liabilities (ROL) measures the appropriateness of financial structure as well as operating profitability and efficiency. The earnings figure used is the same as with the return on assets; to deduct interest would eliminate from the earnings one of the most important items to be serviced and would therefore not illustrate the ability to service it. Thus the difference between ROA and ROL will be in inverse relation to leverage; the higher the leverage, the more nearly equal assets and liabilities will be and the more similar ROA and ROL, while the lower the leverage, the greater the proportion of assets financed by net worth and the greater the difference. ROL will therefore always be higher than ROA (unless the company has a negative net worth); the question as to how much higher is acceptable will depend partly on the return on assets. If assets generate a high return the company can afford (other things being equal) to service a higher amount of liabilities which means a lower net worth and higher leverage. Thus a high ROA allows a greater gap between it and ROL before the latter becomes inadequate. Conversely, if the return on assets is low so is ability to service liabilities, which argues for higher net worth and lower leverage.

English analysts often use return on capital employed (ROCE). Capital employed is roughly equivalent to total borrowed funds plus net worth and is similar to the American concept of return on investment (ROI), though detailed definitions differ. Again the profit used is normally before interest and tax to show the return on funds supplied by outsiders before adjustments for factors which do not arise in the normal course of business.

For most analysts, therefore, a return on borrowed funds (ROBF) will probably be easier to calculate and more familiar. This again is before interest charges, to show whether the company earns enough to justify the cost of borrowing. Unless the return on the present level of borrowings is well above current interest rates, the company cannot afford any new borrowings and should consider ways of reducing borrowings (or increasing earnings).

Finally the return on net worth or equity (ROE) is calculated after all direct financing charges although before dividends. Earnings after tax are commonly used but earnings before tax may be more useful if the tax is distorted by factors out of management's control or when comparing companies with different tax structures. In most cases, however, earnings after tax tell most accurately what is available for the shareholders. Apart from dividends, shareholders benefit from retained earnings which improve the book value of the shares, increase the amount of investment on which future returns can be earned and, in a growing and profitable company, allow further borrowing on which again any return over the interest cost is for the benefit of the shareholders.

The bank is not directly interested in the shareholders' benefit, but is interested in borrowers' access to new capital which a high ROE improves. In addition, a high ROE provides the potential for more retained earnings to supplement net worth. Thus a high ROE at one and the same time improves the balance sheet structure, reduces the dependence on outside capital and makes its availability more reliable.

Each banker/analyst has one or two favourite forms of return. In addition, since they are designed to measure different things, some forms of return are more useful in some situations, some in others. It is rarely necessary to use all the forms of return discussed in analysing one credit. It is necessary to know about them, however, both to choose the right one, and to recognise their significance when others use them.

Example 1

a. The impact of changes in NWI, as a percentage of sales, on leverage and profit requirements.

The Base Case shows a reasonable balance sheet, and certain key ratios and requirements arising from it. Cases 1 and 2 change the balance sheet only by increasing the NWI and financing the increase with short-term bank debt. The Base Case and Case 1 assume a 10% interest rate on both long- and short-term debt; Case 2 leaves long-term rates at 10% but applies a 15% rate to short-term debt.

Balance sheet structure (all items shown as percentage of starting sales) initially is shown in Table 6.1.

b. The impact of growth in sales with unchanged turnover rates. The starting balance sheet is as in the Base Case above. Years 2 and 2a show the sales growth on different assumptions about earnings. In both years sales are assumed to double; in Year 2 they are assumed to generate net profit of 5, which is added to net worth; in Year 2a net profit is 15. In both years depreciation is exactly equal to capital expenditure. No dividends are paid and the increase in NWI in excess of retained earnings is financed by current bank debt at a rate of 10%. All balance sheet figures are shown as a percentage of Year 1's sales (see Table 6.2).

Table 6.1 Starting balance sheet

	Base Case	Case 1	Case 2
Receivables	25	30	35
Inventory	30	35	40
Less Trade payables	20	20	20
NWI	35	45	55
Current bank debt	10	20	30
Dividends	5	5	5
Working capital	20	20	20
Fixed assets	50	50	50
LT debt	25	25	25
Net worth	45	45	45
TL/NW	1.33	1.56	1.78
TBF/NW	0.78	1.00	1.22
TBF % sales	35	45	55
Interest % sales	3.5	4.5	7.0
Operating margin needed for interest cover of 4 times	14	18	28
Current ratio	1.57	1.44	1.25

Table 6.2 Balance sheet structure

	Year 1	Year 2	Year 2a
Receivables	25	50	50
Inventory	30	60	60
Trade payables	20	40	40
NWI	35	70	70
Current bank debt	10	40	30
Dividends	5	5	5
Working capital	20	25	35
Fixed assets	50	50	50
Term debt	25	25	25
Net worth	45	50	60
TL/NW	1.33	2.2	1.47
TBF/NW	0.78	1.3	1.08
TBF % sales	35	33	27.5
Interest % sales	3.5	3.25	2.8
Operating margin for 4 times cover	14	13	11.2
Current ratio	1.57	1.29	1.47

c. Another way of showing the importance of NWI is to look at two companies with sales of $10 million each. The first company has favourable, but reasonable, turnover rates for receivables, inventory and payables (which for simplicity's sake are assumed to be the only components of NWI). The second has unfavourable but still reasonable turnover rates on all three. The difference is assumed to be financed by bank debt at an interest of 10%.

				$
1. Favourable				
	Receivables turnover			
	46 days approx.	= 12½% of sales	=	1,250,000
Plus	Inventory turnover			
	92 days approx.	= 25% of sales	=	2,500,000
Minus	Payable turnover			
	92 days approx.	= 25% of sales	=	2,500,000
NWI			=	1,250,000

Financing cost = $125,000 or 1.25% of sales.
Operating margin required for 4 times cover = 5% of sales.

2. Unfavourable				
	Receivables turnover			
	92 days approx.	= 25% of sales	=	2,500,000
Plus	Inventory turnover			
	146 days approx.	= 40% of sales	=	4,000,000
Minus	Payable turnover			
	46 days approx.	= 12½% of sales	=	1,250,000
NWI			=	5,250,000

Financing cost = $525,000 or 5.25% of sales
Operating margin required for 4 times cover = 21% of sales.

7 Reconciliations

Reconciliations, by a fairly simple arithmetical presentation, enable the analyst to identify which items have caused the specific change in the balance sheet in which he is interested. If the reconciliation is spread over a period of years it also shows whether the causes of change have been fairly consistent or whether there have been differing factors at work.

Reconciliation starts from the basis that the balance sheet must balance and that each item that goes through the profit and loss statement also has an impact on the balance sheet. Thus the analyst can reconcile, in fairly simple form, all relevant items on the balance sheet which cause changes in cash, in working capital or in net worth, or in the source and uses of funds, and allow for the direct impact of the profit and loss statement. However, although the principles behind these reconciliations are quite simple the detailed calculations are sometimes more complex. If the reconciliation does not balance there are two possible reasons. The analyst may have made an error, which can sometimes be desperately difficult to find; or the information provided by the company is in some way either incorrect or incomplete. When dealing with audited figures the latter is unlikely; but in countries where audited accounts are rare, and disclosure poor, it is a real possibility, and a warning of missing information.

A reconciliation looks at changes in everything except the item being reconciled. Therefore, to reconcile cash, look at changes in everything except cash; to reconcile working capital, at changes in everything except current assets and current liabilities. To say, as is sometimes done, that working capital increased or decreased because of a change in receivables is to miss the point. The change in receivables is part of the result; reconciliation seeks the cause, which lies outside working capital.

It is also possible to vary the amount of detail that is

required. For instance in reconciling cash, changes in receivables, inventory or other current assets may be shown separately; or changes in total current assets (except cash) and total current liabilities; or changes in working capital (excluding cash). The net result is the same but the detailed information is different. Similarly, the net change in current liabilities excluding bank borrowing could be shown; since bank borrowing is of particular interest, that change would then be shown on its own.

Before considering a description of each of the four main types of reconciliation (cash, working capital, sources and uses of funds and net worth) the banker should understand the specific value of each.

The reconciliation of cash (or overdraft) is most valuable when liquidity is very tight; the factors which affect cash availability are then crucial to the company's ability to pay its debts. In such a case, a monthly or even weekly reconciliation and projection may be desirable. Over a longer timescale, the reconciliation can cover known specific needs, to judge whether cash availability and/or borrowing facilities will be adequate to meet them, or whether some specific action - such as sale of an asset, issue of equity or arrangement of extra borrowing facilities - is required. A cash reconciliation can also be used to check on the credibility of company budgets.

Working capital reconciliation is more concerned with general liquidity over a longer period when short-term fluctuations in cash are unlikely to be crucial. It shows what have been the main sources of increase in net working capital and therefore of one aspect of liquidity; or what have been the reasons for its decline. This helps to assess the effects of various cross-currents (such as the extent to which heavy capital expenditure is offset by depreciation plus the sale of obsolete fixed assets) on the company's future ability to meet its debts.

A sources and uses of funds provides much the same sort of information as the cash reconciliation, from a slightly different point of view. It shows from where funds have come and for what they have been used and therefore what is the net effect on cash and liquidity.

Finally the reconciliation of net worth distinguishes between those items in the other reconciliations which change cash or working capital but do not change net worth, and those which also increase or reduce net worth. For instance, an increase in term debt, on its own, changes liquidity but not net worth; an increase in share capital increases net worth even if its affect on liquidity is offset because it is used to purchase fixed assets or another company. Perhaps more importantly a net worth reconciliation shows how far net worth is being augmented from earnings and how far it is having to rely on extraordinary or external sources.

Set out in Table 7.1 is a hypothetical reconciliation of working capital. It includes most types of change which can occur. The individual items are numbered and the discussion below refers back to them.

Table 7.1 Reconciliation of working capital

Sources	£000	Uses	£000
(1) Net profit	1,000	(9) F/A expend	500
(2) Depreciation	250	(10) Dividends	500
(3) Increase term debt	500	(11) Increase intangibles	500
(4) Increase deferred taxes	100	(12) Increase investments	500
(5) Increase pension reserves	100	(13) Increase working capital	250
(6) Extraordinary profits	100		
(7) Increase share capital	100		
(8) Increase capital reserve	100		
	2,250		2,250

(1) Net profit is a clear source of working capital, since it represents the difference between the cash value of sales and all the expenses incurred in making the sale. It is only a source of cash to the extent that the receivables generated by the sales have been collected.

(2) Depreciation (or, in full, depreciation, depletion and amortisation, DD & A) picks up the main non-cash item charged in reaching profit. It always includes depreciation of fixed assets but where appropriate covers depletion of mineral assets and amortisation (i.e. the writing off against profits for accounting purposes) of such things as

patents, capitalised interest and goodwill as well. These are all items which reduce reported net profits but without actually changing the flow of cash from operations.

(3) An increase in term debt initially means that the company receives cash; whether it is held as cash or used to reduce a current liability it improves working capital. Where it is used for non-current purposes (such as fixed asset expenditure) an item on the uses side will show this.

(4) Increase deferred taxes. This is a net figure relating to two possible flows in opposite directions. On the one hand, taxes have been charged against net profit but are not expected to be paid in the current year, making the tax to that extent a non-cash charge. But tax which was deferred from a previous year may now have become payable; it will show first as a current liability and then be paid without being charged against profit this year and therefore will be a reduction in working capital. There are two reasons for not showing the two flows separately unless they are large enough to justify an exception. First, in many cases the information is insufficient to break out the exact figures; secondly, the net effect which will always be reflected in the balance sheet is the important one in judging the overall impact on working capital.

(5) An increase in pension reserves works in the same general way as the increase in deferred taxation. On the one hand an addition to the reserves has been charged against earnings but no cash has actually been paid out. On the other hand, if pensions have been paid out of the reserves, that is an actual cash outflow that does not go through the profit and loss account. Here again the net figure is usually the key one but a reconciliation of the various figures if available will enable the analyst to make sure that the information he has is complete. (In both (4) and (5), note that a net decrease shows as a use of working capital, on exactly the reverse arguments.)

(6) Extraordinary profits. It would of course be possible to include these as part of net profit but it is better to break them out to indicate how far the company depends on them to maintain working capital. An extraordinary loss would appear as a use.

(7) Increase in share capital. Normally an increase in the number of shares outstanding generates cash. Occasionally shares are issued in return for non-current assets; in this

case the increase in those assets appears as a use, and the increase in share capital provides balance since it was financed without reduction in working capital.

(8) An increase in capital reserves can arise from the issue of shares at above par value, since only the par value shows as an increase in share capital; the excess shows under capital reserves (possibly under a heading such as share premium account). However, the effect on working capital is the same whether a company issues 200,000 shares at a par value of £1 and a premium of £1 for total consideration of £400,000 or issues 400,000 shares at a par value of £1 and no premium. Capital reserve can increase in various other ways and it may be desirable to show these separately if more than one occurs in any one year:

(a) A revaluation of fixed or other assets with the increase being added to capital reserves. This is a pure accounting transaction with no impact on working capital. Where the information allows, it is quite acceptable to net the increase in capital reserve against the increase in fixed assets; however, precise information may not be available and there may be other changes in capital reserve as well. In this case, the only way to handle it is to include the full amount of both items.

(b) A capital reserve can arise from the sale at a profit of fixed assets, investments or other assets. In this case the proceeds of the sale break down into two parts: the balance sheet will be reduced by the book value at which the asset was carried and this will be picked up as a source of cash. The profit element in the sale price will not show separately on the balance sheet. It may show as an extraordinary profit, but it may be taken directly to reserves. So could a number of other items where some special factor has happened to change the value of an asset or to reduce the size of a liability.

(c) There are various types of special reserve, legal reserve, inventory and other reserves in different countries, which may be classified as capital reserves or may be broken out separately. Changes will affect working capital either because they represent a non-cash charge to profits or because some actual asset has been added to match the reserves. If the asset is current, working capital will increase; if not, then it will show as a use of working capital, balancing the increase in reserve.

(9) Fixed asset expenditure is an obvious use of cash. The detail shown will depend on the information the company gives. Where there is sufficient information and where the analyst thinks it of interest the three components, depreciation (already discussed), sale of fixed assets (a source except to the extent sold at a loss) and fixed asset expenditure, may be shown separately. More commonly depreciation is shown as a source and net fixed asset expenditure as usage. Where companies do not give a figure for capital expenditure, an estimate is quite simple. If there had been no purchase or sale of any fixed assets the difference between the net figure at 31 December 1979 and at 31 December 1980 would be the depreciation charged during the year. Therefore net fixed asset expenditure during 1980 equals the amount by which year-end net fixed assets exceed beginning net fixed assets, minus depreciation (see Table 7.2).

Table 7.2 Calculation of fixed asset expenditure

	£000
Net fixed assets 31 December 1979	1000
Depreciation during 1980	100
NFA at 31 December 1980 if no purchase or sales	900
Actual NFA at 31 December 1980	1050
Therefore net expenditure during year	150

Where no figure is disclosed for capital expenditure or depreciation the analyst uses the change in reported net fixed assets, unsatisfactory though this may be.

(10) Dividends are an obvious usage of cash when paid and create a current liability which reduces working capital between the time they are declared and actual payment.

(11) Increased intangibles use working capital in one of three ways. Either cash has been paid to buy the intangible; or some other means of payment such as a long-term note, which appears as a source and must be balanced; or the intangible increases by capitalising an expense such as interest, so that the company increases reported earnings even though the expense is a drain on cash. Similarly a decrease would be a source of working capital.

(12) Increase in investments uses cash, and therefore reduces working capital, where the increase results from a

purchase. If it arises from revaluation, then there will be an offsetting increase in net worth which, unless separately identified and netted, will show as a source of cash.

(13) Increase in working capital. Since the sources and uses should differ only by the amount of the change in working capital this is a balancing item, and is a check that no item has been omitted or incorrectly stated. A decrease in working capital would show as a source for the same reason.

In the example the company made a profit and assets or liabilities both increase. The calculation works equally well the other way with a loss or a decrease in some or all of the assets or liabilities. The general rule to be followed is that profit is a source of working capital and loss a use; non-cash charges against profit and loss are a source but capitalisation of expenses a use; increase in assets is a use and decrease a source; increase in liabilities is a source and decrease a use; increase in net worth or any net worth item is a source and decrease a use.

The same basic approach applies to the reconciliation of cash rather than working capital except that additional allowance has to be made for changes in individual current assets (other than cash) and current liabilities.

An alternative presentation which is more often used with a sources and uses of funds analysis is a descending one; the first section shows sources and below it uses. The first section can be subdivided to break out operating and other sources and is also an easier form to use for comparisons over several years. A typical sources and uses statement might look like the one illustrated in Table 7.3.

Table 7.3 Typical sources and uses statement

Sources of funds were:	£000
Net profit after taxes	5,000
Depreciation	2,643
Equity issue	1,000
Increase deferred tax	157
Total sources	8,800

continued

Table 7.3 - continued

	£000
Funds were used for:	
Net expenditure fixed assets	6,107
Net reduction term debt	1,200
Dividends	150
Increase working capital	1,343
	8,800

Alternatively, it may look like Table 7.4 which is the same idea presented in more detail to show the difference between natural changes and financing requirements more clearly.

Table 7.4 Alternative format of sources and uses statement

	£000
Sources:	
From operations	
Net profit after taxes	5,000
Depreciation	2,643
Increase deferred tax	157
	7,800
Other: Sale of fixed assets	1,500
Decrease net working investment	100
Total sources	9,400
Uses:	
Purchase fixed assets	7,507
Dividends	150
Increase other current assets	2,500
Decrease other current liabilities	250
Total uses	10,407
Surplus (deficit)	(607)
Financed by:	
Increase short-term debt	807
Decrease long-term debt	(1,200)
Equity issue for cash	1,000
Equity issue for other consideration	- 0 -

(Note: If there is a surplus rather than deficit the rest of Table 7.4 shows what sort of debt or other obligation has been reduced as a result.)

The precise form of presentation is not very important provided it highlights the key aspects. However, the segmented approach which shows the cash flow from various sources, the way in which it is used, and then the result of any surplus or deficit on financing requirements can be quite useful as a predictive tool.

It can also be very informative to run a eye over the "Surplus" (Deficit) line over four or five, or sometimes more years. A company which is consistently in surplus or which alternates between surplus and deficits of comparable size is probably generating enough cash to maintain or improve its balance sheet structure. Consistent large deficits, however, unless they are financed in sufficient part by new equity, suggest a deteriorating position which could quickly become critical if the starting point is weak.

A reconciliation of net worth follows the same basic principle. However, changes in assets and liabilities only affect net worth where they are not offset by a comparable movement on the other side. For instance, if a company uses cash to pay its suppliers, assets and liabilities decline by the same amount and net worth is unchanged. Apart from profit or loss, equity injections and dividends, the main factors affecting net worth are items outside the profit and loss statement which affect one side of the asset/liability balance only, such as a revaluation or write-down of assets. In too many cases companies will show the profits above the line but the losses below it or in a note. One of the main reasons for performing a net worth reconciliation is to find out whether anything has not been fully disclosed; this may show up if the reconciliation does not balance or may be more clearly highlighted even where it does. Identifying and investigating the reason for a substantial discrepancy can be important. A simple reconciliation of net worth is shown in Table 7.5.

Table 7.5 Reconciliation of net worth

	£000
Sources of net worth:	
Net profit	5,000
Revaluation fixed assets	1,000
Profit on sale of investment	500
Equity issue - par value	1,000
Premium on shares issued	2,000
	9,500
Less:	
Dividends	1,000
Extraordinary costs of equity issue	150
Extraordinary costs of closure of factory	1,500
	2,650
Net increase in net worth	6,850

This last figure should of course match the difference between the net worth in the two years. It is failure to do this which warns of hidden changes.

8 Ratio Analysis

Ratio analysis is the use of financial ratios as one among many tools in credit analysis. It does not mean, as it is occasionally taken to, the use of ratios as the sole tool.

The value of ratios, and therefore of ratio analysis, is to sum up relationships in one easy number. They are therefore particularly useful in reviewing trends and can be a useful tool for screening companies with a computer for evidence of deterioration which warrants further enquiry. They also simplify comparison among companies in the same industry or in some other way similar. Above all, however, they are useful in conjunction with verbal analysis to provide clear factual support to the analytical interpretation.

The danger of ratios, on the other hand, is that they suggest a precision which is largely illusory. Financial figures themselves are a shorthand for the assets they represent, so that ratios are a shorthand for a shorthand. Inevitably they leave out a great deal. In particular they pay no attention to the quality of the assets, earnings, liabilities and so on which underlie them. A current ratio, for instance, accurately shows the relationship between the current asset and current liability numbers; it tells nothing about the quality of the current assets or the immediacy of the current liabilities. The same is true about leverage, so that over-emphasis on the ratio tends to encourage the rather superficial judgement that "leverage of 2.25 to 1 is better than the industry average of 2.19 to 1" or worse still "leverage of 3 to 1 is acceptable for this type of company". Neither of these comments is relevant or helpful except as part of a wider analysis which has established the quality of the assets; the reasons why particular companies should be similar or dissimilar to each other; the reasons why a particular type of company justifies a specific leverage; and how the company under review falls into the pattern.

Thus ratio analysis can be a useful tool to the experienced, a snare and delusion for the inexperienced or an excuse for sloppy thinking by the lazy.

This chapter discusses the main ratios and their significance in isolation. The broader use of ratios in analysis will emerge in later chapters.

Balance sheet ratios

Some ratios solely relate individual items or groups of items on the balance sheet to each other. Between them, therefore, they say something about liquidity and leverage but nothing about profitability or cash flow or how they relate to the balance sheet.

Current ratio or working capital ratio (CR). This is current assets (CA) divided by current liabilities (CL), or CA/CL, and is the ratio version of the working capital concept. It does not distinguish the size of the overall position. Thus current assets 15 and current liabilities 10, or current assets 150 and current liabilities 100 both give a ratio of 1.5, but tell nothing about how important current assets are in the total balance sheet. The current ratio relates current assets only to current liabilities, with no indication of the relationship of either, or of working capital, to the rest of the balance sheet. Thus it may be helpful to know whether working capital is 10 or 50, as well as whether the ratio is 1.1 or 1.5.

The ratio is more valuable than an actual working capital figure when comparing the same company over time. Working capital of 10 in 1975 and again in 1980 would, on its own, suggest no change. However, if the company has been growing, working capital should grow too. If the 1975 working capital calculation was 20 - 10, and in 1980 it was 50 - 40, the ratio shows the deterioration which the absolute figure conceals. Thus, a current ratio indicates whether (in the light of what is known or expected about the nature of the components) current assets are adequate to meet current liabilities, with a reasonable safety margin. But it tells nothing about the components or other factors affecting liquidity, and is of limited use except in conjunction with other ratios, or to point to a need to investigate the reasons for a change in it.

However, with all its limitations it is easily calculated and a figure with which many people are closely familiar. Moreover, while it is possible that a change in the underlying quality of assets can allow an apparently stable current ratio to hide a major shift in liquidity, it is probable that a major change in the nature of the assets would affect the current ratio in some way; a stable current ratio is thus a good prima facie indication of liquidity provided not too much weight is put on it. (For instance, a major slowdown in receivables would cause an increase in both receivables and current liabilities. If the starting figures were CA 100, CL 50, current ratio 2.0, and receivables increased by 10, the change would show as CA 110, CL 60, current ratio 1.83. This is not a dramatic deterioration, and the current ratio would not tell the cause of the problem but it would suggest investigation.)

Quick ratio or acid test ratio (QR). Quick assets are defined as cash, near cash and trade receivables (including intercompany receivables only to the extent that they relate to genuine intercompany trade and are payable on normal commercial terms). The ratio relates quick assets to CL and shows the extent to which current liabilities can be met from the combination of cash and those assets which turn into cash quickly and with little or no further cost or work. Receivables sometimes have a minor cost of collection but they represent sales which have been shipped and invoiced, so that normally there is no significant risk or cost involved in turning them into cash. Inventory on the other hand may require time and substantial processing costs before it can be sold, with the risk of a change in the market value. Thus quick assets which cover most or all of current liabilities are safer both in case current liabilities are very short-dated, and because there is less risk of loss. Conversely, a weak or deteriorating quick ratio means that the company has to rely more heavily on fast conversion of inventory, and the analyst needs to be sure this reliance is justified. (A supermarket, for instance, turns its inventory over very fast and has little or no receivables, so that a weak QR is not usually a problem.)

Inventory coverage ratio. This ratio looks at the split between quick assets and inventory from a different angle.

It measures the percentage of inventory which would be required to pay the excess of current liabilities over quick assets; i.e. if QA - CL = 10% of inventory, then liquidity relies to only a minor degree on the speed and quality of inventory; if QA - CL = 50%, then the condition of inventory is a much more important factor in the assessment of liquidity. The ratio originated in liquidation analysis, since it tells how big a discount on book value can be applied to inventory (or alternatively, how important it is that quick assets realise a high percentage of face value) before creditors would have to rely on the value of non-current assets to meet current liabilities.

Current assets to total liabilities (CA/TL). Unlike the first three ratios, CA/TL relates the current position to the whole balance sheet. If current assets alone can repay all or most liabilities, then liquidity is strong and whatever non-current assets there may be are financed with equity. This may be, as with a commodity company, because non-current assets and liabilities are small and the CA/TL ratio is almost a mirror image of the leverage ratio. A manufacturing company, with its investment in fixed assets, is less likely to have a CA/TL ratio above 1 to 1; if it does this suggests not only good liquidity, but low leverage since fixed assets are, by definition, financed wholly by net worth; and vice versa for a weak ratio (which probably means below, say, about 0.7). Deterioration in CA/TL may point either to a loss of liquidity and weakening leverage, or possibly to a change in the nature of its business. A company which had previously been largely a wholesaler, for instance, but started to manufacture would soon show a different CA/TL ratio unless its work in process and fixed assets were wholly financed with equity.

Receivables turnover, collection period or days sales outstanding. The speed at which receivables are collected decides the level of receivables in relation to a given sales volume. The calculation is expressed as sales ÷ receivables = number of times receivables turn over in a year (i.e. if sales are 100, receivables 25, then receivables turn over 4 times a year). Divide 4 (in this example) into the number of days in the year to obtain the collection period (also referred to as "days sales outstanding"). Thus if receivables turn over 4 times a year the average time it takes to collect them is 91 days, rounded to the nearest whole number; or on average at any given time there are receivables outstanding equivalent to 91 days' sales.

Some analysts use an average of the sales for the last two years, but this is not recommended. Indeed, the most accurate ratio would annualise the most recent three months; a change in sales shows through before the corresponding change in receivables, which in turn reflect only the most recent sales. Thus if, during the year, the annual rate of sales doubles, sales for the year will be the average of the annual rate at the beginning of the year and at the end of the year, but receivables at year end will only reflect the rate of sales in the last few months. To illustrate the point in figures: a company actually collects its receivables in 92 days throughout; sales start the year at an annual rate of 100 and then accelerate smoothly to finish the first year at a rate of 200, the second year at 300; thus actual sales are 150 in the first year and 250 in the second. The receivables on the balance sheet at the end of the second year are 75 (one-quarter of the annual rate of 300). A calculation based on 250, which may be the only figure available, shows a turnover of 109 days; an experienced analyst will recognise that some of this slow-down is an illusion due to the growth in sales, even if the exact extent is not clear. To compound this distortion by using a sales figure of 200 (the average of 150 + 250) is simply to create unnecessary problems of interpretation.

The significance of receivable turnover was discussed in Chapter 2 with emphasis on the need for quality and liquidity. The calculation simply provides a tool for assessing and expressing the speed of turnover and drawing the various conclusions about their quality from it. With proper allowance for change of rate in sales (and for any seasonal or other fluctuation affecting the year end) it provides a broad indicator of any change in the liquidity of receivables and through them of overall liquidity and real as opposed to reported cash flow. It also provides a warning of problems such as loss of control or use of extended credit to cover up inadequate marketing or product quality. Thus while, as with most ratios, a receivable turnover figure on its own tells little about the quality of the underlying asset, it is sensitive to changes in that quality. A significant change (a day or two is not significant), after allowing for the affect of changes in the rate of sales, certainly means that something has happened to the receivables. It may reflect a small but widespread change to many of them; this may be the result of a slackening in controls, general reluctance to pay promptly due to tight money, or some form of competitive disadvantage. Or it may reflect a much greater change to one or a small number of customers.

For instance, a company may give a discount for payment in under 20 days, have normal terms requiring payment in 45 days and actual average turnover of 60 days. If one customer, accounting for 25% of sales, for years pays in 20 days and takes the discount, suddenly slows down its payments first to 45 days, then to 60 and perhaps then to 90, there is clearly a risk that the customer is in financial difficulty; if so, not only is the bank's borrower suddenly at risk for a much larger receivable to that company than previously, but it also has a question mark over 25% of its entire future sales; even if neither of these risks crystallise, the slowing down of payment creates a sharp curtailment of cash flow while it is happening, and a permanently higher financing requirement and interest cost once the customer stabilises at 90 days. An increase in average receivable turnover may be the only warning the banker has of this change. Unless he uses it to ask the right questions, he will have no way of distinguishing between the concentrated risk and the more general one; and yet if the concentrated risk crystallises, his borrower could be in deep trouble within a few months.

Where a company gives quarterly figures the calculation can be done quite simply on a quarterly basis by using the latest sales figure multiplied by 4 and then going through the same calculation. The more sensitive warning can be vital if there is concern about the company or if it is known to have a concentration of customers; it can also make it easier to assess whether fluctuations in turnover are real or reflect changing rates of sales.

The sales figure for calculating receivable turnover should normally be net because the items which are deducted from sales do not generate receivables. The argument on whether to use gross or net receivables is less clear-cut; but in most cases is academic because the banker has only one figure. Where a figure for actual bad debts or for a reserve against them is known, this in itself tells something about the quality of the receivables; it is then probably sensible to use the net receivable figure since this is what the company expects to receive and it reflects the position after the company has adjusted for any known problems. However, unless the reserve is known to be very large, in which case a problem has already been identified, the calculation will not differ very much. Receivable turnover is not a precise figure, rather it is an order of magnitude with fluctuations up to four or five days within normal margins of error.

Inventory turnover. Inventory turnover is calculated in the same way as receivable turnover, with one important exception where the information allows. Inventory should relate to the cost of goods sold rather than to total sales, since sales prices cover costs which are not included in inventory and a profit margin. In practice, few companies outside the United States break down costs in a way that allows identification of cost of goods sold and the calculation is much more frequently made on the basis of sales. The significance of inventory turnover was discussed in Chapter 2 and remains the same whether it is expressed as a ratio or in any other way. The comments about fluctuations or growth affecting the apparent rate of turnover apply equally to inventory turnover except that the timing is slightly different. Inventory normally increases in anticipation of higher sales, rather than as a result of higher past sales, so that the use of backward looking averages is even more misleading. Alternatively, it may reflect management's failure to adjust production to an unexpected slowdown in sales.

Cash conversion period. This is a combination of receivable turnover and inventory turnover. It gives an indication of the total period for which cash is tied up from the moment of purchase of inventory (ignoring credit terms) to the collection of the receivable; it is thus a better guide to liquidity than either turnover figure on its own. It is particularly useful where the relationship between inventory and receivables changes more rapidly than the combined figure. For instance, when a company bills a large individual contract and moves it out of inventory into receivables this reflects the recognition of what has happened over the last few weeks or months, rather than a major real change in one day.

Payables turnover. This is calculated in the same way as inventory turnover, with the same comment about using cost of goods sold when available. The ratio gives an idea of the length of time the company takes to pay its trade suppliers, and therefore of the extent to which it finances itself on a self-renewing basis, related to its volume of business and usually non-interest bearing.

The significance of a slow or slowing payable turnover, however, is somewhat different to that of receivable or inventory turnovers. It can be beneficial to obtain a higher proportion of finance from trade suppliers, but too slow a payable turnover may be caused by lack of liquidity. Apart from the overall danger, this can lead to troubles with trade suppliers who may become reluctant to supply unless payment is speeded up; in extreme cases they may demand cash on delivery. Meeting this reluctance uses liquidity when it is already tight, but failure to pay might seriously endanger the company's ability to obtain supplies. Conversely a fast payable turnover may appear to mean that the company is not taking the opportunity to finance itself cheaply, but this too may be deceptive; there may be attractive discounts which more than offset the cost of borrowing (or loss of interest earnings). At the same time, the fast turnover leaves scope to increase the finance taken from suppliers by slowing down payment without running into problems; it can therefore suggest an untapped reservoir of liquidity.

Leverage. There are several ratios which measure leverage. The most common are Total Liabilities ÷ by Net Worth (TL/NW) or Total Borrowed Funds ÷ by Net Worth (TBF/NW). The ratios may also be adjusted by using tangible net worth rather than unadjusted net worth. The significance of leverage was discussed in Chapter 6 but the ratio gives only an incomplete picture. As with other ratios, it does not say anything about the quality of the assets or the nature of the liabilities. Two companies with the same or closely similar leverage ratios therefore may have very different degrees of true leverage; if one has new, well-diversified, high-quality assets and a large amount of pension or other reserves in its liabilities, its leverage will be less than the TL/NW ratio shows; while if the other has old assets, slow-moving receivables, doubtful quality inventory and all its liabilities are current and interest bearing, its true leverage is higher than the ratio suggests.

Although the above two ratios are those most commonly used to measure leverage, particularly in the United States, there are other ways of doing so. One often used in England is net worth as a percentage either of total liabilities or possibly of total capitalisation. While different definitions of capitalisation exist, most include net worth, all long-term borrowing and probably all short-term borrowing although some exclude purely trade-related finance. An alternative is net worth, all long-term liabilities and current bank debt. The difference is not too significant provided the banker knows what is going into the ratio, which is normally expressed as a percentage; thus for net worth to total liabilities a ratio of 50% would be equivalent to TL/NW of 1.0. However, the unwary analyst needs to be careful here; moves below 50% have a more dramatic effect than apparently comparable moves in TL/NW or TBF/NW. Thus a move from 50 to 40% sounds small, but represents a move from 1 to 1.5 in TL/NW; 25% is 3 to 1.

A few hypothetical figures will illustrate the point. For ease of comparison, the definition of total capital is net worth, all long-term liabilities and current bank debt; the companies are assumed to have no long-term liabilities other than borrowed funds (see Table 8.1).

Table 8.1 Presentation of leverage

	Company A	Company B	Company C	Company D
Net worth (000)	1000	1000	1000	100
Long-term debt (000)	500	100	1000	1000
Current bank debt (000)	500	100	1000	1000
TBF/NW	1.0	0.2	2.0	20.0
NW % total capital	50.0	83.3	33.3	4.8

Operating ratios

Operating ratios are those which relate various levels of costs and profits to sales or occasionally to each other, but not to any balance sheet items. The important relationship of profitability to the balance sheet is covered by the combined ratios discussed later. This distinction recognises that the ratios measure two different types of relationship for different purposes; they are too often used without full recognition of this difference.

Operating ratios help to assess the factors which change a company's profits in relation to its sales, i.e. they measure the breakdown of costs and changes in them to see what causes a given change in profits and how likely that change is to continue or accelerate, and they measure the likely importance to the company of known or expected changes. However, this is always in relation to sales; operating ratios tell nothing about the likely movement in sales and therefore nothing directly about the movement in actual rather than proportional profits. Some conclusions can be drawn from them, however, as to the likely impact of a change in sales on total profits. Combined ratios measure the impact of operations on the balance sheet and on the ability of the company to continue to pay its debts and to provide finance for the expansion, R & D, dividends and so on. Thus operating ratios are used mainly to judge whether the present level of profit is sustainable or is likely to increase or decrease and to what factors it is vulnerable. Combined ratios are used to assess whether the level of profitability is adequate in relation to the balance sheet structure and other needs.

Operating ratios permit comparison of developments much more easily than looking at the actual costs. Particularly where sales are changing rapidly, the significance of each cost is difficult to tell by looking at the figures on their own, but ratios make it quite easy to see the trend.

For instance, Table 8.2 does not easily tell the reader whether costs are moving in line with sales or whether an adverse trend is developing.

Table 8.2 Operating ratio (absolute figures)

			£000		
	1976	1977	1978	1979	1980
Sales	200,815	215,320	273,422	250,743	289,987
CGS	191,321	197,123	261,411	239,971	271,214

On the other hand, Table 8.3, which converts the second line of Table 8.2 into two ratios, suggests that gross margin has a fairly stable bottom level but is subject to favourable fluctuations. It raises a question about the reasons for the fluctuations.

Table 8.3 Operating ratio (margins)

	1976	1977	1978	1979	1980
CGS (% sales)	95.3	91.5	95.6	95.9	93.5
Gross margin (% sales)	4.7	8.5	4.3	4.3	6.5

The analyst can calculate a percentage of sales for every type of cost and every level of profit margin. In practice, even where the information is available, it is better to concentrate on the major items, recognising that these differ between companies. Thus raw materials, labour or power and light may well be important and worth breaking out and tracking closely in some cases, but of minor significance in others. Where a cost, or related group of costs, is a high proportion of the total, even a small movement in the relation to sales can have a big impact on ultimate profitability. For instance, material costs may be 90% of the sales of a wholesaling company. Since there is only 10% left for all other costs the net margin will probably be as little as 1 or 2%. An apparently insignificant increase in material costs from 90 to 92% of sales with no change in other percentages can turn a modest profit into a loss. Put another way, it is vital for such a company both to control its other costs and to be able to pass any increase in material costs on in its selling price.

A manufacturing company, depending on the nature of the product, may have raw material costs between 20 and 50% of sales. A company with a pre-tax profit margin of, say, 4% of sales (low, but not catastrophic) would suffer a 25% reduction in pre-tax profit if raw material costs increased from 49 to 50% of stable sales (a 2% change). If at the same time interest costs rose from 1 to 2% of sales, the pre-tax profit would be halved as a result of two apparently trivial movements.

The ratio of costs to sales is also a more general indication of efficiency, where intercompany comparisons may be useful given reasonable assurance of comparing like with like. For instance, two companies may make the same product and sell in direct competition with each other, so that their prices must be competitive. If raw material costs are a significantly lower percentage of sales in one case than in the other, one company is making poor use of its raw materials; this may be due to weak manufacturing techniques, a higher wastage rate, poor purchasing or possibly smaller size and less ability to obtain volume discounts. Whatever the reason, it points to an area of weakness in management or in the company's situation which may need further investigation.

Whether or not he makes a company comparison, the analyst should check trends carefully. Labour costs may gradually increase as a percentage of sales, with perhaps no immediate visible impact on profits because of a modest but unconnected improvement elsewhere. Clearly this cannot go on indefinitely and it is important to know whether the cause is deteriorating efficiency, shortage of labour and therefore a need to pay more, a reduction in the selling price reflecting lower raw material costs, or some temporary factor such as introduction of a new product. This may have a higher labour cost until the benefits of the learning curve come through, or it may be naturally more labour intensive but with offsetting advantages elsewhere. A similar set of questions arises if material or other expenses increase.

The analyst needs to look at the level of profit margins as well as of expenses. Apart from cost of goods sold, expenses are paid from the relevant profit margin, after deduction of prior expenses, and this becomes as important as the percentage of sales. Thus general, selling and administrative (GS & A) expenses are paid out of gross profit. If the gross profit margin declines while GS & A remains stable, GS & A become a higher proportion of the profit margin available to service them and operating profit declines more, proportionately, than the decline in gross margin. Table 8.4 illustrates the point.

Table 8.4 Profit margins

	1976	1977	1978	1979	1980
Gross margin (% sales)	25	20	18	30	28
GS & A (% sales)	15	15	15	15	15
Operating margin (% sales)	10	5	3	15	13

The converse of course is equally true. If gross margin is stable but GS & A fluctuates the impact on operating profit will be greater than the change in GS & A as a percentage of sales would alone suggest.

The same applies even more strongly to interest and financial income. Interest is payable out of operating profit which is smaller than gross profit and can thus be heavily affected by smaller changes in interest or operating margin. Naturally, operating margins vary widely between companies, depending on efficiency and the nature of the business. A company with high operating margins can afford a higher proportion of interest in its costs, and is better protected against fluctuations in interest. For instance, assume that in 1979 interest costs were 5% of sales and in 1980 rose by 50% to 7½% of sales; if the operating margin in both years was 20%, the reduction in pre-tax profit would be from 15 to 12½% - or a reduction of 17% on stable sales, far from disastrous. If the operating margin had been 10% in both years, the drop in pre-tax profit would have been 50%.

The impact of various levels of margins on the volatility of profits is another aspect of operating leverage, in contrast to balance sheet leverage, discussed in Chapter 6. A company with a high level of operating or gross costs and therefore low gross and operating margins cannot afford any significant increase in other costs, while even a modest improvement in gross or operating costs will permit a sharp improvement in pre-tax profit. Conversely, the higher the gross and operating margins (and therefore the lower the gross and operating costs) the more other costs (mostly financial) the company can absorb and the less it needs to be concerned by fluctuations in them.

<u>Interest cover</u>. There is one operating ratio which is not expressed as a percentage of sales: interest cover, also known as "times interest earned". It represents profits, before interest or tax but after all other expenses, divided by interest actually paid. (Capitalised interest is normally included in the interest figure for the calculation even if for accounting reasons it is not treated as a cost.) If the resulting figure is less than 1, then the company is making a pre-tax loss (although it may use extraordinary items to avoid reporting it). If the figure is more than 1, then the company is making a pre-tax profit of the amount in excess

of 1. As this grows, the implications for the company's long-term viability improve.

A company which can barely pay its interest out of profits, and then has to pay taxes on whatever is left, has very little available for building up net worth and liquidity for debt repayment, investment in fixed assets, net working investment and all the other things. It is true that some of this is paid for by cash flow rather than pure profit, but if depreciation has been accurately calculated it will only be sufficient to replace existing fixed assets, and all the other needs must be met from profit, including a dividend for the shareholders. A company can survive a year or two of modestly inadequate interest cover without much harm. However, the longer the inadequacy lasts the greater the likelihood that it is running up requirements, whether of debt service, asset replacement or otherwise, which it will not be able to meet out of earnings; the result is usually either an increase in leverage (compounding the interest cover problem) or a decline in the quality of, particularly, fixed assets as inadequate money is spent on them. Sometimes the decline is in R & D or marketing, reducing the future sales prospects.

Interest cover is probably the most sensitive single warning sign among the purely operating ratios and possibly of all ratios; it takes into account the net changes in all costs above interest, and if either these or interest itself change, the ratio shows the change immediately. There is a danger, however, that interest cover is too sensitive and short-term fluctuations should be treated with caution. Without careful consideration the analyst does not know whether the initial decline in interest cover is a temporary fluctuation or is the first warning of something more serious. He must therefore examine carefully the factors causing the decline to judge whether it is permanent, the beginning of a deteriorating trend or merely a temporary factor which can and probably will be reversed quite quickly.

Combined ratios

Ratios which cover the balance sheet alone or operations alone are important, but the most important ratios in assessing the long-term viability of a company are those which relate the two. The relationships show the extent to which profits are supplying balance sheet needs and/or operational weaknesses are covered by balance sheet strength. A company's present and future financial condition are the result of a mixture of different factors, and the balance between them; ratios which help to assess various aspects of that mixture allow the analyst to draw a fuller picture than any balance sheet or operating ratio on its own can do. They are thus keys to the understanding of a company's future prospects and the most important part of ratio analysis.

Two concepts illustrated by these ratios, coverage and return, have already been discussed in Chapter 6. The purpose of this section is to discuss the individual ratios, how they are calculated and what their significance is within the overall concept. In addition to coverage and return ratios there are some others which do not fit conveniently into any overall concept but which are nevertheless important.

Return on assets (ROA). As discussed in Chapter 6, ROA measures the use the company makes of the assets at its disposal. Since it is concerned with assets, ROA ignores the method by which those assets are financed; the calculation expresses net profit before interest and taxes but after all other costs (NBIT) as a percentage of total assets; the higher the figure the better use the company is making of its assets.

Three things can be deduced (with qualifications) from this ratio. The first is some indication of the efficiency with which management is using the assets at its disposal. The second is the quality of the assets and hence the realism of their value on the balance sheet. Assets which generate a low return are prima facie unlikely to sell for a very high price and may therefore be overvalued. (Put the other way round an asset generating a return of 1 should only show on the balance sheet at 100 if the market accepts a 1% return on comparable assets as reasonable. If the market wants 5% or 10% or more, the asset is almost certainly heavily overvalued.) The low return may reflect poor management rather than poor quality of assets, or poor management may have allowed the quality of assets to decline; this must be judged separately in each case since it will have a bearing on the sale value of the asset, or the ability of new management to improve the return. The reverse points apply when the return is high. A change in trend raises questions as to whether there is a change in the underlying industry conditions rather than, or as well as, a change in the quality of the asset or management. A decline in the return may then not reflect directly on the day-to-day efficiency with which management operates the assets; it may, instead, suggest a strategic weakness and lack of preparedness to adjust to change which, whether foreseen or not, still affects the value of the assets.

ROA also influences the amount and type of debt a company can prudently incur, although its impact will be affected by the present cost of debt and potential future changes in cost. Broadly speaking the lower the return on assets (in relation to interest costs) the lower the proportion of interest-bearing debt which should be used to finance those assets. While low-cost fixed rate debt may partly offset a low ROA, likely future interest on borrowings to replace this debt, or on new borrowings if the total is increasing, is more important in the long run. In this context a low ROA means at best a small increase in net worth from retained earnings. Expansion is therefore more likely to need an external equity contribution, but the low return may reduce the prospect of obtaining it; on the other hand, if financed mainly with debt, expansion will push up leverage fairly rapidly without any assurance that the earnings will be sufficient to service it.

Although ROA is not strictly concerned with leverage it has implications for its adequacy. A very low or very high rate of return, suggesting that the true value of the assets has been mis-stated, also suggest that the true level of leverage has been mis-stated; and by indicating the acceptable level of debt a return on assets also says something about the acceptable level of leverage.

Since the purpose of ROA is to judge the efficiency with which assets are used, rather than how well they are financed, it is sometimes desirable to narrow the ratio a little further by excluding financial income and financial assets. This operating return on assets or OROA may be a better guide as to the effectiveness of the management where the full ROA is affected by the existence of a large financial item on the balance sheet which has little to do with the underlying business of the company. (On the other hand, where the financial income arises from, say, advance payments on contracts, it is fairly closely linked with operations and can be included even in OROA.)

Return on liabilities. This ratio measures the return on liabilities on the same basis as the return on assets, i.e. before financing charges. The difference between it and return on assets will reflect the size of net worth in the total financing package but will not otherwise take account of the method of financing. Return on liabilities should therefore always be larger than ROA; the lower ROA is, the greater the difference should be because the greater the need for equity financing. Apart from this the same comments about the level of return and the ability of that return to cover both current and likely future levels of interest and other financing costs which were made about ROA apply to ROL.

Return on borrowed funds (ROBF). By relating specifically to borrowed funds rather than total liabilities, ROBF points to a present rather than future question. Interest has to be paid on borrowed funds and if the return is less than the actual rate of interest the company is making a loss (again, subject to extraordinary items). Just as ROL should be more than ROA, so ROBF should be higher than ROL; the actual difference reflects the capital structure, while the difference the company can afford varies with the level of ROL. Comparing the actual with the affordable is useful. Remember, too, that the earnings are generated from all the assets, not just those financed with borrowed funds. If ROBF is less than, or only slightly above, the rate of interest, the company could possibly improve its earnings by selling assets and using the proceeds to repay debt.

Return on equity (ROE) or return on net worth. Investment analysts place great weight on ROE, since it indicates the return on shareholders' contribution, and the company's dividend-paying capacity and therefore its attraction to investors. The ratio is net profit after tax as a percentage of equity (although where tax has a distorting effect some analysts will calculate a pre-tax ROE), since all financing and other charges have to be paid before the shareholders, the owners of the equity, receive a penny. ROE is used to measure present and future profit potential for a shareholder, including but not limited to ability to pay dividends. The ratio is less critical to the lender because his return has been covered before the calculation. Nevertheless, it tells him three things. First, how well covered his own and all other prior charges are. Second, the size of the risk that unhappy shareholders will be unwilling to inject new capital if it is needed to support the bank's loans; or that they may even take out excessive dividends. Third, the extent to which the company has the ability to generate new equity on its own, without recourse to outside sources.

Cash flow to total liabilities (CF/TL). CF/TL is the broadest of the coverage ratios showing cash flow as a percentage of total liabilities. It assumes that in the long run all liabilities have to be met in some way; even those which are naturally renewable will only remain so if providers can see adequate cover, and feel confident the company could repay them if they wanted it to. Cash flow is, for most companies, the only continuing internal source of repayment of liabilities; while they can be repaid from disposal of surplus assets or by tighter control of net working investment, neither can be repeated indefinitely. Cash flow, on the other hand, should come in every year in a sound company.

Therefore the size of cash flow in relation to the various requirements for it is crucial. Very few companies pay their total liabilities from the cash flow of any one year, but it is important to know that if cash flow were devoted solely to this purpose the impact would be visible in one year and substantial in as few as two or three. Even where there are virtually no borrowings, or liabilities such as taxes which have to be met on specific dates, it is important to have some ability to reduce the trade payables, advances, pension reserves or whatever substitutes for debt. Most companies have some debt (those that do not rarely need external analysis by bank lenders) and some obligations like dividends or large tax payments which have to be met, and cash flow must provide either a source of payment or of service for the financing used to meet them.

An appropriate level of cash flow is difficult to generalise. However, a lower percentage of liabilities may be safer in countries where it is normal for both receivables and payables to turn over slowly than in countries where a rapid turnover is normal. Similarly, cash flow may safely be a lower percentage of total liabilities in countries where companies commonly carry large pension or liability reserves than in countries where such reserves are unusual; these types of liability rarely appear on Anglo-Saxon balance sheets, so that statistics would not allow for the different characteristics of such liabilities. An acceptable level may also change with the extent to which debt is long-term with very little amortisation or short-medium with heavy amortisation. Nevertheless, although the more refined ratios discussed below are useful as a way of allowing for some of these variations, the general ratio is of real significance. Whatever the nature of the liabilities there must be some cash flow coverage to service them, to prevent them growing so large that the balance sheet becomes top heavy, and to guard against unexpected needs to repay liabilities which are not normally repayable at short notice.

Cash flow as a percentage of total borrowed funds (CF/TBF). CF/TBF, a narrower version of cash flow coverage, relates purely to borrowings since these at least always have to be repaid eventually. Obviously the cash flow coverage of borrowed funds should be higher than that of total liabilities. The difference will reflect the financing structure; the greater the proportion of borrowing in liabilities the less the difference and the greater the need for a high cash flow coverage. Where none of the following ratios are used, CF/TBF should be related to the structure of borrowings too.

Cash flow to term debt (CF/TD). Some (often most) short-term debt is regularly rolled over, and/or repayable from temporary asset fluctuations and is thus not normally a claim on cash flow. CF/TD relates cash flow to debt where there is a specific repayment schedule; the ratio should again be higher than CF/TBF. How much higher depends not only on the proportion of medium- or long-term debt in the total but also on the amortisation pattern. Clearly if there is a smooth and gradual amortisation over the next several years, then the demands on cash flow to meet it or enable it to be refinanced without distorting the balance sheet should not be too great. On the other hand, where there are one or more years of very heavy amortisation, particularly in the near future with little time to rearrange the debt structure, then a high cash flow in relation preferably to total borrowed funds but at least to the particular maturities is crucial. Conversely, if there is no amortisation for several years, a lower cash flow may be acceptable initially, provided it is expected to increase.

Cash flow to total capital expenditure (CF/TCE). Capital expenditure must be financed either from cash flow or from some source which in turn makes demands on cash flow. As one component of cash flow, depreciation is specifically designed to provide for replacement of capital assets; cash flow should therefore be substantially larger than capital expenditure in a company which is not expanding. If such a company reports sizeable profits, but cash flow barely covers average capital expenditure, then depreciation is probably understated and profitability overstated; the value of assets may be overstated as well (although not necessarily so - see Chapter 12).

With an expanding company, depreciation need no longer be expected to cover capital expenditure on its own at least in the early stages of the expansion. An expansion plan may take several years to complete, and even replacement expenditure may come in very large units, so cash flow coverage needs to be considered over several years. If over such a period the company consistently uses more than 100% of cash flow for capital expenditure, this suggests either that profits are inadequate or that the expansion is greater and the profits slower to start, than the capital base justifies. Some outside source of capital, probably equity but possibly long-term debt, is then needed to fund the expansion. Otherwise the expansion and the related increase in NWI will pre-empt the resources needed to maintain the balance sheet, which will deteriorate, and the resulting borrowing may soon run up a larger interest bill than even a profitable expansion can carry.

On the other hand, capital expenditure consistently too far below the level of depreciation suggests the company may be allowing the quality of its assets to deteriorate and, in the long run, undermining its competitive position. The best case is one where a full depreciation charge roughly covers capital expenditure, leaving other substantial elements of cash flow for other purposes.

Cash flow to increase in net working investment (CF/NWI). Net working investment can decrease as well as increase, in which case the coverage by cash flow is academic. However, in a growing company NWI usually also grows and needs to be financed. Here CF/NWI is a useful measure of whether net working investment is pre-empting cash flow, leaving too little for either capital expenditure or for debt service.

It is of course difficult to say which usage "pre-empts" cash flow but, if the total is insufficient to service total usages over a medium period, the company's financial condition will deteriorate and may quite quickly reach the point of no return.

All ratios describing returns and coverage rely on accurate accounting. Among other things they rely on the value of the assets as stated and on the earnings being reliably and consistently reported. Unfortunately, even apart from fraud, there are many cases where this reliance is not justified. This is partly a question of nationality. Some countries require accounts to be prepared wholly for tax purposes rather than to be realistic; tax concessions can distort figures even in countries where this is not true. Other countries impose no accounting standards or inadequate ones which fail to ensure that asset valuations and earnings are stated on any reliable or consistent basis; they rarely require full disclosure of the basis. All the ratios discussed so far become less valuable the less confident the banker can be of the figures.

Cash flow coverage ratios are perhaps slightly less unreliable than return ratios because some of the ways in which companies juggle with their earnings and even with the value of their assets are picked up in cash flow. These were discussed in Chapters 5 and 6 and include such things as changes in pension reserves or deferred taxes, capitalised expenses and liability provisions. However, there can be no certainty that all of the adjustments to earnings are picked up by cash flow and many countries allow allocations to hidden reserves which are not disclosed either in earnings or balance sheets. In such situations other ratios where such distortions are less likely to occur may have to be used. Some of these ratios also have value in their own right.

Total borrowed funds to sales (TBF/S) or interest to sales (I/S). In countries where accounting is unreliable, sales and total borrowed funds are the two items least likely to be distorted. TBF/S and I/S, expressing borrowings and interest as a percentage of sales, are of particular value in such countries but they are useful anywhere. A company with large foreign borrowings, or with large sales billed in foreign currencies, can still distort the figures somewhat due to varying exchange rates. Even with no intention to manipulate, it is misleading to show $1 million of debt at Spanish pesetas 85,000,000 if the exchange rate is now $1 = Pta 115. But if the rate was 85 when the dollars were borrowed, the lower amount will be permitted, even required, under some countries' accounting rules.

With that proviso, I/S tells what operating margin the company needed to cover interest at all, or by whatever margin the bank thinks necessary in the particular case. TBF/S tells what level of debt has to be serviced; while this includes interest it also gives some idea of the amount which needs to be amortised. Moreover, I/S tells only about the interest actually paid; it tells nothing about the vulnerability to future interest rates, as TBF/S does.

Assume, for instance, that a company has sales of 100, interest of 3. This tells the operating profit required to cover interest. However, that 3% could be the result of interest rates of 6% on borrowings of 50% of sales, 12% on 25% and so on; the danger of a sharp increase in interest payments is clearly much greater in the first case. Alternatively the company may be borrowing mainly in strong currencies to keep interest low, in which case the risk of a foreign currency loss is greater.

Moreover, the interest figure on its own may not be reliable in a number of ways. Some result from accounting; the figure may exclude capitalised interest, or net out interest and other financial income. But some are inherent; interest in a year is paid on the borrowings throughout the year, which may not be the same as those reported on the balance sheet at year end. This may be for seasonal or cyclical reasons, in which case the average borrowing (and therefore an interest figure based on it) may indeed be more accurate than a year end figure. But if borrowings are increasing (at least increasing faster than sales), the historical interest figure gives a low reading of the servicing requirement actually being faced.

Moreover, interest rates change as well as borrowing levels. TBF/S gives the analyst the chance to apply current market rates, or even anticipated future rates, in order to generate a notional I/S ratio and see how well the company could cope with it. This is valid when rates are declining as well as when they are rising.

Altogether the TBF/S and I/S ratios are useful pointers even when reliable figures are available. When full balance sheet and profit figures are not available or lack credibility, TBF/S and an actual or imputed I/S can give warning of a top-heavy situation which can quickly become unmanageable. Even before the situation reaches that point, a continuing increase in either or both ratios suggests that the company is not generating sales and profits fast enough to service its debt; in such a case the increasing interest burden can overwhelm a company with moderate operating profits. Even if the increase in borrowing at first results from what is seen as a temporary slowdown in growth, the need to borrow to pay interest can quite quickly build up debt to a level which no likely operating profit will cover.

Sales as a percentage of fixed assets. Where a reliable fixed asset figure is available, or can be deduced, its relationship to sales is a useful pointer in its own right, as well as a help where profit figures are unreliable. Since fixed assets are responsible, at least in manufacturing companies, for an important part of fixed costs, the relationship to sales is at least a partial indicator of the ability to cover them.

If it is known what level of sales to F/A is appropriate in the particular industry, the ratio can also indicate whether the company is operating below capacity, so that improved volume would bring better absorption of fixed costs; or, alternatively, that it is so near capacity that any significant growth will require extra capital expenditure.

Sometimes a company appears to be operating below capacity, but modest expansion in sales triggers off massive capital expenditure; in other cases even a major growth in sales does not improve margins; both of these and other discrepancies suggest that the company is using its fixed assets inefficiently, or there is some other problem which needs to be identified.

Depreciation as a percentage of gross fixed assets. It is important that the company depreciate its assets adequately and therefore that its profits allow for the need to replace them. If the depreciation is consistently low in relation to gross assets this may suggest that profits have been overstated; at least in a low inflationary environment the value of the assets may also be overstated. If, as sometimes happens, the level of depreciation is erratic it can suggest that the company is manipulating reported profits. This may make it difficult to judge whether the depreciation is adequate, taking one year with another, but also raises a question as to the accounting policy of the company, since it may also be manipulating other figures which do not show up so easily.

If, on the other hand, depreciation is both consistent and fairly high in relation to gross fixed assets, this suggests a better quality for the reported earnings, as well as the company's ability to provide for replacement of its fixed assets.

The specific level of depreciation which is appropriate depends on the mix of fixed assets. Land and buildings for instance have a longer life and less depreciation than other assets; some forms of machine and process equipment have a much longer economic life than others; some companies have their own transport, with a relatively short life, while others contract it out, and there are many other variations. Nevertheless, as a broad indication, for a light to medium manufacturing company that owns all its fixed assets (rather than renting or leasing) probably anything under 8% per annum or over 12% per annum (8 to 12 year average life) justifies investigation. For non-manufacturing companies, or for very heavy manufacturing companies, these figures are less relevant.

Conclusion. No banker can or should use all of the above ratios in analysing a single company. Most bankers have a few ratios which they consider particularly significant, and they will rely mainly on these unless there is some suggestion that other ratios are pointing in different directions. Nevertheless, bankers should understand the significance of all these ratios, for three main reasons. They will inevitably, from time to time, have to assess companies where their favourite ratios are not of much value, and should have a portfolio of other approaches they can use. They will read analyses by other bankers who have different pet ratios, and will need to understand their significance. And, finally, in talking with financial management of their customers they will find that these use, and sometimes talk about, ratios in managing their business. Often these are different from those bankers use. Only if the banker has a full understanding of the way in which ratios work will he get full value out of these discussions.

Part III
The Company

9 The Inherent Factors

So far the discussion has covered the financial figures and various developments from them. But the financial figures are only a shorthand for the company itself. Although most liabilities are financial in nature, most assets are not and the features in a company's business which affect its earning capacity, its risk and its ability to withstand risk must be carefully related to the financial figures.

The first step in looking at the nature of the business is to decide whether it is primarily a manufacturing business, a service business, a financial business, distribution or what have you. Only when this has been identified can the analyst begin to develop an understanding of the features which affect the company. For instance, a manufacturing business will usually have a substantial amount of fixed assets, receivables for goods sold and inventory with varying mixes of finished goods, work in process and raw materials. It will have high fixed costs in relation to sales, a labour force to process the inventory and needs for such things as R & D. These will have entirely different balance sheet and P & L features from a service company where the main assets are people and technical skills; or from a distribution company which handles very high volumes of finished goods to which it adds no direct value so that the margin on each sale will be small. On the other hand, distribution requires relatively little in the way of fixed assets or net worth, so that sales will be high in relation to them and even a small margin on sales may provide a large margin on assets and net worth. Equally, its assets will be almost entirely either receivables or finished goods inventory with a ready market, so that its liquidity requirements will be different from a manufacturing company with more or less of its balance sheet tied up in fixed assets or in inventory with a long production process. The rest of this chapter will concentrate mainly on how to look at a manufacturing company but many of the principles discussed can be applied, using common sense, to other types of company as well.

The other distinction which needs to be made in looking at companies is between those features which are inherent in the nature of the business and those which are affected by the quality of management and/or by external factors. The former will broadly be the same in any company in a particular type of business whatever its country and whatever the local conditions; the latter will be specific to the particular company. There is of course substantial overlap between these factors. For instance, certain types of chemical process are prone to produce a high level of pollution; but the impact of this may well depend on local factors (a fast flowing river, for instance, as a cheap method of disposal) and on whether governmental and social restrictions hamper the company's freedom to create pollution or require substantial sums to be spent controlling it. (Where a company is currently exempt from such limitations, the risk of their imposition should be assessed.) Thus the distinction between inherent and external management factors may seem artificial and the question of which category to assign to them may sometimes be very finely balanced. However, the distinction is real; the inherent factors are likely to be impossible to change or avoid, at least in the short run and quite often even in the medium to longer run; the managerial/external factors may be more easily avoided altogether or alleviated.

The nature of the product

There is no one place to start which is the best in every case, but the nature of the product for a manufacturing company is always important. Knowledge about it will lead on naturally to a number of other questions. Discussion of these questions, which are closely interrelated, will inevitably involve some repetition; however, the points are both important, and valid in each context, so repetition should be beneficial.

So the first question is "what does the company do?" If it produces highly complex multi-processed products this has implications for the capital intensity and flexibility of the plant; for the length of the production process and therefore the cash conversion period; for the type of customer to which it is sold and the terms on which it is sold;

for the amount of money which must be spent on research and development and for the risk of technical obsolescence; and for the way in which the product is marketed.

Or it may produce a fairly simple commodity product. This will have different implications for the list of questions above; perhaps the need for tight control of manufacturing costs will be greater; marketing and distribution will be more volume oriented; there will be more risk of new competitors entering the market and competing solely on price.

Or the product may require servicing after it has been sold; there are implications about the cost but also possible profits from the after-sales service and there may be an impact on sales if the company has a particularly good or bad reputation for the quality of its service. There may also be a need for capital investment to supply the service.

The product may be sold direct to the consumer or to other manufacturers for incorporation in their products. This will affect the way it is marketed and perhaps the balance between the importance of cost control, quality control and brand recognition.

The production process

The nature of the product will influence the nature of the production process although there may be external or managerial influences here as well. For instance, factors to be considered include labour and capital intensity, the degree of skill needed and energy intensity. An energy-intensive production process is vulnerable to changes in the price of oil. A management with a choice between two processes which chooses the energy-intensive one at a time of low energy costs can find its calculations falsified if there is a surge in oil prices, as in 1973 and again in 1979/80. On the other hand, a management which chooses the labour-intensive process could suffer equally from a surge in labour costs although good management may be able to offset this by skilful labour relations.

The complexity of the production process is important. A highly complex process may require special-purpose buildings or machinery which may be more expensive to buy and harder to sell in a downturn than a standard light engineering building with standard machinery adaptable to a number of different uses. Similarly, the production process will decide the extent of capital intensity which is discussed below. Its length and the various stages through which it goes will influence the amount of inventory carried and its breakdown between finished goods, work in process and raw materials; the nature of the product combined with the production process may decide whether production is mainly or solely against firm orders or is more speculative and therefore raises a higher inventory risk if the orders disappear.

In general the nature of the product and the production process together will importantly influence flexibility, which is an important feature in considering the credit of any company. The ability to change the level of production quickly to meet changing markets; to shrink the balance sheet, and particularly to reduce borrowings in adverse conditions without damaging the continuing viability of the company; to switch output from one product to another or one market to another to meet changing demand; and in poor conditions the ability to close down or sell off a part of the business, or to delay replacing equipment, without permanently damaging the rest of the business; these are all important defensive elements. A company with high flexibility in these and other ways relies less on protection from a strong balance sheet than one which lacks some of these flexibilities. The less flexible a company is the more it needs to compensate by either balance sheet strength, a particularly high level of earnings and cash flow, stability of sales and costs or some combination. The contribution of most of the subheadings in the rest of this chapter to flexibility is important.

So far the discussion has been of "the" product and "the" production process, but many companies have a wide range of products. Sometimes the production processes will have broadly similar characteristics but some companies use many different processes. (The same may be true of the ultimate market, marketing methods and cost of distribution.) Where this is so the various points must be considered in relation to each main product group with different characteristics and a balance must be struck between the various segments and their relative importance to the business. This can be very difficult where the company does not provide a detailed breakdown but the more the analyst thinks about the underlying nature of each segment of the business the better the chance of understanding the whole credit.

There can be no hard and fast answer to the question of whether a one-product company is sounder than a multi-product company. However, there are some factors which influence the balance sheet in each case. In favour of the single product is simplicity, a single production process, ability of management and all levels of worker in the company to concentrate. This applies to production, to research and development, to marketing, distribution, after-sales service, everything. By contrast, the more products a company has the greater the risk that management attention will be so dispersed that the company will fail to reap the maximum advantage from any product or may fail to notice when one starts to lose ground.

On the other hand, in most cases the diversity of attention carries with it diversity of risk. The main dangers of a single-product company are that something goes wrong with the product, somebody produces a better product or the product's market declines. The company then has no immediate alternative source of revenue and may not have the time or ability to develop one; a company with a range of products can afford to have some decline and even disappear altogether provided the rest continue to do well.

Thus there is no doubt that concentration on a single product is less flexible. The extent to which this matters depends on factors, some of which are common to all products and will be discussed under the appropriate headings below. But a single product is not necessarily sold to a single market so that risk may be diversified with a minimum loss of attention. Moreover, where there are different uses a new product will not necessarily be as effective in all of them. The substitute is likely to have advantages and disadvantages of varying importance to the different end users so that it is less likely that a new product will, in a very short time, put the original product completely out of business. For instance, for many years after the introduction of the transistor some products continued to be made with valves and it was many years after that before replacements ceased to be needed in old equipment. Thus valve-making companies continued to produce at a profit, even if in gradually declining volume, for many years after their product was in a sense obsolete. They therefore had time to generate new products or to run down in an orderly fashion and in the end quietly close down with no loss to any creditors. (To say this is not, of course, to say that all valve manufacturers did so. The ability to recognise the coming end of a market and adapt in time is a management attribute which many companies lack.) On the other hand, a product which has only one or very few end uses is more vulnerable, with the additional risk that the customer industry itself may fail. Even a multi-product company which sells to one market or for one use faces this type of risk. For instance, a company which produces many types of automotive component may be as dependent on the health of the automotive industry as a company with only one product even though it runs less risk that a healthy industry will replace its products with another.

The benefits of concentration of management and so on and a rapid growth rate are greater for shareholders than for bankers, but the risk is borne by the company's balance sheet and through that perhaps by its bankers. Therefore, generally speaking a one-product company requires a strong financial condition and/or high profitability to cover the risk.

Capital intensity

Some products or processes require a higher investment, particularly but not solely in fixed assets, to generate a given level of sales and profits. This is referred to as capital intensity and is usually an inherent factor; the production process broadly determines the extent to which fixed asset investment is necessary and, if sometimes to a lesser degree, the size of NWI needed to support production and to ensure that demand can be met. Some degree of capital intensity can arise from the marketing and distribution requirements; for instance a product which requires many depots throughout the country, or a large amount of finished goods inventory held ready for sale in order to supply demand as soon as it is recognised, can increase capital intensity.

Capital intensity carries implications for the company's balance sheet and profit and loss which need careful consideration. In the first place it means a high level of total assets are illiquid, and should not be financed with short-term liabilities. Thus a high proportion of the capital structure should be either long-term liabilities or net worth. Secondly, to the extent that it is reflected in a high net working investment, a proportion of apparently current assets are not truly liquid and self-renewing, and should be financed long-term. Thus, capital-intensive companies tend to need higher permanent finance, in order to cover the permanent assets; since they also have a higher level of total assets, in relation to sales, more of this finance should be equity, and leverage tends to be lower. Finally, a higher current ratio is usually needed.

There are other reasons which push capital-intensive companies in these directions as well. They tend to have high fixed costs, partly due to high depreciation. Although a non-cash charge, depreciation is a legitimate and continuing deduction from profits because capital assets wear out and have to be replaced. Fixed assets also attract other fixed costs such as maintenance, insurance, taxes, heat and light. They may require a level of skilled labour which is not easily replaced, and therefore cannot be reduced in temporary downturns, so that labour becomes a partly fixed cost. To the extent that assets are financed with borrowed money, interest becomes a fixed cost. As discussed below, fixed costs raise the breakeven point of a company and make it more vulnerable to downward fluctuations in sales. Thus, other things being equal, capital intensity will need to be financed with a higher proportion of equity or other non-interest-bearing finance, to avoid adding to already high fixed costs.

The impact of capital intensity will further depend on the nature of the assets which cause the capital intensity. For instance, two companies may each have fixed assets valued at \$100 million capable of producing sales of \$150 million. However, one may have one very large plant, with integrated production processes and with very high costs involved in running the plant at a minimum safe level or, as in the case of steel mills, in closing it down and then restarting it. Where capital intensity is associated with this type of inflexibility, the tendencies previously described are reinforced.

The other company may have four or five factories, each containing 15 or 20 machines working independently and each capable of being switched from one product to another or stopped temporarily. Here, although depreciation, taxes, insurance remain as true fixed costs, much of the running cost which is fixed in the first example becomes partly variable. Thus although the second company has some of the disadvantages of capital intensity, the implications for its balance sheet and in particular for leverage are less extreme.

Low leverage, or high equity content, represents protection against the ill effects of capital intensity (and other factors). Most companies will fall somewhere between the two extremes described; where exactly they fall will influence the protection they need.

Broadly, the reverse points are valid for a company with low capital intensity; for instance, a commodity company or a pure sales company will have mainly current assets, and an ability to vary its volume of business with little impact on profit margins. Even borrowings will relate mainly to volume, so that interest becomes a variable cost. The company can therefore finance more of its total assets (which will be almost the same as its current assets) with current liabilities and less with equity, since the current assets are mostly fast-moving receivables and inventory which does not need to be financed while being processed. Receivables and inventory need not be replaced if there is a shortfall in demand and will turn into cash quickly and allow a reduction in liabilities. This reduction of both sides of the balance sheet will not impair the company's ability to expand its business again when demand picks up.

The argument then is that non-capital-intensive companies have assets which quickly and easily realise their face value without damaging the business; capital-intensive companies have assets which at best take time to sell, which might well only realise a substantial discount from book value, and the sale of which would damage the long-term future of the company. Until sold, they carry fixed costs. The greater their share in total assets the more important is a strong capital base and a limit on floating rate debt or immediate liabilities (i.e. a strong current ratio is needed to provide liquidity).

Fixed versus variable costs

In the economist's definition, fixed costs are those which continue for a considerable time regardless of the volume of business being transacted, whereas variable costs change with, or as a result of, changes in the volume of business. High fixed costs are often connected with capital intensity, but there are other causes as well.

The word "fixed" is relative. In the long run even a major factory can be closed down. Conversely, even raw material costs can be inflexible if a company is tied to a supply contract which makes it difficult to stop purchasing at short notice. Many items are variable to different degrees. For instance, it may be quite simple to cut back labour costs by reducing overtime working and to that extent labour costs may be genuinely variable costs. But when there is no further overtime to cut, it becomes more difficult. Short-time working is easier to arrange in some countries than in others, depending on the union situation and local laws, but usually has associated costs or inefficiencies in production. Wages used to be considered a variable cost because management could lay people off whenever necessary. However, the development of industrial relations laws in many countries has made this increasingly expensive and sometimes difficult to do at all. The expense means that in many cases companies will find it cheaper to continue to employ the people through what may be a temporary downturn. Even where the law gives a choice, it is often bad labour relations to lay people off at the drop of a hat and in some companies will cause the loss of skills which may be difficult to find when business recovers.

For all these reasons wages (and associated costs) should be investigated carefully, whenever they are important, to see how far they are a fixed cost. In particular, unfunded pension costs relate to the number of existing pensioners and are a fixed cost which will decline only gradually as pensioners die; payments to a fund or trustee, however, relate to present employees and may be cut back with redundancies. However, "last in, first out" is a fairly typical hiring pattern, even when not a union requirement; as a result those kept on will probably account for the bulk of future pension liabilities. In all of this too, the costs of both lay-off and pension are likely to be higher and more fixed for companies which have been good employers in the past, since redundancy payments and pension rights are usually related to the length of service and the level of wages that companies have paid.

Of course, there are cases where none of this is important and wages are genuinely variable. But even in the best countries (for this purpose) there is usually some cost involved in laying people off; and excessive overtime is itself expensive and may be a sign of mismanagement.

Fixed costs related to capital intensity, to fixed assets and to the interest on debt which is funding permanent assets have already been discussed. There are other types of fixed costs as well. Large companies may have substantial office buildings and administrative functions which cannot easily be varied in line with volume; in many cases the marketing costs cannot be easily varied either. Some salesmen are paid largely on commission and this is a variable cost directly related to the volume of business they generate. But there will be marketing managers, there may be distribution depots and a need to carry large stocks of inventory to meet unpredictable demand. Similarly, if the product requires servicing this function cannot easily be cut back and may require the company to hold a stock of spare parts for products which are no longer being produced. Sometimes, too, advertising costs can be considered a relatively fixed cost since a drop in advertising may involve, even in depressed times, a more than proportionate drop in sales and therefore reduction in the coverage of other fixed costs. Finally, the extent to which R & D is a wholly fixed cost varies widely, but even where it can be cut back quite sharply, there is usually a hard core which cannot, and it is rarely closely related to the current level of business.

The importance of fixed costs is that they have to be spread over the total volume of sales. The cost of producing each sale will contain a pro rata share of fixed costs plus the direct or variable costs of that particular unit. A simple mathematical example will illustrate the point. Assume that fixed costs for a particular company are $100 million, that the company can sell the resulting product at a price of $1000 per unit and that the variable costs are $500 per unit. The sale of each item then contributes $500 to fixed costs, which in turn means that the company makes a loss if sales are below 200,000 units. But once unit sales rise above 200,000, each additional sale contributes $500 directly to pre-tax profit. Thus if unit sales are 250,000, pre-tax profits are $25 million. A drop in unit sales, with no other change, from 250,000 to 225,000 (or by 10%) will cause a 50% drop in pre-tax profits from $25 million to $12.5 million. (A similar calculation using $10 million for fixed costs and the same variable costs of $500 with the same sales price shows a dramatically different picture.)

This has interesting implications for the company's pricing policies. Suppose that to avoid a reduction in unit sales, the company has the choice of reducing the unit price from 1000 to 950 and maintaining volume at 250,000 units; the reduction in contribution to overhead would be 10% and sales of 250,000 units at this price would generate $237.5 million in revenue, a decline of 5% instead of 10%, and leave a pre-tax profit of $18.75 million, a decline of 25% instead of 50%. Thus the importance of high fixed costs depends at least partly on the degree of the price elasticity in the product. Obviously if the cut in prices leaves sales at 225,000 items, it simply aggravates the problem. It is for this sort of reason that chemical companies and others with high fixed costs cut their prices substantially in a downturn in an attempt to continue to cover fixed costs even if by a smaller margin. Steel and airlines are two recent examples of these attempts being carried to self-defeating extremes.

Of course, although a particular line of business may involve inherently high fixed costs, management has some ability to control them, as will be discussed in the following chapter. However, the importance of high fixed costs on the balance sheet is seen in two ways. Where interest is a fixed cost, management can reduce it by changing the capital structure more towards equity or other forms of non-interest-bearing finance. Moreover, the risk involved in the multiplier effect is clearly appropriate for the shareholders to bear. There is therefore a general tendency for both reasons to require a higher proportion of equity, or lower leverage, the higher the fixed costs.

The example of a commodity or sales company given in the discussion of capital intensity applies equally well in looking at the difference between fixed and variable costs. Such a company has little in the way of fixed assets or other sources of fixed costs. The two largest cost items will almost always be the cost of goods sold which may be from 75-90%, or even 95%, of total sales, and interest on borrowings used to finance inventory and receivables.

(Because inventory and receivables turn over rapidly, the borrowing will be a relatively low proportion of sales.) In a volume decline, the receivables are collected rapidly, purchases are cut back, debt reduced proportionately and the business continues to operate at a lower volume with approximately the same margins on sales; this may mean reduced total profits before fixed costs, but fixed costs are very small so the net margin only declines modestly if at all and the company's ability to service its liabilities remains unimpaired.

As with capital intensity there is a wide range of different combinations of fixed and variable costs between these two extremes. Particularly when analysing multi-product businesses it is rarely possible to break out exactly which costs are wholly fixed, which are fixed over the short- to medium-term only, and which are fully variable. Nevertheless the analyst needs at least a general idea of their relative importance and must relate this to the various other risks and strengths to come up with an overall assessment.

Nature of fixed assets

Something has already been said about the nature of fixed assets under capital intensity. But they vary widely, not only in their nature but also in their purpose, and this variation can have a substantial effect both on the company's flexibility in managing them and on the return which it can get from all or particular types of them.

Only if it is recognised that different types of business have different requirements will factual information be of much assistance. For instance, to say that a particular company has factories in five different parts of France can be to identify anything from a serious criticism to a major source of strength. For some types of business, it will suggest that the plants are small, old-fashioned and uneconomic and would be better replaced by one or two modern central plants; other types of business may need to have plants close to the customer either because of the cost of transporting the product (cement, for instance) or for marketing, service and similar reasons.

Similarly, fixed assets are not only used in the production process. Some types of distribution require heavy investment in warehouses and depots; others may require a heavy investment in servicing equipment; yet others in cars and/or lorries for the salesmen and delivery of the product. Finally a company may have a large headquarters staff housed in an expensive office block in a prime site in the most expensive part of the capital of its country.

The general nature of fixed assets and their value in relation to sales may be inherent in the nature of the business. However, there is room for good management to ensure that the actual fixed assets are as economical as possible within the range needed. For instance, shift working, either permanently, or in peak periods, may reduce the volume of fixed assets; good maintenance techniques can keep machines running more continuously and reduce the number needed. In some businesses, such as construction, equipment may be hired as needed for specific contracts and so on. An unnecessarily expensive headquarters building can tie up a lot of capital - although with the inflationary tendency for prime property values to increase, its sale at the right time can release cash into productive use in the rest of the business.

Thus there is really no overall guideline to the nature of assets appropriate to different types of company, except to take the trouble to understand the nature of the business and resulting assets and to think through their implications on the financial figures. Consider the flexibility or otherwise, the way in which it arises, the form it takes. Consider how adaptable the assets are, how saleable if no longer needed; consider whether they are old or new and how much it matters. Some assets last longer than others; some are obsolete before they wear out, others are replaced regularly by virtually identical equipment. Relate all of this to the balance sheet and its impact on costs and profits.

The market

A key factor in many aspects of a company's business is the market or markets to which it sells. It may be a mass market or a much more individually tailored market; it may need more or less after-sales service; the product may sell on price, on quality and reliability, on technical advance, on brand loyalty or on a combination of these and other factors; it may need heavy advertising expense or sell on reputation; its distribution may involve investment in fixed assets or in a large labour force.

The difference between mass markets or individual production has implications for a wide range of other factors. Mass markets suggest volume production which in turn suggests capital intensity. For instance, millions of cars and hundreds of millions of pins are produced each year. The motor industry invests billions of dollars in equipment and design for new products and the pin industry probably only a few millions; nevertheless pins are produced on a machine the cost of which is a large multiple of that of the pin, so that an enormous number of pins must be sold to cover fixed costs.

Mass-produced products may thus be commodity products with no brand loyalty. Pins are very much like each other and few consumers can tell the difference enough to ask for a particular brand. Here the market is the retailer, who must be persuaded to stock one company's product rather than another's. Cars are mass-produced, but very much brand oriented so that the end purchaser must be persuaded to approach a particular dealer. Hi-fi sets are different again; dealers will carry several brands and a customer may go in for a particular brand, or for a quality and price which he will check by listening.

These different markets require different types of marketing approach and costs, different inventory levels, all of which affect the risk, the balance sheet and the profitability. And all are different again from the risks and requirements of selling raw materials or sophisticated machinery to major industrial companies.

These differences affect some particular points.

For instance, while pins need no after-sales service both cars and hi-fi sets do, as do many other products both for the mass market and for industry. The nature of the after-sales service required can vary quite widely, however, as can its impact on the company's business. Cars are mostly serviced by the garages that sell them or by other independent garages and the manufacturer may to some extent lose control of the quality of service but at least has very little investment tied up in it. Manufacturers arrange special training programmes for their dealers and insist that the cars be serviced only by them, but the quality of the service is largely outside their control and yet the customer's perception of it may be an important factor in selling the car.

There is also the question of spare parts. The better the quality and more durable the car the longer the maker will need a good stock of spare parts close to wherever the car is sold, which can be expensive unless the dealers take on the cost. But with a model still in production and with some other products (aero engines are perhaps the prime example) the continuing sale of spares over many years is a source of extremely profitable business and may provide a contra-cyclical defence; when customers refrain from buying new cars or aircraft, they have to spend more on spares.

For some products it may be necessary to establish a network of servicing units perhaps equipped with sophisticated machinery which adds to capital intensity and fixed cost; or to ensure that engineers are always available at short notice, which may mean that they are under-employed. A product which needs continual after-service has helpful or harmful characteristics depending how the service is provided; the impact of good or bad service on sales of the original product and the ability of the manufacturer to control its quality; the need to maintain a large range of spares, equipment or people which may tie up money for a long time; and the possibility that service and spare part business may be a continuing source of profit.

The basis on which a product is sold is important. Some products sell almost entirely on price with very little differentiation for quality, reliability and so on. In these cases a company needs efficient and cost-effective manufacturing and distribution facilities to keep the price down. This may require capital-intensive investment in the most modern and up-to-date machinery, pushing the breakeven point higher. Where demand for this type of product is vulnerable to economic decline, which may cause price cutting as producers strive to keep volume above high breakeven points, this adds one more element of risk.

Some products sell largely on impulse buying, so that the seller needs to have products in as many outlets as possible to take advantage of favourable impulses. As well as increasing the volume of inventory to be financed, this may affect the amount and type of advertising, with costs involved, to ensure that the impulse is to buy the company's product rather than a competitor's.

Some products sell more on quality and reliability than on price. These include some sold to the consumer markets but also a range of products sold to industry; this may be equipment used in production, or a component or raw material. A small measuring device sold for inclusion in a large piece of sophisticated equipment may well account for only a tiny proportion of the latter's total cost but may be crucial to its performance. The customer is unlikely to quibble unduly about its price but will insist on complete reliability and technical equality or superiority to anything else on the market. This will require sophisticated quality control, perhaps high-quality R & D and after-sales service; design may be most crucial of all. But clearly the risks of loss of market to competition are very different here than when selling digital watches, cosmetics or bicycles.

Other products sell because technical superiority gives one or more specific advantages over the competition. They may be cheaper, more reliable, lighter where weight is important, faster, or they may have any one of a number of other qualities important in the specific use. But the more they sell on one specific quality rather than a range of qualities, the greater the risk that a new product will outmatch them in this particular quality.

Many products sell on fashion, of which there are broadly three relevant types. Spasmodic crazes such as those for hoolahoops or skate boards enable a company to make a substantial profit for a while but the life of the craze is unpredictable and so is what follows when the craze is over; demand may disappear altogether or settle at a lower level so that some companies at least can make a profit from the product. Then there is fashion for clothing and other items of this type; the basic product is always in demand but the exact form in fashion changes frequently and unpredictably. Here a prime quality for survival is the feel of designers or other people for the way in which fashion is going to develop; a close second is flexibility in manufacturing and distribution so that changes can be made to meet fashion quickly when the first attempt gets it wrong.

The third type of fashion is technological fashion, which usually applies to new products, although sometimes established but minor products (medicines, for instance) suddenly become the "in" product for a particular use. This fashion may continue for longer than the other type, but eventually either a new product will come in or new research suggests that the foundations for the fashion were not well laid. Here, the market may not completely disappear since there is usually a sound continuing use, regardless of fashion, but a company which mistakes fashion for true underlying demand can find itself in a difficult position.

All three types of fashion carry a high risk reward ratio. A company whose product is in fashion sells a high volume usually at good margins; when the product goes out of fashion, volume declines rapidly with little prior warning. In the short run this can leave large stocks of virtually unsaleable products; in the medium to longer run it can mean surplus productive capacity and unmanageable overheads. There are various forms of protection against this risk: diversity of product, to avoid over-dependence on any one; flexibility of manufacturing; perhaps sub-contracting of production to pass the fixed costs on to a third party; and others as appropriate to the particular product. But one protection is a strong balance sheet, with limited reliance on borrowed money.

Distribution

One feature affected by the nature of the product and of its market is the form of distribution, and the various types of cost, risk and investment which it requires. For instance, a company which sells wholly through wholesalers or agents may be able to reduce its direct costs in salesmen, warehouses etc., but will have to cede part of its profit margin to the middle man, and loses control of the enthusiasm with which the product is sold; it may, however, get access to expertise not otherwise available. Whether the use of a middle man is inherent or the result of a management decision and whether it is a plus or minus can only be decided case by case.

Some products require substantial investment in distribution, in the form of warehouses or smaller depots scattered throughout the country to act as central delivery points; or of lorries or vans for the actual transport; or the more indirect form of keeping the factories relatively small and scattered because the product has a low value to weight ratio and therefore cannot be economically transported long distances.

Impact on receivable and inventory turnover and quality

Chapters 2 and 8 discuss the importance of receivable and inventory turnover. This can be affected by the nature of the product and also by the market to which the product is sold. Taking receivables first, as a broad generalisation very large products which take months or years to produce - i.e. usually capital items - are often sold on long credit terms. Sometimes this can be offset by receiving interest, which still involves a credit risk. More often the company has to absorb the whole burden of carrying the receivables and in an inflationary environment this can be costly. Moreover, where the individual sales are very large the risk is concentrated. A single customer failing to pay can then have a much more dramatic impact on the company than when sales are to hundreds or even thousands of customers, so that no one accounts for more than 1 or 2% of total receivables. Concentration of sales to a relatively small number of customers has other risks; a creditworthy customer may use his importance to obtain longer payment terms or lower prices than normal in the industry, or a large customer may decide to make the product itself. However, selling to a few strong companies can reduce the credit risk, the cost of collection and the need for advertising and other marketing costs.

A company whose products are sold in very small amounts to many customers has the protection of diversification but will probably need a more expensive collection and credit-checking procedure to ensure continuing prompt payment, and will almost always suffer some credit losses. It cannot be hard hit by any one defection but can be hit by many if it allows its quality or credit controls to slip.

Products sold mainly to governments or government agencies are nearly always subject to slow payment. Defence items, school books and equipment, in some countries medicine, and some other items are sold mainly to governments, and many others have government as a major but not sole customer. Depending on the country, the tendency to pay slowly may be more or less extreme. In Italy, for instance, the hospital system rarely pays in less than a year, sometimes nearer two years. Thus although the credit risk in selling to governments is usually good, the risk of slow payment and consequent interest cost, erosion of value by inflation and so on is often damaging.

Exports tend to have a longer collection period than domestic sales. This depends to some extent on the countries from and to which goods are exported. Exporting from a country where payments are usually slow, such as Italy or Spain, to one where they are faster, such as Germany, may even improve turnover. But more often the longer period between shipment and receipt of the goods, the need to buy foreign currency and the sheer distance and difficulty of pressing for payment tend to cause exports to turn over more slowly than domestic receivables. It may also be harder for the exporter to check on the quality of the importer; even if he can do so before the initial sale he may find it difficult to keep doing so as sales grow. As protection it is often possible to get either government-backed or private enterprise export insurance which covers most of the risk of an overseas customer, and the analyst should know whether, and if so in what form, this has been done. Finally, exports may be denominated in foreign currencies; if so which ones, and the steps the company takes to cover the exchange risk, can decide whether there is risk of loss or even chance of profit due to currency movements.

The nature of the business, the product and the marketing and distribution can also have an affect on inventory turnover and quality. The retailer or wholesaler who simply takes finished goods in, displays them and sells them has a fast turnover; for perishable food, the turnover may be as little as a week but even items such as clothes or white goods should have a fairly rapid turnover.

Manufacturing processes of varying degrees of complexity have needs for large stocks of raw materials or semi-finished components at each stage in the process; there is also a considerable difference in the actual time spent in the manufacturing process itself before the product moves from one stage to another and is finally completed. If it is manufactured against specific orders it will be shipped as soon as completed; if for sale off the shelf it may be held in the factory, or in warehouses or depots throughout the country, or placed with retailers on consignment or under sale and return contracts, so that the risk and the financing cost remains with the manufacturer until final sale.

The size and nature of the inventory can also depend on whether the company is making a number of closely related products so that raw materials and perhaps components and even semi-finished goods can be switched quickly from one product to another if demand fluctuates; or whether the products are so differentiated that a full reserve of raw materials or components has to be held for each one.

Technology and R & D

The level of technology required has several implications for both the balance sheet and profit and loss and the degree of risk.

As a generalisation, to which there are exceptions in both directions, high technology products require larger R & D spending as a proportion of sales. While it is undoubtedly necessary for many companies to spend money to keep up with technology and ensure that their product remains competitive, the quality of R & D is one of the hardest things for an outsider to judge. It is not too difficult to compare the amount spent on R & D with competitors' spending, as a percentage of sales or in absolute terms. (This can be one area where size is extremely important. IBM spends more in R & D annually than many computer companies generate in sales. The advantage this gives hardly needs stressing.) But the amount spent tells very little about the value received for it, particularly since R & D often aims at long-term rather than short-term results. So a company with a liquidity shortage may look at R & D as an expense which can be cut fairly quickly without doing much damage in the short-term; by doing so it may damage its longer-term chance of survival. In the reverse situation some companies obstinately persist in R & D which has no prospect of an immediate return, so ensuring that they do not remain in existence long enough to exploit the outcome.

There is no way of discovering from the figures alone whether R & D is effective. The annual report or possibly even the technical page of the Financial Times and other similar publications may show that the company is introducing new products, which at least suggests that it is getting something from the R & D. But this is one area where a company visit can show something about the quality of the R & D and about its practicality and the likely timing of any benefit. Is the company technically behind the competition and struggling to catch up? Is the R & D simply aimed at minor improvements to existing products and methods or is it aimed at a breakthrough into a completely new product or process for producing the same product? If the R & D is successful, will it merely stem loss of market share, increase share of existing markets or open up new markets which had not previously been available to the company? If so, will there be any beneficial side-effects on existing products? Although companies should have enthusiasts in their R & D departments, who may in good faith oversell the advantages of the work they are doing, nevertheless answers to these types of questions can be a useful beginning to understanding R & D in a particular company.

Bankers can also talk to suppliers, customers and competitors. This has to be extremely carefully handled if there is any reason to fear that the company is in any sort of trouble; the last thing a banker wishes to do with such an enquiry is to make the problem worse. For these reasons specific questioning about one company is not very common but discussions about the industry and state of the art as a whole can often be informative. The point is not just to have good scientists; good management of R & D ensures that it leads to marketable products, to improvements in existing products or in the manufacture of existing products. The most common benefit is larger sales, but R & D can also be an effective defence against the competitive inroads, or can help to reduce costs and so improve margins on a stable volume of sales. R & D into the manufacturing process may be as important as R & D into the product itself.

Altogether, then, R & D is a fixed cost in the sense that it does not vary with today's volume of business, but it is sometimes one which can be cut back sharply without damaging the immediate business of the company. There is a danger therefore that in difficult times R & D gets cut back sharply with adverse long-term results. There is an equal danger, however, that bankers who are aware of the first danger allow the company to go on spending money freely on R & D without being sure the money is well spent.

Although a certain speculative element in R & D spending is inevitable, nevertheless R & D, like anything else, should be able to justify itself by results over the medium to longer term. Management should be able to satisfy its bankers that the amount of money currently being spent is commensurate with the potential rewards in the future and is being spent in a controlled way most likely to obtain results. Finally, the longer the time before the benefits are felt, the greater the combination of profitability and balance sheet strength required to carry the R & D.

Because of the difficulty of all this, too many bankers judge a company's R & D spending purely by the percentage of sales, compared with other companies in the same industry, rather than by actual and potential results.

Advances

Advances are inherent rather than external in the sense that they arise mostly in situations where the completion period of a product and the costs involved during that completion are substantial. Probably the most important case of this is various types of construction project, but it can also apply to heavy equipment, arms and so on. Occasionally it can arise in other situations such as the producer of mineral waters who receives deposits on the bottles which are repayable only when the bottles are returned for refilling.

However the advances arise, they have a substantial affect on the balance sheet and on the company's profitability. This affect is particularly important in times of high interest rates, but can sometimes be exaggerated where a company accounts on the completed contract basis. Amounts may be shown as advances which in fact are progress payments for work already done rather than advance payments for work to be done. Although they may show as advances, and the work done as inventory, in fact the goods have been shipped or the work on site has reached a certain stage and therefore all the expenses related to them have been incurred before the payment is made. In this case the effects discussed below either do not occur at all or are limited.

A genuine advance payment first reduces and sometimes eliminates the need to borrow to finance inventory and receivables; i.e. it reduces or eliminates net working investment. In extreme cases it creates a cash surplus which can be invested in short-term money market or sometimes longer-term instruments to earn a significant return. The result, particularly where cash balances are generated, is to make the balance sheet more liquid. Even without cash balances, replacing borrowings with advances improves liquidity, since an advance does not have to be repaid in the normal course of business, unlike borrowing.

On the profit and loss statement the result is at least a reduction in interest cost and sometimes its replacement by interest or other financial income. Thus, whereas normally operating profit has to be sufficient to cover financial expenses as well as taxes and extraordinary items, a company with large advances can afford a lower operating profit. Indeed, a company which is sure of getting a given percentage advance on a contract and which is able to predict with some confidence the return on the advance, can afford to reduce its price and its gross and operating margins in order to obtain the contract and still make a satisfactory overall return.

However, there are some dangers in relying too heavily or uncritically on the continuance of advances. They are made against future deliveries and therefore inventory must be purchased and processed, wages paid and so on without any further income. Secondly, if for any reason the supplier fails to deliver in accordance with his contract, the advance is repayable; thus it is definitely a liability even if it is normally met by delivery of goods or work rather than cash. The value of advances fluctuates with interest rates; in a time of high interest rates the amount saved on borrowing or earned on investment will be correspondingly large, but if interest rates drop sharply so will the return. This may put the company in a dangerous position if it has allowed its operating margins to decline in order to obtain the advances. Or a change in customers' finances may make advances harder to obtain, as happened in several areas in the early 1980s. It usually happens in tight competitive conditions so that it is difficult to raise operating margins to offset the decline in advances; and the company may find itself with a sharp decrease in liquidity, a sharp increase in interest costs (or decrease in interest income) and pressure on operating margins, all at the same time.

Thus, although advances are useful and desirable, analysts and managements must be aware of the dangers and able to assess their profitability and the risk of their loss against the company's balance sheet strength and profitability. This may require the analyst to know whether the company receives relatively small percentage advances across a range of products or whether it receives large advances on a relatively small number of projects. The danger of concentration applies to advances as much as to other aspects.

10 The Managerial and External Factors

The quality of management is always an important factor in corporate credit and often the most important single factor, but is very difficult to judge objectively. J. P. Morgan was thought to be able to judge a man's ability and integrity on the basis of one meeting and there may be some bankers today who pride themselves on the same ability; but most have to look for other criteria.

The number of companies dependent on one man, whose ability decides the quality of the whole management, is these days small. Often, however, the banker's personal knowledge is confined to financial management only, or perhaps the managing director or chairman. But a good financial management may not be influential in a company dominated by engineers or marketing men; and even a competent chairman or managing director may lack support. The bank needs to assess the quality of management in all areas; finance certainly, but also production, marketing, R & D, personnel and labour relations to mention only the most important. Moreover, the management needs to be competent not merely at the top but in depth. In a large company, even the ablest manager cannot do everything himself, indeed the ablest manager is usually the one who delegates the most successfully. A one-man band, whether running the company as a whole, or a particular function within it, can prove disastrous if the one man leaves the scene or if the managerial requirements change. But a delegator needs to recruit sound managers to whom to delegate, and the bank can only judge whether he has done this by meeting the people, which is often not a practical proposition.

The quality of management may show in the past record; however, an unbroken record of success may simply reflect favourable conditions. It may even lead to a situation where, since the management has never had to deal with unfavourable conditions, it loses the ability to adapt to them. Many companies have collapsed apparently overnight after a long run of success and been shown to be rather poorly managed. Indeed, a record with some setbacks from which management has recovered well may be a better indication of management's resilience and adaptability than an unbroken upward trend. But even then the record is only the past history and does not say very much about the present or the future.

There is no certain method of judging management, but a close look at the various factors which affect the company's wellbeing and how they have been handled can help, as well as giving an indication of how soundly based the company is operationally and financially.

The factors outlined in Chapter 8 which are inherent to a company are only so within a more or less broad range. The quality of management will decide where within that range the particular company falls.

Financial controls

Although very few companies make much money from financial controls, many lose it and some go out of business because of weak financial controls. Some aspects of them have been touched on in earlier chapters; for instance, receivable turnover, within the parameters of the particular business, is a direct reflection of financial controls; so is the quality and concentration of receivables and thus the risk of bad debts as opposed to slow payment. Inventory turnover may not be a direct result of financial controls, more often it requires good production management, reliable suppliers or occasionally even location close to suppliers. For instance, few European companies keep such low stocks of raw materials and components as Japanese companies because European suppliers will rarely guarantee the frequency or reliability of delivery to make it possible. Nevertheless, a well-managed company will ensure that its suppliers are reliable and deliver often, allowing lower holdings of inventory and related financing costs. It will also organise its production to ensure the smallest possible stock of raw materials etc. awaiting each stage of processing. A less well-managed company or one which is less lucky in its suppliers may find that it has to accept less frequent but larger deliveries, or to buy from two or more suppliers to ensure it never runs out. This may increase the purchase price, since neither supplier can spread its overheads over the maximum possible volume, and even then the customer may have to keep higher stocks than it likes. Much of this is outside the area of financial controls strictly defined, but good financial controls will highlight the success or failure of measures to control inventory levels.

Much the same can be said about various types of cost. One directly related to inventory which can be very expensive is wastage. Companies which use a large amount of expensive raw material in their product can have widely varying wastage rates which can be expensive; financial controls should pinpoint the need for a reduction even though the wastage itself may be the result of poor manufacturing techniques. More generally, companies need good cost control systems which enable them to pinpoint quickly changes in the relative level of various costs to sales and the reason for them. They also need to allocate costs, particularly overheads, correctly. Controls should allow them to identify those products which are showing good margins and those where a price increase or a change in manufacturing technique is needed or where the company should consider ending production altogether. Too many companies do not have a clear idea of the breakdown of their costs either between different types of material, component etc. or between products. As a result they may put too much marketing and manufacturing effort behind the less profitable products and neglect the more profitable; or they may use a more expensive raw material or component than is necessary for the product or justified by the price they are getting.

Limited information as to these features is available in published annual or interim reports; even management accounts rarely give a clear picture. While poor control of costs usually shows up in operating results, it will rarely be possible to tell that this is due to poor financial controls rather than some other aspect. Thus the analyst who senses that something is wrong has to rely on discussions with management in most cases, or perhaps intercompany comparisons of those costs which are broken out, to try to identify the weakness and management's handling of it.

Any going concern banker should be doing this in all of his contacts with the company. Although many contacts may be to market the bank's services or solve particular problems, nevertheless the banker should be taking every opportunity to discuss the business with the financial and other management and to assess different aspects of it. Even without reviewing the full paraphernalia of cost controls he should aim for a feel as to financial management's skill in monitoring costs.

Good financial controls are also important to ensure that forecasts and budgets are realistic. (Realism, or lack of it, in budgets is a prime indicator to the quality of management.) Although the main input as to the sales volume should come from the marketing units, financial controls must ensure that they are realistic and that the company can accurately budget the costs arising from them, and thus the balance sheet and the subsequent financial costs or income arising from that. In other words, to forecast receivable turnover accurately it must be controlled; without such control, management can neither forecast nor control interest costs.

Altogether, then, financial controls are an important managerial mechanism for operating as effectively as possible within the inherent requirements. As a means of judging management, it is less satisfactory because it is harder to assess on the information available. There are pointers, however, even though they are often inconclusive. Do receivable and inventory turnover, for instance, expand when sales increase, but fail to contract when sales decline? Are budgets consistently optimistic? Are debt and interest increasing as a percentage of sales, and increasing faster when sales are growing than when they are declining? Is the company fuzzy on what are its most, or least, profitable products or what is its cost structure? Is it reluctant to eliminate loss-making products? Worse still, does it claim to have done so, but still margins fall? These and similar questions should be reviewed in the light of the figures, but also of the information gleaned in conversations with the company and about the industry.

It may be tempting to feel that really large companies with massive financial resources which invest hundreds of millions of pounds a year do not require tight controls or are so sophisticated that they automatically have them. In fact, the reverse is true. Even where controls only make a difference of 1% or less of costs, this amounts to millions, even tens of millions, of dollars for a large company. Moreover, the very size which makes control essential risks creating a "control bureaucracy" which cancels out the benefits. Controls must be effective, but their cost too must be controlled.

Quality and amount of capital expenditure

The nature of the business decides the nature of the capital assets, but there is considerable scope for management to improve the quality of capital expenditure and to control the amount. It should never be more in any period than the company's finance can reasonably handle. Nor should it be so small in some years that the company falls behind and then has to have a great catching-up period. Clearly the extent to which it should be completely even year by year depends on the nature of the capital items being financed, and particularly the minimum economic units of capacity. Investment can also be timed to avoid coming on stream at the beginning of a slump. Within the scope of what is practicable, quite wide variations in management occur.

Quite apart from the amount of capital expenditure there is the question of its purpose and quality. If the company is investing for growth, rather than replacement, then it should have satisfied itself that there will be a market for the higher output at prices which will ensure a satisfactory return. The banker rarely can or should double-check the decision in detail, but he should be satisfied that the company has sound techniques to control expenditure and appraise investments and minimise the room for doubt. All the information in the world cannot replace commercial judgement, and it is not a banker's job to stop a company taking sensible risks. But companies should take risks consciously, not by mistake, and the expenditure and related financing should not be so large that a failure, perhaps even a partial failure, could endanger the company's whole future.

The quality of investment is harder for a banker to judge. To do so, he needs to know about its purpose, the marketing opportunity for which it is designed, and the technical or other risks which might cause it to go wrong; and in many cases the company will invest in a mix of assets with different combinations of factors. The banker may be able to judge whether the purpose itself is a sound one and whether the investment is well designed to meet it, but often he will have to take management's word for it so that his assessment of management's competence is that much more important. He should be better able to judge the prospects of the markets for which the investment is aimed, and whether the company's position will be enhanced sufficiently to justify the investment. And finally, he should have some idea of the risks; the equipment may already be, or soon become, obsolete; on the other hand, if it is breaking new technical frontiers it may not work according to specification; it may be more expensive to buy, or to run, than the improved volume justifies, and so on.

Within the overall amount spent there are three types of purpose for capital which affect the quality. They are replacement of worn-out equipment with no improvement; replacement of existing equipment, whether fully worn out or not, with better assets which improve production techniques, save labour or some other factor; and completely new capacity to expand volume, or perhaps introduce a new product. Very few companies invest solely in pure replacement, but when they do the main risk is of obsolescence. A mixture of replacement and improvement is quite common, with the balance varying widely; there is some risk of obsolescence here, and some of technical failure, but if the investment is in improved equipment, rather than in a technical breakthrough, the risk is moderate.

There is a wide difference in risk between relatively small accretions of new capacity to take advantage of a growing market, or of greater market penetration in existing products, and large units of new capacity to break into a new market or introduce a new product. Companies do not always have a free choice as to which type of investment strategy to follow, but when they take the riskier one, the risk should be controlled. This is partly a question of size, of familiarity. A company expanding its existing capacity for a well-known product with well-known manufacturing processes is unlikely to run into any technical or other unexpected problems; on the other hand there are examples of companies nearly bankrupting themselves with a new and costly process which has not worked as expected.

But there is also the question of whether the expenditure is the best for the purpose. Companies which consistently spend their money on out-of-date machine tools, for instance, because they do not have either the expertise or imagination to buy and use the most advanced, are soon at a competitive disadvantage. Other companies which buy the latest gadget regardless of whether or not it is necessary for their particular business and/or whether they can earn a decent return on it will run into trouble for the opposite reason. To some extent both of these problems relate to financial controls, since these should certainly ensure that adequate economic justification is identified before major expenditure is authorised.

Conversely, financial controls which pay too much attention to cost and not enough to return and competitiveness may result in buying machinery that is cheap, rather than the most cost-effective for the purpose. But although financial controls can have an influence on the quality of capital expenditure, it is not primarily a financial matter. The finance director can only look at the capital proposals that are put up and test them for economic viability. He will rarely know what alternative equipment is available and even if he does will not be well placed to make a case for it if the people who will use it do not want it.

Much the same is true for the banker, who cannot measure the quality of fixed asset spending closely, but can get some pointers from the figures. At one extreme, a fairly steady increase in capital expenditure, perhaps above depreciation but consistently related to it, which generates a high return and little or no increase in leverage suggests good quality expenditure. At the other extreme is a company which after years of low capital expenditure, generating poor returns, suddenly launches into a large re-equipment programme; this increases leverage sharply, but the banker may well wonder why the management which achieved such poor returns on the old equipment should do any better now. If the return on assets remains weak, it may soon create a problem in servicing the debt; it will then be too late to refuse to lend, however.

Few companies in fact fall at either of these clear-cut extremes, and where there are mixed indications the conflict may arise wholly or mainly from the quality of the capital expenditure or may reflect problems or advantages elsewhere in the business. Nevertheless, study the relationship between capital expenditure, depreciation and the trend in return on assets (lagged if necessary to allow for a delay between starting to spend the money and actually going into production and selling the output); these trends, in the light of changes in the capital structure, at least give a pointer as to the quality of management decisions. Again, it may be too late to decide the current programme was badly thought out after it fails; the company's past record may indicate whether it has ever attempted a comparable expansion and if so how well it was managed.

The time lag is important both in assessing the effects of capital expenditure and in managing it in the best possible way. Some companies can buy a machine tool off the peg, install it and have it producing within a matter of weeks; others can tailor their expenditure programmes very closely to demand, and only need to tie up funds in a non-producing investment for a short time, if at all. Particularly when a company is in a weak financial condition, the ability to get a quick return on investment can be a very substantial advantage, partly inherent, but also subject to management action.

On the other hand, some companies invest in larger units which may only start to produce months or even years after they are ordered. This type of investment requires careful advance planning and a strong balance sheet. To commit large amounts of money knowing that the return is at least two years off involves a greater risk that demand will no longer exist, or that a new process will make the one being installed obsolete before it starts to produce; or simply that other people may have the same idea, so that the plant comes on stream facing massive overcapacity. If earnings are low at the beginning, this compounds the risk, and if their weakness is due to poor demand there is the additional fear that they may not recover. On the other hand, to fail to spend the money may condemn a company which is already suffering because of inadequate capital expenditure to permanent decline and eventual liquidation.

Thus the quality of capital expenditure and of the financial controls relating to it is very important in the company's long-term future. A banker can rarely have detailed knowledge of how the decisions are taken and whether they are right, but should aim for at least a general feel. The more capital-intensive the company, the more important the quality of its capital spending.

Quality of assets

The quality of assets is important to the lending banker, even though the bank rarely looks to them as its primary source of repayment. Banks always want a possible second way out if the primary way (usually cash flow or refinancing based on cash flow) fails, and high-quality assets help to provide it. Their quality, moreover, may well be a feature in helping the company to generate the cash flow which will provide the first way out and make the second unnecessary. Although quality can be defined in several ways, one is certainly the ability to generate a return which services all the debt used to finance the assets, with a satisfactory margin for contingencies, re-investment, return to shareholders and so on.

The quality of fixed assets is largely a reflection of the quality of the capital expenditure over previous years. If it has been correctly judged in amount and wise in direction, then the quality of the fixed assets will probably be good, at least initially. They still can be badly operated or badly maintained but this is very difficult for a bank to judge directly, and it is usually necessary to assume that companies which buy well probably use and maintain well and the reverse may also be true. Good purchasing does not enable a company to avoid its assets becoming obsolescent in a fast-moving industry, since even a well-judged purchase may be superseded. However, a well-managed company will recognise this early, depreciate the asset rapidly and phase it out quickly.

But some of the features which affect the ease or difficulty of planning a capital expenditure programme also affect the quality of the assets. For instance a company which operates standard machine tools or looms in general light engineering buildings has more flexibility than the one which has to use an enormous integrated process in a purpose-built building costing tens of millions of pounds; the former are better-quality assets than the latter in this if no other sense. A slump will undermine the value of most assets to some extent; a slump in a specialist industry may make assets designed solely for it virtually valueless, whereas more general-purpose equipment may only lose 10, 20 or 30% of its value, damaging but less likely to be fatal.

Furthermore, a company which could realise its assets in

small units at a relatively modest discount in a slump is less likely to be forced to do so. Banks will be more willing to give it time because they recognise that the amount they can lose by doing so if the recovery attempt is unsuccessful is limited; to sell the assets six months, a year or even two years later will recover almost as much as selling now, and the company need earn only enough to pay the interest for the banks to be little or no worse off by waiting. On the other hand, a company whose fixed assets are liable to lose value very rapidly in bad times may find it harder to persuade the bank to give it time to sort out its problems. The bank can see that time costing a great deal of money as the market value of the assets shrinks. The existence of a satisfactory second way out therefore may help to make it less likely that it will in fact have to be used.

The features making for quality of receivables and inventory have already been discussed. Their quality is crucial both because they are the vital mechanism through which the company generates earnings and cash flow and because they are prime elements in liquidity. Moreover, in liquidation receivables, and sometimes inventory, are the assets most likely to be collected at little or no discount. They are thus an important part of the second way out, and again a bank is less likely to take early protective action if it knows they are of good quality.

The risk of liquidation, however, makes it desirable to look at them from a slightly different point of view. Not all receivables are as collectible in liquidation as on a going concern basis. The customer may argue that he bought the goods expecting the producer to be able to service them; if it is not, he does not want them and will return them unpaid. In such a situation it is also unlikely that finished goods inventory, at least, will be saleable at anything approaching cost. On the other hand there is no reason why anybody should refuse to pay for plywood and any inventory of it should sell at close to book value.

Some of these factors are inherent in the nature of the business, but a great deal is managerial and some external. For instance, two companies making the same type of chemical product and creating the same degree of pollution may be faced with different requirements for pollution control. One company may have to finance substantial assets and resulting costs solely for this purpose, contributing nothing directly to the saleability of the product. This can leave it at a competitive disadvantage, on top of which the anti-pollution equipment may be specifically designed to meet either local regulations or a particular environment and have little or no value to anybody else.

In other cases, however, management may have a choice between two types of process, one of which is less polluting but perhaps has other drawbacks. There are also products, such as cement, which can be made in a more or less energy-intensive way. Companies which installed the more energy-intensive method before 1973, or even 1979, now have to generate enough earnings to be able to afford the alternative method. Otherwise they will see their costs become steadily less competitive as more and more companies change to the energy-efficient process. There can be an element of luck here; companies at different stages in their re-equipment cycles when the new process is first discovered may be more or less able to convert it. Mainly, however, it is a question of having the technical knowledge and management foresight to recognise the size of the advantage the new process gives, and the cash flow to take the opportunity.

Where the equipment comes in relatively small accretions, then it is more a question of recognising the better equipment before the competition. If a company is spending a stable amount each year, it is important that it buy the right assets, but one or two years' delay may be less damaging than spending five years' cash flow on a plant which is obsolete before it comes on stream.

Labour relations and wage costs

Labour relations cannot be analysed from the balance sheet or profit and loss statement. However, they can be vital to the health of a company and it is important (although often difficult) to have an idea of their quality, the extent to which the company is unionised and whether by one union or a number which have conflicting points of view; in some countries the political complexion of the union will be important, in others the frame of mind of the shop stewards or men on the shop floor, in others the union leadership. Labour relations decide more than just whether the company has a large number of strikes or other forms of industrial action; they are crucial to the effective use of manpower and to obtaining the best results from modern equipment. Indeed it can be argued that good labour relations can improve the quality of capital assets by allowing effective use so that they reach their full potential. In some cases it affects the quality of expenditure too, since there may be no point in buying the best equipment if the labour force refuses to operate it.

Talking to management can help to give a feel about labour relations; a management which is proud of its labour relations and feels it has a good workforce will usually say so; conversely, a management which is continually criticising the quality of its people, their unwillingness to work, their stupidity or lack of training may indirectly be criticising itself. Lack of training in particular is a reflection on management's failure either to recruit the right people or train them in the right way. While not all companies can afford some of the amenities which the most enlightened companies provide, generally speaking a management which is considerate of its labour force, provided it is not too paternal, is likely to have better labour relations than one which is not.

Factory visits or office visits for service companies can also help in judging labour relations, as part of the wider judgement of how well set out the plant is, the flow of goods through it, the quality of equipment and so on. Unless a banker is experienced, however, it is easy to be taken in by an impression of activity and goodwill which may only reflect that the particular person taking him round is quite well liked.

Many companies give a figure for wages which should, ideally, include related payments such as social security and pension reserves and so on. It is possible then to see what proportion of sales this is and whether it is increasing, decreasing or stable. While this may reflect changes in pricing, or in fixed assets, it also gives an indication of unit labour costs and indirectly of how well labour is being used. Industry comparisons can be useful if the banker can find a company in a similar line of business. If the number of employees is known as well as the total bill this can give an average per employee. Industry comparisons will then show not only the unit costs, but whether the company is paying more or less than competitors and thus how likely it is to lose good people. It can be difficult for a company to refuse to match wages offered elsewhere without risking losing a lot of its people. Good labour relations and other tangible or intangible benefits in working for a particular company may partly offset a wage differential but management cannot rely on this for more than a short time. Therefore it comes down to making the best use of the labour; if skilled workers command £100 per week in a particular locality or industry, the company which employs them must use them well enough to justify the wage. The higher wages are as a percentage of total costs, the more important it is to ensure good usage of labour to reduce unit labour costs.

High wage costs as a percentage of sales, and certainly a deterioration in this figure, warn the analyst to ask questions about possible reasons, including labour relations. A favourable or improving figure may allow the analyst to concentrate more on other problems, since it appears that any labour problems there may be are not damaging operations. However, the analyst should be alert to the possibility that apparently good labour relations result from buying off problems, so that costs are high or inflexible. It may be possible to absorb such cost in higher volume while business is going well, but they may become unacceptable and the lack of flexibility much more damaging in a decline. It is then that the trust that arises from dealing with problems constructively rather than buying them off is most needed.

Redundancy costs and labour costs

Even in a growing economy the need to adapt to changing conditions may require a company to close some plants while expanding others; to do this effectively it may need to lay off people. Companies in declining industries and almost all companies in a recession often need to reduce the total number of people they employ. Good financial controls combined with good planning and forecasting should allow management to foresee this need and to smoothe it by not replacing workers who leave or retire, often known as "natural wastage". Where this is not enough they may also make generous provisions for early retirement or find other ways of persuading people to leave voluntarily. However, this is obviously more effective in an expanding economy where other jobs are readily available; in a declining economy less people will leave naturally or be prepared to go with only a gentle push. And even the best-managed companies are hit by sudden changes in business conditions or in competitive position and demand for particular types of product; this may arise for instance from a change in the price of raw materials such as oil. In these circumstances, and for less farsighted companies in other circumstances, the ease and cost of redundancy can be vital to a company's long-term creditworthiness; this depends on the laws and social climate of the country in which the company operates.

The extent of any restraint varies from country to country. In a few, ability to lay people off with little or no legal cost is almost unfettered. Although good managements often treat their people better than the legal minimum requirement, this approach allows management the most flexibility. In some countries there may be some legal constraints but the main ones result from union requirements. These can be very onerous and can be affected by the negotiating climate in the country or industry concerned over which management has little control. Nevertheless good managements have been able to negotiate arrangements which are workable with even the most difficult unions. The worst position is where labour laws make it virtually impossible to lay people off, or prescribe very high minimum payments for doing so, which are often prohibitive. In this situation the cost of being a good employer can be greatest because the statutory requirements often relate to length of service.

This type of labour law or union practice may not apply solely to redundancy (or the need to reduce the overall number of people because of lower volume). There may be union or legally-imposed restrictions on dismissing people for incompetence, or for any reason short of proven dishonesty. There may even be a prescriptive right to a particular job so that an employee cannot easily be moved from one job to another, even at the same pay, or have the job definition changed. These are all external constraints, which good management can partly alleviate, depending on their nature and source. The analyst needs to be aware of them in assessing the company, and particularly of their possible impact if the company is in a declining industry or weak economy.

Thus redundancy costs and labour laws are a serious problem when things go wrong but can be an important constraint even to a stable or expanding company. They may also be a factor in the level of inflation, the availability of skilled labour, and the possibility of training more; they can restrict the flow of skilled men on to the market and push up their cost; overmanning in heavily unionised industries may also reduce the availability and increase the cost of people to non-unionised companies.

Management can use skill to make the best of the particular environment in which it works, but a poor environment must make its task harder and the risks that it will fail greater than a favourable environment.

Quality of the product and of service

The quality of the product and its reputation for value clearly are within management's control. However, quality usually has a cost attached, and there is often a limit to the extra price people are willing to pay for quality. Balancing the demand for quality against the cost of obtaining it and producing something that will sell on both bases is a major management skill. The balance will depend on the complexity of the manufacturing process, whether quality involves more expensive materials or greater precision in production, the general nature of the use and the particular requirements of the customer. The owner of a mini car has lower expectations about quality than the owner of a Rolls Royce, and pays less; but if his expectations are not met he will not buy from the same manufacturer again even if its product is cheaper than other mini cars.

There are a wide number of individual factors which affect the ability to achieve the right quality at the right price; the design of the product and of the manufacturing process; the control of labour and of raw materials and components, to mention only a few. The banker can rarely expect to judge for himself how well management handles each individual item, but should try to obtain an overall feel as to the company's success. Some of this can come from market surveys, conversations with competitors or suppliers, or newspaper or magazine articles. The banker may even use the product himself or have friends who do. If any of these sources raises a serious question as to the company's quality/price mix, it can be worth discussing with management.

The standard of service affects the customer's view of quality where service is needed. Many consumer goods tend to be important financially to the consumer, who purchases them relatively infrequently. A car, a hi-fi set, a dishwasher or clothes washer, a refrigerator are all things which the consumer uses regularly, relies on, in some cases heavily, and expects to work (which is part of the quality). Recognising that nothing can work without any possibility of failure, consumers expect a prompt repair service. And repeat buying of a particular product may well be heavily affected by the consumer's view of quality, which in turn is heavily influenced by service. The size and infrequency of the purchase means that once a customer is lost, recovery is slow.

Where the product is sold to industry or commerce the servicing requirement can be just as important. Whether it is a machine tool or lathe, a copying machine, a computer or typewriter the company wants to be able to use it continuously and its breakdown may affect many other parts of the business. Again the customer looks first to reliability to ensure that it does not break down frequently, but recognises that some breakdown and some maintenance are inevitable, and expects fast service. In some products service can be a very profitable sideline, particularly if it involves sale of replacement parts, but the main point is usually to ensure satisfied customers and repeat buying. A company with an inadequate service network or a reputation for poor service is often at a significant competitive disadvantage, while one with a reputation for exceptional service may be able to charge a premium price and thus improve its margins as well as its volume.

Position in the market

Position in the market exists in two different senses. One is the importance of the company in the market, its market share, degree of price and even fashion leadership. The other is the segment or segments of the market it chooses to penetrate. Cars range in price and quality from a Rolls Royce, through a Volvo or BMW to various qualities and sizes of mass-produced car to the Mini; there are also specialist cars such as sports cars, Land Rovers etc. Most other consumer products have a similar range of price and quality and so do many industrial products. A company has to decide in each case whether it needs to offer the whole range, or whether to go for a specialist niche, or to aim for volume and low costs, quality and high margins, or some compromise. The correct judgement of which segment or segments a company should cover is complex and depends on both the factors relating to the product and the company's own areas of advantage and disadvantage; again a banker cannot expect to make the judgement himself, but can look for pointers which support or question the company's judgement.

A market leader should have a high volume over which to spread overheads; should be high on the learning curve, with efficient operations, and may well be in a strong bargaining position vis-à-vis its suppliers. If it is also a price leader the rest of the industry may have to follow its decisions on price, giving a significant element of control over margins. Absolute price leadership is relatively rare but it is common for two or three companies to be dominant, and a major company can often influence even though not control the trend of prices. Leadership may also allow influence over credit terms, length of warranty and other factors which affect profits.

The ability to influence the price still leaves a difficult judgement as to the best combination of margin and volume for the particular productive process and requires good management to strike the balance. Moreover, market leadership can be and often is challenged; beating off the challenge may be expensive but a company which is unchallenged for too long may become complacent and start to lose market leadership without realising it. As with many factors, market leadership is normally desirable but carries risks of which the analyst should be aware, and which he should be prepared to assess carefully in the minority of cases where the risk actively threatens to become a reality.

To do so he must consider the basis for market leadership in each case. It may be price and manufacturing skill; quality of product or service; innovativeness and technical excellence; a strong brand name and imaginative advertising; or some combination of these and other factors. If the product is important to the viability of the purchaser, security may be an important factor. A company installing a computer for the first time knows from the experiences of others that getting it wrong can be a disaster. It is much harder to criticise that company or the particular manager for buying the appropriate IBM machine than that of a smaller competitor, even though the latter may be cheaper and better fitted to the specific use.

In many products, too, customer loyalty is important; a company which already holds market leadership can expect that most of its customers will buy its product again, so that to some extent market leadership is self-reinforcing.

These factors, and the risks that they can change, need to be understood in all industries the nature of which allows market leadership, whether or not the borrower is a market leader. If it is, the bank needs to understand the advantages of the position, the types of risk which could cause it to be lost, and the likelihood of their occurring; if the risk is at all imminent, it is particularly important that management be aware of it and doing everything possible to protect against it.

If the borrower is not a market leader, the bank needs equally to understand how serious is the disadvantage, what is the possibility of overcoming it, whether management should be trying for market leadership, and if so what are the risks in doing so. There are many sound companies which have no ambitions to be a market leader, and by definition only a minority can be. The market leader is, however, more likely to survive and be profitable; the importance of this difference varies from industry to industry.

The possibility that market leadership can change hands can arise from three types of development. The market leader can begin to lose the quality that made it market leader (or that kept it there); or a challenger can outperform it; or the requirements can change and the market leader not change fast enough with them. Often, two or three of these factors will combine, and the banker must be alert to the possibility and able to assess whether an initial challenge is likely to be successful or whether the leader can recover and retain its leadership. In this case the unsuccessful challenge may substantially weaken the challenger, which will also be the customer of a bank.

Market position can also refer to the product's position in the spectrum of price and quality. Broadly speaking, although the exact extent depends on the product, products at the top of the market are higher quality, higher priced, give the producer a better margin on sales, but attract less volume. They may also require particularly high skills, making it harder for new competition to enter. As the product goes down market, emphasis tends to switch from quality to price, margins on sales reduce but volume increases, requiring tight cost controls to profit from the volume. This in turn may require a heavy investment in sophisticated machinery, generating a degree of capital intensiveness which makes the company more vulnerable to changes in price or volume. Alternatively, the lower end of the market in some products is open to a much wider range of competition, with lower labour costs, lower overheads and perhaps lower costs of safety or environmental controls.

In some products, a company can choose the market sector which suits its particular skills; in others it may be necessary to cover the whole market, either to absorb overhead costs and perhaps produce common components, to provide a full service, or to develop customer loyalty early. Again, the best approach in each case is a matter of fine judgement. The banker rarely could, or should, try to second guess management; but if management gets the decision wrong, it can put the bank's money at risk, so the banker should aim to know enough to assess the quality of the decisions and to identify early signs that a major decision is being proved wrong.

Information on these points is rarely included in, or evident from, published material. The analyst must try to obtain background knowledge about his customer's product range and that of actual and potential competitors, and use this knowledge to assess the risks or advantages of his customer's stance, and the dangers of competitive inroads.

Price sensitivity

The degree of price sensitivity of the product will affect a number of company decisions as well as its vulnerability to adverse conditions. Sales volume in some products can be dramatically reduced by a small price increase or vice versa. Their producer is open to different pressures and risks than if the product sells largely on some other feature; a producer whose product is not price-sensitive can afford to adjust prices in line with costs at least up to a point and often completely as long as its costs stay in line with those of competitors.

For most products price sensitivity varies with the actual price and is affected by other features. Thus a company with a well-established brand name may find that a 2 or 3% change in price makes little difference to volume but a 10% change in price changes volume by 15%. Or a market follower may find that it can only obtain a given volume by pricing lower than the market leader; volume may be sensitive to the differential rather than, or as well as, the actual price. There are therefore two aspects to price sensitivity: the ease with which a given volume of sales moves between competitors, and the affect on the total volume of sales of the product. Recognising the degree and type of sensitivity and pricing appropriately is an important marketing skill; it must be supported by the production skill to produce at a satisfactory profit margin without weakening the selling features of the product. As with other elements the analyst can rarely make a precise judgement as to the right strategy, but if he understands the problem he has a better chance of assessing the quality of management's thinking. Price sensitivity also indicates a type of vulnerability which may require offsetting strengths elsewhere.

Governmental involvement

There are a number of ways in which governments become involved in business directly, or indirectly create conditions which help or hinder business. These include company law and taxes which vary quite widely from country to country but do not normally differ very much between individual companies in the same country. While the analyst should certainly be aware of them, it would take a book, not a section of a chapter, to discuss the variations.

There are many areas in which some governments interfere more than others and interfere with some companies more than others. They are too numerous to list in detail, but a few examples should indicate the sort of thing for which the analyst should be alert.

Price controls became increasingly frequent in more and more countries during the 1970s. In some countries they are selective and only apply to certain products; in others, they will apply across the board; in yet others there will be exemptions for certain types of cost, perhaps those of imported raw materials. Selective controls are often aimed at influencing the retail price index or local equivalent; some products are considered to have a high social and/or political visibility, such as grain or rice in some under-developed countries and beer or wine in more developed countries. Even when price controls are not in force the risk of their introduction exists. Its probability depends on the economic, social and political climate of the country as well as the nature of the product.

The likely impact of price controls also varies; at one extreme a product offering good margins and with its costs subject to the same controls may suffer only slightly, at least unless the controls are unusually rigid and long-lasting. At the other extreme a commodity product selling in high volume at low margins and with its main cost a raw material priced in the world markets may be severely hit; if, as is quite probable, the price freeze coincides with a weakening of the currency, the problem is redoubled. Instant coffee is a good example of a product which suffers from price controls in this way.

In many countries and for many products, price controls are of academic interest only. Where they are a genuine risk, however, the analyst must consider the impact on the borrower and what defences it either has or could develop.

Environmental and pollution controls are becoming more frequent and more burdensome, but their impact is very uneven. Two otherwise identical companies may be subject to different regulations and different costs as a result. The analyst should always question whether a company produces a product with a high pollution content. If it does, he should ask about the current regulations in his country and those in other countries; these may tell something about the competitive impact and give a pointer to future requirements domestically. A banker does not wish to finance a project which at the time the loan is made is free from pollution controls, but when the money has been committed and spent is suddenly subjected to strict controls. The project then cannot operate without large items of control equipment and other costs which may make it uncompetitive.

Other types of government control which can affect individual companies include import and export controls, exchange controls, quality standards, the need to get safety approval for drugs and so on. These can either be exactly what they seem, or a device to favour domestic companies. There are also subsidies to state-owned competitors, buy-domestic policies and so on. Where any of these exist the analyst should assess their importance; where they are only a possibility, assess the risk of introduction and the likely impact.

The nature of competition

Very few companies are complete monopolies and the nature of the competition, actual and potential, is of vital importance.

Actual competition may come from companies as large or larger than the bank's customer, or smaller but trying aggressively to gain market share. They may compete across the board or they may be a different group for each product, in which case the strength of each must be assessed. Even where national competition is weak, international competition may come from major multi-nationals, or from less developed countries with cheap labour, or foreign specialists. The earlier analysis of the basis for market strength (technology, position in the market, price sensitivity and so on) will be useful in judging whether competition is a serious threat to the borrower's viability. Pointers to potential future competition can be found in looking at the factors which make competition easier or harder, as well as the competing companies. Again these tie back with various other points about the nature of the product and manufacturing process. Defensive features include high capital intensity, which makes it expensive to enter the market; high manufacturing skills or R & D; need for a well-spread distribution or servicing network; high brand loyalty and so on. Features which make a product more vulnerable to new competition include low technological content; high labour intensity; commodity nature of product and lack of brand loyalty; simple manufacturing requirements and so on. None of the defensive characteristics give complete protection from competition but they make it both less likely and easier to foresee.

Competition can also come from different products; just as steel lost market to aluminium and plastics, cotton and wool to synthetics and beer to wine and vice versa. The likelihood of such a challenge, its probable speed and breadth should all be reviewed periodically, since an apparently entrenched product can lose ground as a result of technical, price or fashion change.

Selection

Chapters 9 and 10 have discussed features which can affect a company's financial needs, balance sheet structure and earnings potential and requirements. No two chapters could cover all aspects of all companies, nor would it be desirable to do so. No company will be affected by all of the aspects discussed nor will those which apply be of equal importance in each case. The purpose of the chapters therefore is not to provide a checklist which the analyst solemnly ticks off to make sure he has covered everything; rather it is to illustrate the ways in which different aspects of a company can affect the credit risk of lending to it. Thus it may stimulate the analyst to think imaginatively about each company in the light of what he knows and equally important can infer about the actual features of each borrower. A good analyst will select the two or three (or maybe four or five) features which are of particular importance to each company and weigh up their effect on its credit.

Equally, the information will often not allow detailed understanding of how a company works, and the analyst will have to draw inferences from inadequate information and apply general knowledge to specific cases. He will not do this successfully unless he is thinking about all of the ways in which the business features interact with each other and with the financial condition.

The Duke of Wellington is reported to have said: "All the business of war, and indeed all the business of life, is to endeavour to find out what you don't know by what you do; that's what I call 'guessing what was at the other side of the hill' ". That could serve as a motto for bankers and credit analysts.

Part IV
Striking a Balance

11 Recognizing the Trade-Offs

Credit analysis involves the intelligent dissection of the balance sheet, of relationships within and between it and profit and loss, of management and of the various features discussed in the previous chapters. The aim is to reach a balanced view of the company's strengths and weaknesses, to identify the risks, to assess their probability and the company's ability to survive them. To do this banks almost always need more information on the finances and on the nature of the business than companies publish or are willing to disclose. The banker must therefore constantly seek to expand his information in contacts with the company, with others in the same industry, customers and other outside analysts. Much of this information also helps the banker to market his bank's services to best advantage; indeed, credit and marketing are in this as in other areas closely interlinked rather than conflicting as some bankers, and many customers, seem to see them.

The best way to seek information is not to ask the company a long list of questions once a year; rather during each contact with the company the banker should be alert to gather information, to ask intelligent questions arising from the conversation or to make comments designed to encourage provision of specific information rather than demanding it. It is particularly important, because few companies have only one product or line of business, to persuade management to talk about the importance, and strengths and weaknesses, of various product lines or markets. Many companies have a range of products with different characteristics and in most countries published information about the breakdown is woefully inadequate. Even where a breakdown of sales and profits is given, the balance sheet items relating to each segment of business are not. So that when companies have a mixture of manufacturing or trading, capital-intensive or labour-intensive products, it is harder to judge the balance and to assess the trade-offs discussed later in the chapter. The banker must therefore use every opportunity to learn about the way the company operates.

The subject of this book is not the marketing of credit or how to obtain information, but both are tools of sound credit judgement and important skills which all bankers and analysts should cultivate. A skilled analyst may reach a sensible conclusion even with inadequate information, but there is a limit to how many bricks can be made with no straw; the quality of the ultimate decision will be affected by the quality of information the banker has been able to glean. Sometimes lack of information will on its own justify a refusal to lend.

Strengths, weaknesses, risks and structure

All companies have certain types of requirement and of weakness which need to be offset by strengths elsewhere. Very strong companies are those where the weaknesses are minor and/or the company is well protected against them. Even with these the banker must understand the nature of the weakness to assess the risk that it could increase and overwhelm the strengths. Equally he must grasp why the strengths are important, from what base they spring and what could, by threatening them, undermine the borrower's overall standing.

In general terms this means understanding how the financial structure of a company should compensate for weaknesses arising from the nature of the borrower, and checking to ensure that it actually does so. Thus, the features which make for capital intensity often, but not always, carry other features which add to the need for certain types of balance sheet strength. There may also, however, be other factors which partly offset this need. For instance, a manufacturer of heavy machinery needs a large factory, has a long manufacturing cycle with massive amounts tied up in inventory, and a relatively small number of large receivables. Its payables are unlikely to be any slower than average, so that it has a high net working investment which, as discussed in Chapter 6, is a form of capital intensity. Thus at best its fixed costs are fairly high, and since almost all its assets are fairly illiquid any interest on borrowings merely adds more fixed costs. Furthermore, since its sales are in large individual items it is quite likely that volume of sales can vary as a result of quite minor changes in end demand. If it is selling to cyclical industries, variations in demand may be quite sharp.

Some pointers to the profit and loss statement emerge from this discussion. Annual sales will be relatively low in relation to fixed assets - in some cases less than the balance sheet figure, so that a fairly high operating margin on sales is required to obtain a respectable ROA. And if a high proportion of assets are financed with debt, interest will be a larger percentage of sales, requiring high gross and operating margins to cover it.

On the positive side, the company may well be able to obtain firm orders before starting production. This makes planning easier and, provided the sales terms are appropriate, reduces the risk of having large amounts tied up in finished goods. The very capital intensity, particularly if it is combined with high technical skill in manufacturing, makes it less likely that new competition will enter the picture. These factors, and the likelihood that the product will be a vital part of the customer's manufacturing process, may mean that he will be more concerned that the machine is delivered on time, and meets specification, than with the last penny on price. This in turn should enable the seller to obtain reasonable margins.

Thus the overall picture is of a company which requires a high capital base and rather low borrowing, particularly short-term, or low leverage and a high current ratio. This need is based on the relatively illiquid assets, the high fixed costs and vulnerability to even minor loss of demand, and the low sales/asset ratio which makes the cost of assets financed with debt a fairly high percentage of sales. The company also needs, for the same reasons, sound profit margin on sales and some of the same factors make it likely that, at least as long as sufficient demand exists, such margins will be available. Depreciation will also be important so that cash flow should be well above reported profit, thus improving the quality of earnings. Any major deviation from this broad pattern needs to be explained.

At the other end of the corporate spectrum a commodity company, since it adds no value to the goods in which it trades, can command only a very small margin on sales; however, nor does it tie up capital in fixed assets or inventory being processed; its inventory turns over fast and usually so do its receivables. Thus the features which make for a low margin on sales will also tend to ensure that sales are high in relation to total assets, and therefore permit a respectable ROA.

The balance sheet will therefore consist almost entirely of receivables and inventory, financed by a mixture of trade payables and short-term bank debt. The bank debt will be related directly to the volume of sales, and the interest will be a factor the company can calculate into its margins. The high liquidity of the assets and ease with which they can be turned into cash mean that only a modest net worth is required as a cushion against loss of value on some of the assets; this in turn means that even the very narrow margins left on sales after deducting interest can give a reasonable ROE. With few fixed assets there is little or no depreciation; cash flow is almost identical to net profit after tax and is unlikely to be a major source of repayment of debt. This, in fact, is one of the asset-based companies discussed in Chapter 12.

The acceptability of such a low net worth depends almost entirely on the quality of the key assets, receivables and inventory. If receivables are slow moving or, worse still, of doubtful collectibility, the cost of financing them increases sharply; losses can eat into a small net worth very fast, so that a considerably higher net worth is needed. Similarly, inventory is normally made up of goods which are highly marketable, but often very volatile in price. A company can protect itself against this volatility either by hedging on a commodity exchange, or by buying only where it has a firm sales contract. If it does neither, it will make much larger profits if the price moves in its favour, but it can make equally large losses; banks do not share in the profits and, if they were prepared to lend at all, would expect a substantial net worth to protect against the losses.

These two rather extreme examples show that an analyst should be able to obtain a general idea of what the balance sheet and profit and loss statement look like, just by knowing the type of company. Of course there are many qualifications and modifications; for instance, capital intensity always raises the fixed costs and break-even point, but the importance of this depends on a range of other factors. A company with a very stable demand and sure of its ability to pass on costs in the price does not need to worry about the risk of a downturn; it may be able to borrow substantially more (provided it can obtain a fixed rate) than a company with more volatile demand and costs. The US utilities industry is (or was) a good example of this.

The general assessment of what the company should look like must be adjusted when more detailed facts are available. The picture must also be compared with the actual balance sheet and profit and loss. Only when the analyst understands what protection the company needs and why can he begin to assess whether the actual financial condition is sound.

Quality

One aspect which needs to be considered in assessing various strengths and weaknesses is that of quality, as it applies to the assets and to cash flow and earnings. Part of the quality of fixed assets is inherent in their nature and in the types of flexibility and adaptability discussed in Chapter 10; the greater the quality in this sense, the more leverage is acceptable in relation to a given degree of capital intensity and other risks. But quality also relates to reliability, suitability for the particular function and age - or perhaps remaining economic life. This reflects the extent to which money has recently been spent and/or is likely to be required in the future. A company which has just completed a major capital investment programme and has modern, efficient fixed assets enabling it to produce low cost, high quality goods has strengthened its position; it may therefore be able to afford a relatively high level of leverage (in relation to the nature of its business and other factors discussed). It has spent the proceeds of the borrowing which caused the high leverage but either has not yet, or has only just, begun to get the benefits from the assets. If the money has been well spent, the result should start to show in higher earnings and cash flow which can be used to build up net worth, service debt and generally improve the balance sheet. Its need to spend money on fixed assets in the next few years will probably be relatively small so that both the increase in cash flow as a result of the programme and some of the cash flow which existed before can be used mainly to service debt.

The opposite is true of a company which has neglected its capital spending or perhaps been overtaken by advances in production technology. It may have a high proportion of old machinery and equipment which needs to be replaced and now is running inefficiently and reducing margins. It must almost certainly increase its capital spending substantially in the next few years, and perhaps then wait several years before it begins to obtain the benefit; there must be some doubt about the ability of a management which gets into this position to choose and use the fixed assets to the best advantage. These factors tend to make the safe level of leverage much lower than in the first case; if such a company starts from a position of high leverage, its chances of survival may be rather poor. Certainly it has no reserve strength if demand declines or some other factor puts more than normal pressure on its profitability.

In practice, of course, most companies fall between these extremes. The analyst should however consider where between them each company is, and what are the implications both as to the present level of leverage and likely future demands on cash flow, either to fund capital expenditure directly or to service debt used to fund it. Capital spending represents an important potential use of cash flow and of other sources of funds and can weaken a balance sheet if there are no offsetting strengths. Old and inefficient machinery offers a poor second way out and, at the same time, it makes the need for one that much more likely.

The same general comments apply to the quality of current assets. If they are naturally slow moving, they need more long-term finance; if there is any doubt that they will turn into cash, then the reported liquidity and leverage ratios need to be stronger to cover the possibility that the figures overstate them. Similarly a slow inventory turnover may be inherent in the business or may also conceal a part which, for various reasons (out of fashion, overpriced, underdesigned, obsolete), either cannot be sold at all or only at a price well below book value. In both cases, too, the doubts about quality may imply that profits are overstated. Thus, any question as to the quality of receivables and inventory must be offset by strengths elsewhere (such as lower leverage, higher current ratio or strong earnings).

The quality of other assets, particularly investments, is also important. Investments in other companies may be a necessary means of extending control over important aspects of a company's own business and if so must be judged in the light of how effectively they do that. Or they may just be a use of funds to diversify; in that case the extent to which they generate income and the ease with which they could be sold if necessary are important factors in considering the overall balance sheet and earnings strength of the company.

These are the major assets in most companies but where other assets exist their quality must also be assessed.

The quality of the earnings and cash flow, also important, has two slightly different meanings in this context. The first relates to the way in which the profit is reached which includes, although it is not confined to, accounting considerations. For instance a high depreciation charge makes for better quality earnings than a low one, because it provides an element of stability and a more favourable cash flow in relation to earnings. Depreciation may be high because there are substantial fixed assets or because the company chooses to depreciate smaller fixed assets fast. Conversely it may be low to reflect relatively minor fixed assets or because it is manipulated to show a stable or growing pattern of earnings, in which case it clearly reduces quality. Capitalised interest or R & D, unequal treatment of favourable or unfavourable "extraordinary" items or other forms of manipulation are examples of poor accounting quality, but in many companies manipulation is less obvious. The quality and trustworthiness of the information affect the perceived quality of earnings.

But there are some inherent qualities as well. In brief, stable or growing earnings are better than cyclical ones; predictable fluctuations are better than erratic jumps; earnings from the company's main line of business are higher quality than those from a temporarily favourable cash balance or from an activity which, while perfectly sound, is peripheral to, or less stable than, the company's main business. For instance, property investment companies in the United Kingdom make their main profits from rental income and a sound portfolio will generate a stable income, rising with or slightly ahead of inflation. But companies can make more dramatic profits by developing properties and selling them after they are let for a capital gain, or trading in them. However, leases protect against downward fluctuations in rental income but not necessarily in capital values, and development or trading can generate large losses as well as large profits.

Balance sheet passive; earnings active

Overall then the analyst must balance the strengths and weaknesses in the company. He can perhaps accept higher leverage, or tighter liquidity, in relation to the nature of the company, if it is offset by a high and sustainable cash flow; relatively low ROA can still be satisfactory if quality is good and/or capital intensity is low. Apparently strong positions can be undermined by poor quality assets or earnings, or by known or suspected needs for future cash. Even apparently sound borrowing totals can be dangerous if maturities are bunched in one or two years or interest is floating and rates are rising sharply. The company characteristics outlined in Chapters 9 and 10 and the requirements for financial strength or defences against financial weakness can make sharply differing demands on the balance sheet and on cash flow.

Moreover, balance sheet strength, while desirable, is largely passive. Ample liquidity and low leverage provide defensive strength; they allow time and perhaps supply resources to reduce costs, develop and market new products, install new equipment and adapt to changing competitive or other conditions. However, a strong balance sheet will not achieve any of these ends on its own, nor ensure that attempts to do so are successful. It will not improve poor labour relations although it may make the cost of a strike more bearable; it cannot ensure that capital expenditure is wisely directed or well managed and the investment well used.

Earnings and cash flow are much more active. Earnings can be reinvested, building up net worth and improving leverage, either by actually reducing debt or by ensuring that it grows more slowly than assets and net worth. Cash flow can reduce short-term debt or increase current assets or some combination of the two and thus improve both liquidity and leverage. Or it can pay off maturing term debt, improving leverage without harming liquidity; or be used to purchase fixed assets, pay for R & D, or finance increased NWI needs which would otherwise weaken leverage, liquidity or both.

Inadequate earnings, particularly in an expansionary or

inflationary environment, mean that net worth grows more slowly than assets and the difference has to be financed, increasing leverage. Losses actually reduce net worth, and must be offset either by higher liabilities or by realisation of assets. Companies may improve their balance sheets by liquidating surplus assets while making an operating loss, and if they start with a sound balance sheet may survive for a surprisingly long time. Indeed, a short period of loss may be salutary if management was a little relaxed about its financial controls and consequently borrowing more than desirable. Clearly, however, there is a limit to this particular exercise and sooner or later a company losing money reaches the point of no return.

The same process applies to liquidity and net working investment; strong earnings will both help to finance the growing receivables and inventory directly and make sure that any additional borrowings needed for the purpose will be comfortably serviced.

Earnings and cash flow are particularly important if the company is growing fast rather than gradually expanding as a result of inflation or natural increase in business. A conscious chase for growth may well involve taking on business at low margins and thus may compound any existing problem of inadequate earnings or a weak balance sheet. It is particularly important that the returns on assets, liabilities and net worth be solid when a company is expanding rapidly. If the company starts off with a strong balance sheet and consciously accepts the need for a few years of relatively weak earnings as an investment while new capacity is brought on stream or while a new product is introduced and builds up market share, this may well be acceptable. But if the earnings do not begin to come through within a reasonable period or if the company's strategy is not clearly thought out and based on obtaining an increase in margins as a result of the growth, then rapid growth can be positively dangerous.

Flexibility versus rigidity

Earlier chapters talked about the desirability of flexibility in certain aspects of the business such as fixed assets. But flexibility is desirable in all aspects of the business and rigidity is correspondingly dangerous. Thus, broadly speaking the more flexible the company is the greater the other weaknesses which can be accepted while rigidity in any aspect requires an offset, perhaps in the balance sheet.

The ways in which fixed assets can be flexible or rigid was discussed in earlier chapters; certainly flexible assets can partly offset the dangers of high leverage. High leverage is itself a form of rigidity and so is capital intensity, so that they should rarely appear together. A high cash flow gives considerable flexibility in its use whereas a low cash flow must be dedicated to the most demanding creditors and gives little or no ability to put the money to positive but perhaps longer-term uses. A wide range of products and/or a wider range of customers, and still more customers in many countries, gives greater flexibility than dependence on a single product, country or customer industry or on a small number of major individual customers. The ability to switch marketing and other efforts from one country or product to another, to expand investment in one area and contract in another, and perhaps to take advantageous currency positions, all provide defence against a deterioration in one area of the business. This is also true of sources of supply and raw materials. Heavy reliance on one or a small number of major suppliers with no competition gives little ability to resist price increases, obtain discounts for volume, insist on frequent deliveries and other helpful factors; access to a wide range of suppliers competing strongly for the business improves flexibility in all these factors. A product or process which can only use one particular raw material or type of fuel is vulnerable to unexpected shortages or sharp increases in price, while ability to substitute provides some protection. The 1973/4 and 1979/80 oil price increases provide the most dramatic but by no means the only examples of this point.

Some of these sources of flexibility or rigidity may be inherent in the business; in many, however, management has a choice and must weigh the advantages of flexibility against the extra costs that may be necessary to obtain them, and vice versa. (For instance, a plant which can use several types of fuel may be more expensive to install, or to run, than one designed for only one fuel.) But part of the price for rigidity must normally be an offsetting strength to provide protection if the lack of flexibility becomes a real, rather than merely potential, disadvantage. This offsetting strength may appear in the balance sheet as low leverage or high liquidity or some combination; or it may appear as higher margins and returns (for instance, committing to one supplier may enable that supplier to spread his fixed costs over a higher volume and perhaps reduce his other costs and thus the price at which he supplies). The analyst must be aware not only of the general dangers of rigidity but of the specific dangers of each type of rigidity, and whether a counter feature provides a direct offset against it, or is just a general source of strength.

Stability and predictability

The stability or otherwise of earnings and cash flow powerfully affect the overall balance. The more stable and the more predictable earnings and cash flow are, the greater the likelihood that the assessment of their ability to meet future needs will be correct. It is important to understand the causes and timing of fluctuations; to assess whether a high level of earnings is likely to be sustained or whether it is the peak of the cycle with not merely a probable decline next year but a lower average over time; this changes the view as to the company's ability to finance expansion, pay off maturing debt and so on. It is equally important to distinguish whether low or declining earnings are due to a cycle which can be expected to reverse itself in a recognisable pattern or whether they result from a longer-term weakness which the down cycle has exposed rather more dramatically than would otherwise have been the case.

Thus to call a company stable or cyclical is too simple; it does not account for the extent to which the stability is soundly based or the possibility that the base may be threatened, and more fragile than appears at first sight. Moreover, stability may make slightly lower earnings acceptable, but earnings which are stable but inadequate are worse than more erratic earnings which at least part of the time generate a high return, since this can be used to protect against the downturn. Indeed, in all cases the question is not just the general one of "are earnings and cash flow high or low, stable or cyclical?" Rather the question is "how do actual and expected cash flow and profits relate to the present balance sheet structure and to expected future needs for cash to maintain the company in sound condition?"

Seasonal or cyclical variations affect the balance sheet as well as, indeed because of, sales and margins. With seasonal companies inventory builds up during the slack sales season, when profits are poor, and converts into sales and profits later in the year; a review of the company at the low point would, if appropriate allowance were not made, give an entirely different impression from that a few months later. In longer cycles there may be a comparable tendency for inventory turnover to appear to slow down due to slack sales and for profits to decline. In a general economic downturn the effect on NWI may be aggravated by suppliers trying to collect their receivables, which are the company's payables, more quickly. Where the cycle is fairly predictable, management should be able to adjust its rate of sales and production appropriately; in some cases it may cut back the growth in inventory, in others perhaps it will deliberately stockpile low cost materials to be in a better position to take advantage when demand recovers; to do this, however, it needs a strong balance sheet before the downturn begins, in case it lasts longer than expected. A management which fails to control inventory in a cyclical decline gives a warning that perhaps its controls are not very good. A disproportionate build-up in a relatively shallow cycle might raise a question as to how great the build-up would be, and how manageable, if the cycle became more pronounced. There will also be a tendency for debt to increase early in the down cycle to finance the increase in inventory; receivables may increase while customers with similar problems pay more slowly; the reduction in cash flow will also reduce debt-servicing ability and may cause debt to rise as a result.

But fluctuations are not all cyclical. Some companies and industries have an erratic rather than cyclical record. It may be vital to assess whether the erratic earnings are due to factors outside management's control, and if so what protective measures are possible; or whether they arise from management weakness. For instance some companies, dependent on the ordering cycle of a government department, find most of their orders come in the final quarter of the government's financial year, as the department rushes to spend its budget before it loses it; the size of the orders depends on political rather than economic factors. Construction and other companies involved in a small number of large projects naturally tend to be influenced by the exact date an order is received or completed; completion accounting may exaggerate this tendency.

A sound reason, out of the company's control, for erratic earnings and no reason to suspect management weakness still points to a need for a stronger financial condition, a stronger capital base and better earnings, however assessed, in the good periods than a company with stable or growing profits would need.

However, the other side of this coin is that, since strength is required to protect against known risks, the use (or consumption) of that strength for the purpose for which it is needed is not in itself a danger sign. The analysis must ensure that the amount of protection which has been, so to speak, consumed is not disproportionate to the depth of the cycle and more importantly that sufficient protection remains for the rest of the downward fluctuation expected. There are two traps to avoid: a panic because of an apparent deterioration which is in reality a normal fluctuation; and the complacent assumption that every fluctuation is normal. There are three main points to consider, some of the answers to which relate to broader industry or general economic conditions. First, is the fluctuation in fact normal or does it either conceal or represent a broader or deeper weakening of the company? Secondly, is the company taking all prudent steps to cope with it? And thirdly, if the fluctuation proves to be of unusual depth, how soon could it exhaust the defences?

The predictability of some industrial cycles, and their link with either the general economic cycle or some particular aspect of it, provides management with some tools. Its financial controls and marketing strategy should be designed to give as much advance warning as possible, so that production, labour levels, marketing tactics can be quickly adjusted. Receivables, for instance, should rarely increase when sales decline. Inventory should only do so as a result of a conscious decision; perhaps to take advantage of lower raw material prices, perhaps to provide stable employment in return for higher productivity in the upturn; perhaps to maintain or improve market share by offering faster delivery than was possible in the boom period. The marketing tactics may also be adapted; to spend more on advertising, to offer better volume discounts, to slow the introduction of new, more expensive products; these are all possible adjustments, but only an alert management can have the right one ready for use when needed. Similarly, an investment strategy should be capable of adjustment, so that expenditure does the least damage to the balance sheet and earnings and the investment comes on stream during an upturn. A company which consistently brings new capital investment on stream just as the market turns down or cuts back its capital investment during the downturn so that it has inadequate capacity in the next upturn aggravates the effect of the cycle rather than compensates for it. (A bank may have an opportunity to improve the quality of its credit and learn more about some of its smaller customers by offering economic counselling to those companies which are too small to be able to afford to employ economists themselves.)

One result of cyclicality is that comparison with the previous year and often even with the previous two or three years can give a distorted view of the trend. It is often better to compare the company in the same phase of as many different cycles as possible, rather than at different phases in the same cycle. Particularly in a recovery, it is important that the recovery be as strong or even stronger than in previous cycles; a company which is weaker at the bottom of each successive cycle and recovers more slowly and to a lesser extent at the top suggests a deteriorating long-term trend; the analyst must not allow the cyclical overlay to cause him to miss the trend.

Adequacy of returns

Profits should give an adequate return not only on assets or liabilities but also on risk. The relationship of risk to different types of earning patterns has an arithmetic element. A high sales to assets ratio means that a low margin on sales may give satisfactory returns on assets, liabilities, or net worth etc. but also that a small decline in the margin on sales will have a disproportionate impact on the returns; thus the risk of this small change may be more important than at first appears. At the other extreme, a low sales/assets ratio requires a much higher margin on sales to produce sound returns, and the risk of a decline in sales may be more important than a decline in margins of the same proportion.

This is another way of looking at the questions of capital intensity, the break-even level and fixed costs. A high sales/asset ratio is another way of describing low capital intensity and (usually) low fixed costs; since variable costs are thus a high proportion of total costs, a change in them is an important risk. This risk may be offset by an ability to pass on such costs to the customer; if it is not, some other protection must be identified. Conversely, of course, a company with a low sales/asset ratio is likely to be capital intensive, unless it is under-using its fixed assets. It therefore needs wider margins to compensate for the risk of a drop in sales which, with a high break-even point, is more dangerous than a drop in margins. Of course, a drop in sales may cause a drop in margins; again the relationship depends on the mix of costs, but it is the combination which does the damage. Most companies are situated somewhere between the two extremes described above and the various pressures need to be carefully balanced. The important thing is to check the extent to which a particular risk or mix of risks threatens a change in volume and margins which together constitute a serious danger. The wider the combination required before the danger is serious, the better the defensive quality of the company.

Chapter 14 talks more specifically about risk; here the main point is that any risk is only worth taking if there is a return, and the higher the risk the greater the return should be.

Defensive qualities are important to the correct overall balance. Some companies produce necessities, demand for which continues almost regardless of economic conditions; a few even benefit from recession because their products are cheaper than their substitutes and easier to afford in bad times; other companies have an inherent flexibility which enables them to ride out any but the most general recession; yet others use management and financial controls to resist pressure on sales and to maintain sound margins and balance sheets.

On the other hand, some products are luxuries, are subject to sharp changes in fashion, or are in danger of supercession by a new generation of technology. Clearly, if these features are combined with capital intensity, high fixed costs and perhaps weak management controls, only very high profitability will be sufficient to justify the risks, and probably then only to shareholders rather than lenders. Put another way, companies in unusually risky businesses probably should not borrow at all, however high the profits which compensate for the risks; if they do borrow, it should be on a genuinely short-term basis with a specific source of repayment.

Refinancing ability

The availability of sources of new equity or forms of long-term fixed rate financing offer a partial offset to some types of risk. Banks, which used to finance only short-term requirements, now provide medium-term debt as well. They are providing "permanent" working capital and sometimes other types of capital to industry; partly as a result, good companies increasingly believe that they never need to pay off their debt but only to continue servicing it. By no means all bankers accept that this is desirable, but it is undoubtedly happening, desirable or not. This makes companies more like banks, which could never repay all their deposits en masse, and will never need to as long as each depositor is confident of being able to withdraw if necessary. The ability to raise equity (or refinance in other ways) is thus often crucial to continued confidence by bankers, and since it is harder to raise equity when making a loss, the management must be prepared to strengthen the balance sheet before there is a problem. Reluctance or inability to do so can be a serious weakness, and is one reason why a private company, with no access to capital markets, needs a strong balance sheet.

The banking system as a whole cannot pay itself off but an individual bank can be paid from loans by other banks. Thus if a bank expects to be repaid by being more alert than its peers it must understand the borrower better than they do. It must also understand what will cause other banks to become alarmed, which for an international bank means being familiar with a wide range of local banking systems, risk preferences, analytical approaches and legal constraints. "Refinancing ability" then refers to the continuing willingness of other sources of finance voluntarily to provide funds with which to repay a lender. It must not be confused with, or allowed to shade into, what might be called "restructuring ability"; this is the ability, often with the help of other lenders or even government, to persuade a reluctant bank to forego its right to demand payment; in extreme cases to force the bank to convert debt into equity, extend the life of debt for long periods, or accept a below market rate of interest, all on the grounds more or less openly stated that the bank will lose less this way than by putting the company into liquidation. In brief, refinancing ability refers to the ability to avoid loss altogether; restructuring ability to the ability to limit it or change its timing or form. To confuse the two can be very costly.

Selection

Finally, the analyst has to select those factors, financial, industrial and economic, managerial and others, which affect the particular company and draw a conclusion as to whether the balance is sound or not. Particularly where the company is a new customer, but whenever the analyst is not already familiar with it, it can help to focus on areas which appear inconsistent with what is known or which suggest unexpected strengths or weaknesses which may influence the final conclusion. The suggested exercise is simple to state, more complex to do; it is to draw up an outline balance sheet and P & L statement before looking at the actual figures provided and then compare the actual with the expected. This may be more easily done in terms of percentages of sales initially rather than absolute figures but may then need to be converted into figures for ease of comparison with the actuals. To compare this outline with the actual figures gives a useful starting point to an analysis, or even to an investigation prior to analysis. It will be helpful in highlighting any misconceptions about the implications of various aspects of the company's business or any unusual features which were not obvious from the background information available. An outline which coincides reasonably closely with the actual figures does not eliminate the prospect of hidden features altogether, but it certainly reduces the probability. Conversely, major discrepancies, or an inability to estimate certain figures on the information available, gives a starting point for further investigation. If the analyst had not understood the company's business or had missed some inference, this exercise will at least improve his understanding. Otherwise, it will help to draw his attention to specific problem areas and in investigating the significance of these he may learn a good deal more about how the company works.

This approach will be most effective when the borrower provides consolidated figures or most of the operations and assets are in the top company so that unconsolidated figures give a reasonably full picture. With unconsolidated figures, the inherent nature of the assets, liabilities and risks may well be concealed; all the parent needs to show is a net figure for its investment in subsidiaries with no indication of how the figure is made up or even whether it reflects a true figure rather than an out-of-date cost. Similarly, on the income statement all that shows is often dividend income, with no knowledge of how well the dividend is covered by earnings - or uncovered by losses.

The general approach is one which an experienced analyst performs in less detail almost without thinking, as was illustrated at the beginning of this chapter. However, the suggestion here is for something more detailed. The following examples cover three types of company and some only of the many variations which can occur. They are intended to be illustrative, not definitive. They assume Anglo-Saxon accounting, payment terms etc., and would need adapting to conditions in each country, although the basic principles do not change.

Example 1 - Heavy industry

The first example uses the machinery company described at the beginning of the chapter. The products are machine tools for use in the automotive and related industries, such as tractors, construction machinery etc., with some sales also going to the white goods industry.

Using sales as 100%, the three major assets can be estimated quite quickly. Receivables are to a relatively small number of large customers, who will probably use their muscle to delay payment but will pay; say 90-100 day turnover or receivables 25. The production cycle will be quite long, but on the other hand all production will be against firm orders; say a 120 day turnover or inventory 33. Sales will probably be less than total assets, but closer to that figure than to fixed assets; say fixed assets 55. If the company is an American company, add perhaps 3 for cash, and in any case another 3-5 for other current assets. Unless information suggests other non-current assets such as intangibles or investments, the asset side of the balance sheet should then look something like Table 11.1.

Table 11.1 Asset side of balance sheet

	(% of sales)
Cash	3
Receivables	25
Inventory	33
Other C/A	3
	64
Fixed assets	55
Total assets	119

On the liabilities side, trade payables probably turn over in real terms at about the same speed as receivables, but because they represent only raw materials and components, they will be a smaller percentage of sales, perhaps 17-20%. This will leave a high NWI which, assuming no unusual earnings pattern, suggests that net worth and long-term liabilities should cover fixed assets and a substantial part of NWI; say 75-80% of sales in all. Bearing in mind that high fixed costs make a high interest burden undesirable, term debt should not be more than, say, 10%.

At this stage a partial balance sheet looks as shown in Table 11.2.

There is still 20 of liabilities to account for to make it balance. Most of this will probably be current bank debt; while in practice there may be items such as dividends or minority interest these are not crucial. The final B/S then looks like the Estimated column in Table 11.3, and can be compared with the actual figures. Two rather different sets of actuals are shown to illustrate various points (Table 11.3).

In A, the company seems to have exceptionally fast receivable turnover for this type of business, raising the possibility that some may have been discounted, perhaps with a remaining contingent liability which has not been disclosed. Inventory turnover is somewhat slower than expected

Table 11.2 Partial balance sheet

Assets	(% of sales)	Liabilities	(% of sales)
Cash	3		
Receivables	25	Trade payables	20
Inventory	33		
Other C/A	3	Total C/L	?
Total C/A	64	Term debt	10
F/A	55	Total liabilities	?
	119	Net worth	69
		Total liabilities + NW	119

Table 11.3 Presentation of different balance sheets

	(% of sales) Actuals				(% of sales) Actuals		
Assets	A	B	Estimated	Liabilities	A	B	Estimated
Cash	3	-	3	Bank debt	25	15	15
Receivables	15	35	25	Trade payables	5	35	20
Inventory	40	50	33	Other current liabilities	5	5	5
Other C/A	1	-	3	Total C/L	35	55	40
Total C/A	59	85	64	Term debt	19	5	10
F/A	45	55	55	Total liab	54	60	50
Total asset	104	140	119	Net worth	50	80	69
				Total liabs & NW	104	140	119
Current ratio	1.69	1.55	1.6				
TBF/NW	0.88	0.25	0.36				

but, provided this is stable rather than a declining trend, the 26-day difference between actual and estimate is as likely to be due to a mistaken estimate as to any major weakness. The faster receivable turnover and slightly higher current ratio provide a sufficient offset in purely balance sheet terms. The company also appears to be using its fixed assets effectively, assuming they are accurately stated.

The main worries here come from the liabilities side. While the very fast payable turnover suggests the company is earning discounts and partly justifies the short-term borrowing, this is still high, and term debt has no such justification. TBF/NW of 0.88 is very high for this type of company and can really only be justified if the returns are unusually high.

Actual B shows a receivable and inventory turnover which, if the original estimates were about right, suggests the possibility of real problems in either or both areas. The higher trade payables suggest that perhaps industry terms are more relaxed than the estimate so that the receivables may not be as bad as they seem at first sight, but overall there is a real question mark here. The use of fixed assets seems about right, and the high net worth and low TBF/NW mean that the company is in fair shape in the short run; the bank can take the time to sort out whether there is a real problem and how serious. Much will of course depend on the earnings and cash flow.

The estimated balance sheet assumed gives some pointers to the P & L. First, depreciation should probably be about 7 or 8% of gross fixed assets. With an estimated net fixed asset figure, and no knowledge of how much has already been depreciated, 12-14% of net F/A, say 6% of sales, seems reasonable. Similarly, the known amount of debt makes it possible at least to estimate the interest burden; at a 12% rate this is about 3% of sales.

To provide a decent ROE, net profit should be at least 8 or 9% of sales, preferably higher. Assuming a 50% tax rate, this means pre-tax profit of 18-20. Unless the analyst knows a good deal about the machine tool business, he probably cannot produce much of a breakdown between the individual costs, apart from this, but could perhaps guess that general, selling and administrative costs should not be more than 10-12% of sales and R & D another 1 or 2%. The outline P & L then looks something like Table 11.4.

Table 11.4 Outline profit and loss statement (% of sales)

	Actual A	Actual B	Estimate
Sales	100	100	100
Cost of goods sold	55	62	60
Gross profit	45	38	40
G S & A	9	11	10
R & D	1	1	1
Depreciation	5	6	6
Operating profit	30	20	23
Interest	5	2	3
Pre-tax profit	25	18	20
Net profit	13	9	10
Interest cover	6.0	10.0	7.3
Return on assets	28.8	14.3	19.3
Return on equity	26.0	11.3	14.5
Cash flow to TBF	40.9	75.0	64.0

It appears that Actual A is able to offset its high leverage with better than expected profits, giving strong interest cover and good returns on assets and equity. Although cash flow covers TBF less well than in the other cases, it is still good enough to permit significant reductions in debt quite quickly; provided this is not a freak year at the top of the cycle there seems no reason to worry about Actual A. It can be seen, too, that Actual B's strong balance sheet is required to offset a weaker operating performance; again, providing this is a typical year, there seems no reason why Actual B should not chug along as a sound but unexciting company.

However, if we reverse the first part of Actual's A & B, so that the higher CGS and GS & A figures apply to the weak Actual A balance sheet, the position then looks like Table 11.5.

Even the combination is no disaster, but the safety margin is clearly much reduced. An increase in interest rates from 12 to 20%, combined with only a small drop in gross margin, could produce the pessimistic figures set out in Table 11.5. At this level, although the company is not yet in serious trouble it is teetering on the edge; an increase in borrowing (which is quite likely with such low cash flow) and a small further deterioration in gross margin could together quickly push it

Table 11.5 Profit and loss statement

	Pro-Formas (% of sales)	
	A & B Combined	Pessimistic
Sales	100	100
Cost of goods sold	62	64
Gross profit	38	36
GS & A	11	11
R & D	1	1
Depreciation	5	5
Operating profit	21	19
Interest	5	9
Pre-tax profit	16	10
Net profit	8	5
Interest cover	4.2	2.1
Return on assets	20.2	18.3
Return on equity	16.0	10.0
OCF/TBF	29.5	22.7

into a loss and its balance sheet then gives little support.

The assumptions so far have been fairly simple. There are a number of factors which could modify these figures. For instance, if over 50% of sales were exports, the receivable figure might well be closer to 30% of sales than 25%; this would require extra finance, but if it were known to be guaranteed by a government export credit agency, the quality might justify debt finance. This would in turn increase the interest bill, and perhaps require a higher operating margin, particularly desirable if exports were billed in a weak currency (and/or raw material imports billed in a strong currency), in view of the risk of loss, or cost of covering to avoid one. Price competitiveness is also important here; if the exporter's currency strengthens, this may reduce exports, and total sales, quite sharply. If it were known that the company had a technical edge, and its operating margins were high as a result, it might be possible to modify the balance sheet by increasing debt and reducing net worth somewhat and adjusting the P & L appropriately.

Finally, if the analyst knew that advance payments were common, these might wholly or partially replace bank debt, reducing interest costs. In extreme cases they might eliminate all debt and allow a much larger cash balance. This in turn would allow the company to accept lower operating margins.

Example 2 - Light manufacturing

The second example is a producer of plastic mouldings, sold to a wide range of industries for incorporation in their products. Products using them include cars, radio, hi-fi and television sets, refrigerators, dish and clothes washers and driers, computers and electronic instruments and many others. The factory is a standard building on a trading estate, easily adaptable to any one of a number of light engineering uses. Machinery is specialised to moulding, but by the use of interchangeable moulds (often owned by the customer) can be used for a wide range of different moulded products and plastic compounds. Most production is to order, in batches of 1000 mouldings or more, but a few standard mouldings are produced for stock. Most of the mouldings can be produced by anybody with the right machinery, but a minority demand considerable skill. Nevertheless, there are many companies in the business, the customer can move his mould at short notice and orders are very price sensitive. Particularly in bad times there are a considerable number of orders given at the last minute for rush delivery, so a supply of the most common raw materials has to be on hand at all times.

Taking sales as 100 again, clearly receivables should turn over faster than with a heavy machinery company; on the other hand the competitive position and the large number of customers, some of whom are small and not too strong, may limit the advantage. Say a 60-day turnover, giving 17% of sales. Inventory would include almost no finished goods, and with a short manufacturing cycle, not much work in progress. The bulk of inventory would be plastic raw materials, probably in powder or pellet form, but since there would be perhaps half a dozen main ingredients which would be used in combination to produce different mouldings, even this would be relatively small; say, 22% of sales in all. Fixed assets are unlikely to be more than 25-30% of sales (i.e. sales are several times fixed assets, and perhaps 120-130% of total assets). Trade payables are likely to be somewhat smaller than receivables, despite the slower inventory turnover, but the lower fixed assets and better working capital turnover makes a higher debt level acceptable - if operations are profitable enough to carry the interest. An outline balance sheet should then look approximately as shown in Table 11.6.

Table 11.6 Outline of balance sheet

	(% of sales)		(% of sales)
Cash	2	Trade payables	14
Receivables	17	Bank debt	15
Inventory	22	Total C/L	29
Other C/A	1	Term debt	15
	42	Total liabilities	44
F/A	30	Net worth	28
T/A	72		72
Current ratio	1.45		
TBF/NW	1.07		

There are always minor unpredictable items such as dividends, and allowance must be made for liability reserves, pension funds etc. in countries where they are common. Nevertheless, this is a fairly typical balance sheet (except that both current ratio and TBF/NW are a little weak, even allowing for fast turnover of assets) for a moderately profitable company with the type of characteristics outlined. Any substantial weakening of a major item would need to be offset by strength elsewhere - or by unusually high profitability - if it were not to raise at least a minor question as to the overall creditworthiness of the company.

The relation of sales to assets and net worth means that a net profit after taxes of 10% of sales gives a return of 36% of net worth; a net profit of somewhere around 3-6% of sales (11-21% return on net worth) therefore seems more likely, given the other characteristics of the company. This in turn suggests pre-tax profit of 6-10% of sales. Add back 4% of sales for interest, which gives NBIT of 12-14% of sales or interest cover of 3-4 times.

The same approach to depreciation used in the last example suggests a figure of 4-5% of sales. Starting from the other end, fixed costs other than interest and depreciation will be low, but raw material and labour costs relatively high. With a mass of small customers marketing, distribution and collection costs will be fairly high. R & D is a bit of an unknown quantity since the customers may pay for some of it (directly or by supplying the moulds). Probably most of what there is will be development rather than research. This leads to a P & L something like that shown in Table 11.7.

Table 11.7 Profit and loss statement

	(% of sales)
Sales	100
Cost of materials	30
Labour	35
Gross profit	35
G S & A	15
R & D	1
Depreciation	4
Operating profit	15
Interest	4
Pre-tax profit	11
Net profit	6

	(% of sales)
Interest cover	3.75
Return on assets	20.8
Return on equity	21.4
OCF/TBF	33.3

The breakdown between G S & A, labour and raw materials will vary among light manufacturing companies, but otherwise something along these lines will fit most of them. In many countries the profitability will tend to be lower, and borrowing somewhat higher. This may be acceptable provided profits are reasonably reliable and interest rates low and stable. As many German companies found in 1981/2, a change in economic conditions which undermines both those assumptions at the same time can be crippling.

In both of the first two examples the analyst has to allow for possible cyclical variations. The figures have been built up on assumptions about the relationship of sales to other items which may well be valid in a normal year, but change at either the peaks or valleys of the cycle. In the low period, sales decline in relation to fixed assets, receivable and inventory turnover tend to slow down while pressure from suppliers to pay may mean that NWI increases more than proportionately. The extra borrowing may carry a lower rate of interest due to low credit demand in a slack economy, but the inflationary experience of the 1970s and early 1980s makes that less likely than it used to be. Because of lower sales, fixed costs reduce margins just when the reduction can be least afforded; there may be substantial lay-off or redundancy costs, or the staff may have a guaranteed week which makes labour costs 100% fixed. Even the cost of raw materials may not drop as fast as the price at which the product can be sold, and any drop in prices involves possible inventory losses.

While roughly the reverse is true at the peak of the cycle, it is very easy for a company to lose control of its receivable or inventory levels in a rapid expansion, allowing its borrowings to expand just as interest rates rise rapidly. A boom can also cause loss of control on other costs, and if a cyclical company does not make high profits in a boom it will never build up the strength to ride out a bust.

The analyst should therefore check what phase of the cycle the company is in, and adjust his estimated figures accordingly. He should also check whether the present condition allows sufficient margin to ride out the other stages.

A similar comparison with actual figures to that carried out in the first example will again help the analyst judge how well the company is actually doing.

<u>Example 3 - Retailing</u>

The third example is a chain of supermarkets. These sell food and household goods, many of which are perishable, for cash. They thus carry no receivables and turn their inventory over at least once a month. However, they pay their payables (which are the same as inventory except for the profit margin) on average after 70-75 days. As a result, they have a negative NWI, i.e. they can finance a part of their fixed assets with trade payables, an unusual situation. Their fixed assets, moreover, are prime sites in as many as several hundred different towns, readily adaptable to other uses. Some are leased rather than owned outright. Where the analyst does not know the exact proportion, he has to make a guess; to the extent that he gets it wrong, fixed assets will decline but fixed cash costs, in the form of rental payments, will increase or vice versa.

For the P & L, obviously the largest item in costs is materials; fixed costs relating to buildings (whether depreciation or lease payments) and labour are relatively minor; normally, there should be little or no interest cost, and unless the company is using all its cash for expansion, there may even be some financial income. Apart from that, operating profit and pre-tax profit will be the same, and since sales are many times assets and net worth, a pre-tax margin on sales of 1-2%, and net after tax of 0.5-1%, is satisfactory.

The balance sheet and P & L then look something like Table 11.8.

Table 11.8 Balance sheet and profit and loss statement

	(% of sales)		(% of sales)
Cash	6	Trade payables	19
		Misc. current liabilities	2
Inventory	9	Total liabilities	21
Total C/A	15		
Fixed assets	20	Net worth	14
Total assets	35	TL & NW	35
Current ratio	0.8		
TBF/NW	-0-		
Sales	100		
Materials	88		
Gross profit	12		
Depreciation & rental	6		
Wages, heat etc.	4		
Operating profit	2		
Net before tax	2		
Net after tax	1		

These examples are all predicated on Anglo-Saxon attitudes and would need to be adjusted for use in other countries: to take account of pension reserves for instance; or of the faster and slower payment habits of Germany or Italy; or of the greater willingness - perhaps predicated on historically high profits and/or low interest rates - to permit bank borrowing in particular and borrowing in general to be higher than seems safe in England or America.

The analyst, in adjusting for these differences, must distinguish between mere accounting difference, and differences of substance. With the latter, he must be sure to understand the underlying conditions which justify the difference, and the likely impact if those conditions change. The traditionally high leverage of German companies, for instance, based on good profits, low interest rates and unfunded pension reserves, looked less than sound in the conditions of the early 1980s.

The balance

Each company needs a balance between its requirements and its strengths. There are some aspects of the balance which are fairly obvious and apply in many cases: capital intensity requires a good capital base; high risk requires a combination of high returns and low leverage; high fixed costs require some combination of stable demand, high margins/returns or low leverage; a high NWI requires a sound current ratio; and other similar combinations. But each company also has its own features which either add strength or require protection.

No company actually strikes the ideal balance; but the analyst must have a clear idea of what it would be like and why. Without such a benchmark, he will not easily know how serious are the variations, or their impact on the overall credit. While understanding of the various financial concepts is vital to assessing this balance, they cannot be used in a vacuum. The balance reflects the nature of the company's business, markets, economic and even social environment, risk factors and many other items. Financial analysis cannot assess a company without taking at least the major features into account; on the other hand, a description of the business without relating it fully to the financial analysis is also incomplete.

To strike the balance, therefore, the analyst must have an intelligent understanding of financial analysis, but must develop as much knowledge as possible about the company as well, and think about the relations between the two.

12 Asset-Based Lending

Most manufacturing and trading companies are properly analysed as cash flow situations; cash flow is the main source of debt repayment and the realisation of assets (other than inventory and receivables) would mean either the outright liquidation of the company or at least a major reduction in its ability to do business. However, this is not true for a limited but important range of borrowers.

Just as it is important to recognise that most companies do not repay debt from realisation of assets, we must also recognise those which do; for them cash flow is a secondary source of debt repayment and the correct approach is to analyse the asset base.

Seasonal lending

There are several types of asset companies. Seasonal companies may have a continuing need for finance with a fluctuating need in addition. Although the main analysis of the company will concentrate on the cash flow, their ability to reduce the annual peak borrowing relies on asset reduction. A fertiliser company, whose borrowings probably peak in February, does not reduce that level from cash flow, but rather by converting inventory into receivables in its peak selling period during the spring; it collects the receivables after the harvest and reduces both sides of the balance sheet. Because of the seasonal nature of the business this can be done without damaging the ability of the company to stay in business.

When analysing a seasonal company, therefore, the analyst needs to know the stage in the cycle. If it is the peak borrowing period then, in addition to his normal cash flow analysis, he must check that the inventory and receivables are high enough to repay borrowing as they run down from the seasonal peak. Conversely, at a low seasonal period the debt as well as the assets should be much lower; and in both cases appropriate allowances are needed in assessing leverage, cash flow coverage, return on assets and so on. He will still need to ensure that cash flow is sufficient to cover any borrowing which cannot be paid by seasonal asset reduction.

Financial companies

Some companies' assets are purely financial and they earn a profit by the differential between interest income and expense. Banks, finance companies, leasing companies and in a slightly different way insurance companies all come into this category. Although the interest differential and the degree of risk they will accept on their assets differs, the first three are all lenders of other people's money for a profit and all thus incur financial liabilities as the main source of cash with which to fund financial assets. Because, as with commodity companies, they provide the use of a product - money - without adding to its value, they receive a relatively small return. There is thus no expectation of a bank or a finance or leasing company repaying its debts from cash flow. On the other hand, all of its assets are themselves loans or other forms of credit which are expected to be repaid at some stage. Provided this expectation is met they can use the capital proceeds to repay the deposit. In practice, a sound financial institution normally replaces maturing loans with new ones rather than reduce its total deposits or other liabilities; the point is that the assets mature in a steady stream which gives the bank or finance company a source of repayment which does not impair its ability to continue in business. It is analogous to the way in which a manufacturing company uses proceeds of its receivables to meet trade payables, but nearly all of a bank's assets fit this pattern.

As a result, the quality of assets is even more important with asset-based companies than with a cash flow-based company. If the assets are not good, then they will not generate the funds to repay the deposits. In practice, banks and finance companies take such a large spread of risks that it is inevitable that some will prove unsound; but a healthy portfolio will generate a level of earnings high enough to absorb a normal level of bad debts; indeed, most banks charge a specific amount to earnings to build up a reserve for this purpose. Nevertheless, key questions which the analyst can usually only answer in the most general terms cover the quality of the loan portfolio and of the credit assessment procedures, controls and monitoring which decide its future as well as its present quality. It is usually impossible to review the portfolio in depth, but more and more banks are beginning to reveal at least some information on their bad debts and problem loans which makes an assessment more practicable. It is often possible for other banks to obtain a feel, through joint lending or competition for loans, about the quality of their competitor's credit procedures.

Finance companies in the United States are required to provide fairly detailed information on bad debts, recoveries and slow payers which is an important factor in the bank's decision as to whether to lend. Such information is harder to get outside the United States but is still essential; banks lending to finance companies should make a considerable effort to get it and should refuse to lend if they do not get at least some information.

However, the quality of a bank's assets is not the only factor in its creditworthiness, although it will always be important. It is important to know whether banks or finance companies finance themselves by deposits from the general public and/or from the money markets and the mix where they use both; also their vulnerability to withdrawal because of a loss of confidence or of interest sensitivity. In recent years depositors of all types have become more sophisticated and interest conscious, so that there is a real danger of a large movement of deposits even where soundness is not in question. Therefore either the bulk of deposits must be matched fairly closely against assets so that they will run off together; or if there is a deliberate policy of mismatching then it must be carefully handled; there must be diversified sources of deposits and a spread of maturities so that no one deposit proves impossible, or unduly expensive, to replace.

There are two types of risk in mismatching; one is the loss of the deposit altogether and the other is of its replacement only at an interest rate higher than that on the asset financed. Thus asset quality in a bank relates not only to the individual asset, but to the interest structure. Some finance companies which lend at fixed rates are endangered if rates move up rapidly; the longer the term for which they lend the greater the danger. For instance, hire purchase companies in the United Kingdom normally lend for a period of two to three years with monthly amortisation, so that although the interest rate on each loan is fixed, loans run off steadily and are replaced by new loans at a higher rate when the cost of money increases. Thus, hire purchase companies tend to do badly in periods of rising rates and well when rates decline, but their problem solves itself reasonably quickly unless rates continue moving upwards for an unusually long time. On the other hand, savings and loans associations in the United States provide mortgages for twenty or thirty years at fixed rates. Amortisation is so slow that the sharp increases in US interest rates under Presidents Carter and Reagan broke a significant number and threatened to bankrupt the entire industry. The building societies in the United Kingdom perform a very similar function but have always lent on an adjustable rate of interest; they still flourish despite growing competition from the clearing banks.

But while the general pattern of a bank's deposits may be known (the proportions of current account and of interest-bearing deposits, possibly broken between domestic and overseas offices) the exact structure is likely to be complex and to change fast in line with changes in the bank's views of future interest rates. The analyst should therefore be more concerned with the management philosophy, with the ability of a bank's traders to keep it out of trouble and with the quality of its controls; if the traders start to go off on the wrong track they must be reined in before much damage can be done.

Banks and other asset-based companies can also lose money on foreign exchange trading and other specialist activities, and each borrower is exposed to different specific risks related to its business. In many cases it will be impossible to assess the imminence of such a risk; for instance no outsider can know clearly what a bank's foreign exchange position is. However, the market will usually have a view about the competence of the bank's foreign exchange traders and whether the bank takes major positions which could undermine its profits and/or balance sheet if they went wrong.

Profitability, net worth and return on assets and net worth remain important. Net worth represents the margin of safety should any of the assets turn out to be overvalued (i.e. bad debts) or should the bank make losses for any other reason.

Profitability is necessary both in itself and as an indication of the value of the assets. Assets which yield an inadequate profit throw doubt on their true value. While the link between profitability and value works differently for each type of asset, it exists for all. For a marketable asset like a government bond or a CD there is a direct mathematical relationship between the market price and yield. Loans are not marketable and therefore do not have a market value, but a portfolio of loans can fail to generate sufficient interest to cover the costs of establishing and policing it for one or a mixture of three causes. A significant number of the loans may be paying a below market rate of interest (or no interest) for credit reasons (which almost certainly means that some of the principal will not be recovered either); or a high proportion of fixed rate loans may have rates below the current market rate and not have been matched to eliminate the risk; or floating rate loans may have been made at margins so low that they do not cover operating costs and bad debt losses. In one sense the last two types of loan may be full value since the borrower will meet his contract in full; it is the contract itself which is poor value. Even if it can be argued that loss is the result of an increase in interest liabilities rather than a lower value for the assets, the relationship between assets and liabilities is unsound, and must be covered by net worth.

The danger of this type of loss, and the need to maintain a cushion of net worth against it, makes the profitability of banks and finance companies important even though it is not sufficient to pay the liabilities. Profits must be adequate to demonstrate and maintain the ability of the assets to pay all debts; they must build up the net worth cushion to allow the bank to grow over time; and give the shareholders a return which will enable the banks to raise additional capital if faster growth makes this necessary. Although banks deal almost entirely in money, even modest inflation will balloon the nominal values of a bank's balance sheet; net worth must match this growth or the bank's ability to provide support to its customers will be reduced. Thus growth for banks is necessary if their customers are to grow; growth in net worth is necessary even where the bank has no excessive ambitions for rapid real growth; and in the long run, growth in net worth depends on profits.

Leasing companies

Leasing companies are a form of financial institution with something in common with banks or finance companies but also some differences. They have most in common with a finance company when they lease a wide variety of small items to small users, even consumers, where many of the considerations are the same as in consumer lending. Leasing major items, particularly where confined to a single type of product, requires different skills. Banks often lend to companies secured against the lease contract but the value of the security depends on that of the asset, which has two different features. In one sense it is a purely financial asset, a contract with the user of the equipment to make regular payments to the leasing company which, in turn, pays all or the major part of these to the bank. As long as the contract is watertight and the user of the equipment creditworthy, the bank will be paid in full even if other customers of the leasing company run into trouble and perhaps even if the company itself collapses. However, if the lessee becomes unable to meet the lease payments then, from both the lessor's and the bank's point of view, the asset ceases to be financial and becomes the underlying piece of equipment. Its value depends on the ability to find another lessee or outright purchaser, which in turn will depend on the nature of the equipment and why the previous lessee failed to pay. If it was using the equipment in a way which is no longer economic then it is unlikely to be worth much to anyone else; if the leasing company specialises in this one line it may well have a number of other failures and will not itself be a likely source of payment.

These leases are full payout leases, i.e. covering a period and at a rate which would allow the original cost of the equipment plus interest to be paid from the first lease. Partial payout leases are also common; equipment with an economic life of five to seven years may be leased initially for, say, three years and the lease payments on the initial contract meet perhaps 60%, occasionally less, of the lessor's cost. The lessor expects to renew the lease with the same lessee or failing that to find another. This exposes it (and the bank) to the risk that a better or cheaper product will make this impossible, or possible only at too low a rental to repay the debt, even though the original lessee meets its legal obligations completely.

The more specialised the nature of the equipment and the more concentrated the leasing company's business on one type, the greater the danger that high non-renewals will bankrupt the borrower and cause a bad debt for the bank. Therefore banks rarely finance partial payout leases for more than the value of the original lease, thus ensuring a higher equity contribution from the lessor to cover the greater risk. In the rare cases where a bank finances the full value of equipment on a partial payout lease, the borrower must have an adequate equity cushion; it should also have, and the bank take as its collateral, a diversified portfolio of leased equipment. The obsolescence of any one product, or problems of one customer, is then less likely to have a fatal effect overall.

Although the bank expects to be paid from the cash generated by the lease payments, this is not cash flow in the normal sense. The cash represents, to a large extent, payment of capital and only to a small extent the profit from the lease. Thus provided the lessor has enough original equity in the lease, the bank can be paid in full from lease payments even though the lessee company makes no profit or even a small loss.

There are other forms of asset-based companies with mainly financial assets; insurance companies for one. But the examples should enable even the fairly inexperienced banker to apply the basic principle to all asset-based companies and assess how the loan is expected to be paid, and the risks which could prevent payment.

Asset-based companies which deal in real rather than financial assets can be broken into two main types. In one type, the asset is self-liquidating in a fairly short time so that any finance can be paid out from the normal completion of the transaction. Commodity companies, for instance, often arrange bank financing for specific transactions; indeed, a letter of credit and the related acceptance finance may be an integral part of the transaction. The product is bought from a producer against a letter of credit, sold to a consumer who pays on receipt of shipping documents and the payment meets the maturing acceptance drawn under the letter of credit. This is a simple example and is not by any means the only form of self-liquidating finance possible. But again the purpose here is not to list all types of trade finance (see Chapter 4 of Lending in International Commercial Banking by T. H. Donaldson) but to highlight the features of asset-based companies and lending. The margins which commodity companies earn on sales and the borrowing in relation to them are respectively so small and so large that there is no possibility of paying out from cash flow.

Property and shipping

There are several types of asset companies where the assets are individually large and generate cash over a long period. Lending in such cases is related to the individual asset and repayment is either from its cash flow or from refinancing which can only be repaid over a period longer than a bank is prepared to extend a loan. The two main examples of this are shipping and property. There are some major companies in each industry with diversified portfolios which generate sufficient cash flow to provide a base for unsecured or non-specific lending. Even these companies usually borrow to finance individual assets and the repayment comes primarily from their earnings; and a high proportion of borrowers are entrepreneurs or single ship or single property companies borrowing on the basis of those assets.

A ship only generates a secure cash flow if it has a long-term charter; not all types of shipping business lend themselves to charters. Without a charter the ship's value is normally a reflection of the rate at which it can now be chartered and the expected rate in the foreseeable future; or of the expected cash flow if it is employed in one of the uses which does not provide a charter, but nevertheless generates revenue. If value of the charter or earnings from other employment decline, the capital value of the asset will follow. It may drop by the same proportion as earnings, by less if the reduction is seen as temporary, or more if a further fall seems likely. If earnings decline below operating costs, the ship may have to be laid up; the value should logically become negative because the ship is at least temporarily unsaleable, but laying it up incurs significant costs. It is therefore normally only laid up if it is expected to be able to earn again in the future; otherwise it will be sold for scrap, and scrap value is usually considered the minimum value. But the point is that the finance of a specific asset relies either on the cash flow from that asset or on the ability to sell it to realise its capital value; this will be a multiple of actual or expected cash flow.

The same general principle is true of property which, however, has a much longer economic life and rarely generates sufficient cash flow in the lifetime of a bank loan to repay it. Nor does property have scrap value although land often has more value than the cost of demolishing a building. A building may generate enough cash to pay rental interest and possibly even a small amount of the principal over seven or ten years, but the bank almost certainly relies on either the sale of the asset or on the provision of longer-term finance (mortgage finance of twenty-five or thirty years in many countries) which will be used to pay out the bank loan and serviced from rental or from capital values based on rental. The value of the property and therefore the price at which it can be sold or for which the longer-term debt can be raised will again be linked to the income it earns; it will also be affected by the type of building, the location, the quality of the tenant and so on. The precise linkage between the income and the capital value will vary from country to country reflecting methods of setting rent, the types of buyers and the extent to which they are interested in immediate yield or capital gain. Nevertheless, although the relationship may vary not only between markets but with different conditions in the same markets, it will always be there.

Secured lending

Chapter 1 suggested that banks which traditionally use the liquidation approach and look more at the value of assets often rely more heavily on security than banks looking mainly to cash flow. The latter argue, for reasons given later in the chapter, that a charge on assets in a cash flow company is at best of secondary value and that over-reliance on it can be positively dangerous. However, the situation is different with an asset-based borrower. Here the bank is not relying directly on cash flow, but on the quality of assets in general or in some cases of specific assets. There are several general and one specific argument for taking security in these situations; not all of the arguments apply to every case but there is considerable overlap.

First, the asset generated by the project being financed provides the source of repayment. One purpose of the security is therefore to establish a claim on that asset ahead of other lenders which have contributed nothing to its value. Secondly, the bank may find it easier to analyse the likely value or success of the particular project or asset than of the company as a whole. Alternatively, or additionally, even though the bank may see real substance in the rest of the business, nevertheless its prime reason for lending is the particular asset; the security enables it to control use of the asset and cash it generates, to ensure that they are in fact applied to the loan and not to any other lender or purpose. And finally no bank can afford to be unsecured if most, or sometimes if any, of the other creditors are secured ahead of it; secured lenders then pre-empt the asset base and even the cash flow in certain circumstances. If these are insufficient to pay all the creditors, the unsecured lender may find that other banks are paid in full while it gets nothing. This is the reverse of the first reason, and applies equally to cash flow lending.

There is, however, considerable danger in relying on security which is not the primary source of repayment; nevertheless some banks lend secured to a cash flow company as a substitute for sound analysis, or as an easy way out where analysis suggests that the company is unsound but the loan is very profitable. (Bankers too easily forget that profits on lending are normally unusually high for a good reason only; this is often that the market has identified an unusual element of risk and requires special compensation. Banks which understand the nature of the risk can analyse the individual situations, accept sound ones or take protective measures (including well-judged security). They may well be justified in taking a recognised risk which they have recognised and guarded against and for which they are well paid. Banks which take the reward without understanding the risk or even without recognising that it exists deserve the losses they will undoubtedly get.)

It is unsound to rely on assets in a cash flow company for the same reason for which assets have to be carefully analysed in an asset company; broadly speaking they are only as valuable as the profits that they generate. Thus a bank has no real need for a charge over the assets of a manufacturing company as long as it continues to generate the cash flow necessary to service its debt. Once profits cease, the assets begin to lose their value and in extreme cases may have none at all. Liquidation approach analysis recognises this to some extent by assigning various discounts to the value of the assets before using them as cover for a loan. However, this is a very subjective valuation because no bank can tell what the mix of assets will be at the time the company runs into trouble, nor what will cause the trouble. If it is caused by management incompetence, other people may be able to make a better profit from the assets and be willing to pay a price high enough to repay most of the borrowing. Often, however, even badly managed companies fail because of general problems in the industry or economy, which make the assets of little value to anybody.

Some of the factors, such as flexibility, which were discussed in earlier chapters for the going concern may reduce the likelihood of a dramatic decline in asset value and analysis can help to assess this. But conditions can change and this form of asset lending will only be successful if the quality of the assets and therefore of the earnings they produce is carefully monitored. In other words at this stage security is no longer a way of avoiding analysis and monitoring but rather a support to a different approach to them. Going concern bankers prefer their own approach, but will readily agree that the most important point is that there should be a serious attempt to analyse, and to monitor once the loan has been made. The argument therefore is not that taking security in a cash flow company is always wrong; rather it is wrong where it substitutes for, instead of supporting the conclusions of, analysis and monitoring. The danger is that however good the intentions, the banker will be lulled into a false sense of "security" and relax his analytical standards.

Lending secured by certain types of assets, such as receivables or inventory, in weak cash flow companies can be a relatively sound form of lending which actually helps to improve the quality of the credit. Receivable lending in the United States, for instance, involves the bank in careful monitoring of the quality of the receivables and in setting standards below which it will not accept a receivable as collateral at all. This can supplement a small company's controls or cause it to institute them for the first time; this in turn could prevent it from extending excessive credit to the wrong names in aiming for faster growth and collapsing as a result.

The same general principle that security supports analysis and does not substitute for it needs to be applied in deciding whether and if so how and why the bank needs security in lending to asset-based companies. The bank must identify the source of repayment and then use the security at least to ensure that the proceeds are used to repay the loan and not diverted to excessive expansion or dividend payments. In lending to a commodity company, for instance, it is better to have a claim on goods already resold to a strong buyer than a floating charge over produce which has not been sold and the value of which can fluctuate dramatically overnight. Thus where the bank is financing on a collection basis or by documentary letters of credit it can review each transaction; if its collection procedures are better than average it may even improve the chance that the payment will be made. With a sound transaction the bank will probably be paid even if the company fails.

Conversely, if the company takes positions on the market, the value of the collateral can change rapidly and without a firm buyer the company has no protection unless it has hedged on the appropriate exchange. The bank can rarely be sure there is an effective hedge and is more vulnerable to a position going badly wrong and wiping out the limited equity. A general or even a specific charge over unsold assets in a warehouse does not protect the bank against loss of market value; although close policing of values and the ability to call for additional security, or sell what is already held, may.

The same general point is true of major items like ships or property. A bank may lend to finance construction or purchase of an asset because there is a clear source of income either already in place or clearly arising in the future. This is expected to be used directly or indirectly to repay the loan and the charge ensures that it does so.

Capital values will fluctuate less if the assets have an assured flow of cash than if the projects speculate on the ability to obtain charters or tenants when they are completed. The capital value is also less important if the income can service the loan.

Where the loan is against a property or ship under construction, a firm lease or charter may still assure its future value. In some markets it may be possible to make bridging finance against a firm institutional take out to provide long-term capital. If this is sufficiently tightly written then the risk can be confined to that of the institution failing, which is unlikely, or of a failure to construct in accordance with the terms of the take out; banks can normally assess this risk fairly accurately against the known capabilities of the constructor. Indeed it is often possible to get a bank guarantee against failure to deliver a ship on time.

The point then is the need for an asset which will provide a specific source of repayment. It is not easy to take general charges against all the assets of property or shipping companies but even if it were to do so would not give a great deal of extra security. A general charge assures that if the company gets into trouble the bank will do at least as well as any other bank and perhaps better. It does nothing to increase the chances that the company will survive. In asset companies it is almost a matter of indifference to the bank whether it has a general charge because everybody else does or whether neither it nor anybody else does. If all the charges rank equally all of those holding them will recover the same as if nobody had a charge. (This is not true in manufacturing companies where there may be fairly large amounts of trade and other credit which would rank pari passu with an unsecured bank but behind a secured bank. But where the banks are virtually the only creditors it is valid.)

The right way to look at security is as a means of ensuring that the previously identified source of repayment will be kept in as good a condition as possible and will be used for a specific purpose, i.e. repaying bank debt, rather than anything else. As far as possible security, and the policing or monitoring which goes with it, should actually aim to improve the quality of the asset and therefore of the underlying credit although usually only a minor improvement is possible. In a few cases it is possible to finance a specific project which will not be affected by financial or operational problems of the rest of the business. In most cases it is necessary to analyse the business carefully and recognise that its failure may either be symptomatic of a weakness which also applies to the security; or it may so divert management's attention and even funds that the bank's security is prejudiced.

The basic principle remains the same whether taking security to support cash flow or charging assets which are the main source of repayment. The source of repayment must be identified and the security must be a means of controlling it. Security is never an automatic way out in its own right without the need to analyse how and why it will provide for repayment.

Valuation - some examples

Thus the valuation of assets for security purposes can often be misleading. A property or ship valuer gives a valuation under today's circumstances and in today's market. If the market today is favourable and the borrower has a charter or tenant which is well regarded, this will give a high value. If the charter expires or if the tenant goes bankrupt and cannot pay the rent, suddenly the value of the asset depends on the ability to find a new charter. Unless the banker has assessed the factors which make the particular ship or building attractive to tenants or charterers, it will have no way of assessing its value because it will have no idea of its earning capacity.

Example 1. A company purchased a property for £2 million. It planned to spend about £750,000 renovating the building and then to re-let it. On the basis of these plans a reputable firm of real estate valuers valued the property at £3.5 million. A bank lent the purchase price and agreed to lend the cost of the refurbishment.

However, while the refurbishment was at a very early stage - indeed some of the old tenants were still in the building - market conditions changed dramatically. It became clear that market rentals would no longer justify the cost of refurbishing, but the property was in no state to re-let without it. The company was on the verge of bankruptcy, and unable to pay the interest; the bank considered financing a minimum refurbishment, but could not justify even this. Eventually the property was sold for £400,000 - a loss to the bank of £1.6 million plus nearly three years' interest.

Example 2. A syndicate of banks lent £20 million to finance the purchase of a freehold; the property was let to a pension fund, which in turn let it on more favourable terms to a British government agency. The purchaser agreed to buy the head lease from the pension fund in order to get the benefit of the more favourable sub-lease. It made a down payment but, because of the same change in conditions which was so damaging in the first example, was unable to make the later payments. The pension fund therefore refused to pay the rent until it had withheld the amount due; the banks put a receiver into the property who sued the pension fund. He won, but the pension fund appealed; since the property was unsaleable with the litigation hanging over it, the receiver settled for a smaller amount than the original judgement.

At the time of the purchase, interest rates were low; the rent was about £850,000 p.a. but was due for review in two years, at which time it was expected to rise to over £1.4 million. On this basis, the property was valued at £28 million. However, with the market deteriorating, the new rent was in fact set at £1.1 million. At the same time yields which buyers expected to receive rose rapidly. The combination of lower than forecast rental income and higher yield expectations more than halved the value, and the property was sold for £12.5 million. Allowing for the payment from the litigation the banks lost over £5 million of principal and three years' interest.

Example 3. A bank lent $10 million to buy a ship; the ship was chartered to a major trading company at a rate which would pay interest and principal on the loan over seven years. Unfortunately, when the loan had been reduced to $8 million, the trading company went into liquidation; part of the reason was a dramatic fall in the rates at which it could re-charter a number of similar ships it had chartered in. The owner was unable to find a new charter at a rate which would even cover the interest. Although the owner was thought to be a wealthy man, he had no assets in Britain in his own name and the bank was advised that the chances of enforcing a judgement were small. In the end it accepted a payment of $4 million and wrote off the remaining $4 million.

These examples illustrate the importance of cash generation in capital values. In the last example, the loan would have been paid in full if the trading company had remained solvent, which in turn it probably would have if demand for that type of ship had not slumped. In the first example, the value depended on a set of assumptions which, while apparently reasonable when made, indicated more of an equity risk; if the assumptions were right the borrower made a fortune and the bank a spread; if they were wrong the bank lost money. The size of the loss, compared with either of the other two, shows the vital importance of a stream of income.

In the second example, the original valuation was based on a capitalisation of a mixture of assured present income and assumed future income. The assumption proved optimistic, and the capitalisation factor applied by the market changed adversely. Despite this the banks could possibly have avoided any loss, and certainly reduced the actual loss, if they had been able to sell when market conditions began to move against them. The litigation made this impossible, however.

The lessons

The lessons, in lending against security which is not completely self-liquidating, are:

(i) Long-term asset values depend on streams of income.
(ii) The market value of a stream of income can change. Any doubts as to the right to the income can make the asset temporarily unsaleable at any price.
(iii) Even apparently conservative estimates of future streams of income can prove optimistic.
(iv) If (ii) and (iii) weaken together as they often do, the impact on capital values can be devastating.
(v) Even where the stream of income is contractually assured, the contract is no stronger than its obligor. Conditions which cause him to fail are very likely to make it impossible to find a replacement at anywhere close to the same level.

(vi) For all these reasons, secured lending requires at least as much analysis as unsecured, and often additional specialised knowledge.

(vii) Secured lending usually carries higher margins than unsecured. Although there are other contributing factors, the main reason is that the need to lend secured often arises from the risky nature of the loan. It may be possible to offset the risk by greater skill, but this too has to be paid for.

13 Using Inadequate Information

One of the major problems in all analysis is the lack of detailed and reliable information on most of the points discussed in the rest of the book. Even where full accounts are available, the number of ways in which they can mislead, intentionally or by accident, for good motives or bad, would fill several books each longer than this one. The banker must be aware of the danger and of the significance of different types of presentation or concealment.

Accounts are a shorthand; they neither borrow nor repay debt. The balance sheet merely represents more or less accurately the money value of assets which can generate cash and the liabilities which have to be repaid; the P & L, because it uses accrual rather than cash accounting, does not distinguish fully between profits which generate cash today and those which may generate cash at some time in the future or even, occasionally, those which have generated cash in the past. Thus in interpreting accounts the banker must be familiar with the accounting technicalities but must not allow himself to become too absorbed in them. It is dangerous to let interest in the justification (or otherwise) for a particular accounting treatment take priority over understanding the underlying strength or weakness. A company with conservative accounting can lose money; a company which deliberately manipulates its accounts to show a particular picture is dangerous, however intellectually elegant the manipulation; and some highly competent and honest managers have what seem to bankers extremely odd ideas about how to account for certain items.

Where the information is inadequate or suspect, the banker must understand the borrower's business and the type of impact it is likely to have on the balance sheet and profit and loss. By comparing what the company should look like with the actual figures, the bank can get at least an approximate idea of whether the figures are misleading.

A knowledge of local accounting criteria is essential. Is

it tax-based or is it genuinely intended to assist management? Are there any particular types of reserve, hidden or otherwise, which may be deducted from profits and perhaps from one or more assets to obtain special tax or other treatment? How does the local accounting system treat items such as the revaluation of fixed assets, the valuation of investments, the treatment of foreign currency items? Is the treatment different for investments in overseas subsidiaries, debt and current items like trade payables and receivables? A general knowledge of all of these items is essential in interpreting the figures of each country.

Lack of consolidated figures

One of the greatest barriers to the understanding of corporate credit is the failure in many countries to provide consolidated figures. In an extreme case figures may be solely those of a holding company with all of the assets and operations of the subsidiaries shown simply as investments. In less extreme cases the holding company may also be a fairly substantial operating company in its own right with anything from 20% upwards of assets, sales and profits of the total group. Or domestic consolidated figures may be given, with overseas subsidiaries shown as investments. Even where substantial operating assets are disclosed, the importance of the investments and their valuation can be unclear; so can the extent to which the parent company is manipulating its profits and balance sheet by putting unfavourable items which would otherwise weaken its credit into the non-consolidated subsidiaries. For instance, transfer pricing can make the sales to subsidiaries appear more profitable than they really are. Only the dividend of non-consolidated subsidiaries appears in the parent statement; it can be manipulated to keep the parent profits stable almost regardless of the subsidiaries' ability to earn and finance it, for a time at least. The subsidiary may be required to pay for purchases from the parent very rapidly while the parent pays it very slowly for upstream sales, thus transferring borrowing out of the parent balance sheet and improving the parent's reported leverage and liquidity. Similar means can be used to transfer profits between subsidiaries.

Of course to say that a parent can conceal a weakness in

these and other ways is not to say that it always does. Indeed a strong parent may act in the opposite way. It may pay its subsidiary quickly and allow it long payment terms; or may require no dividend even where earnings justify one, thus strengthening the subsidiary's balance sheet, reducing its borrowings and interest charges and improving its earnings. The parent may then show higher leverage and lower earnings than fully consolidated figures would reveal.

The decision as to which of these various approaches to take is rarely based wholly or even mainly on a desire to conceal. It may reflect sensible tax planning, a means of covering or reducing foreign exchange exposure, direction of borrowing where interest rates are lowest or a sound allocation of funds to the country where the return is highest. Nevertheless the result is to make it harder for the bank to judge the true position.

There is only a limited amount the bank can do if a company will not cooperate in providing information. Just how much will depend on the country or countries in which the subsidiaries are located. Some countries require all companies to publish figures in some sort of official monitor (Belgium for instance) or to provide copies to a central point where they are available for inspection (as in the United Kingdom). Or the bank may be lending to a subsidiary through its local branch and obtain figures to support the loan. However the figures are obtained, they give at least some idea as to whether the subsidiaries are more or less highly leveraged and more or less profitable than the parent. In particular they should show whether the parent is taking more dividends, royalties etc. than the subsidiary can truly afford and overstating the parent's profitability. Given the vagaries of accounting in many countries such indications can never be wholly reliable but some information is usually better than none.

If major subsidiaries are in countries where reasonably detailed and reliable information is available, it may be possible to perform a rough and ready consolidation. This requires some knowledge of the intercompany sales and payment terms, but even if this cannot be obtained precisely from the figures some estimate may be possible. Even a partial consolidation gives some pointer to the direction of the effect; it is helpful to know whether leverage is overstated or understated, for instance, even if it would be more helpful to know by how much.

If the subsidiary is a pure sales company its material costs or costs of goods sold will roughly represent parent sales to it and can be eliminated in consolidation, so that only its gross profit is added to total sales. If a gross profit figure is not available, add what seems a reasonable proportion of operating profit. Some subsidiaries manufacture in their own right; if there is no information as to the extent to which they import from or export to the parent it may be possible to extrapolate from the proportion of total payables and receivables which are intercompany. Certainly, disclosed royalties, commissions or management fees paid to the parent can be eliminated. Set out in Tables 13.1 and 13.2 is an example of how this approach might work. (For simplicity's sake, all figures are assumed to be in the same currency; in practice it will often be necessary to convert.)

A is the parent; B is a subsidiary known to manufacture; C is a pure sales company. Items not relevant to consolidation such as pension funds and liability reserves are ignored.

Table 13.1 Sample rough consolidation of balance sheet

	A	B	C	Eliminations	Consolidated
Cash	150	10	5	-	165
Trade receivables	5,000	1,500	100	-	6,600
Intercompany receivables	500	50	-	550 (1)	-
Inventory	6,000	1,600	150	-	7,750
Total current assets	11,650	3,160	225	550	14,515
Fixed assets	7,000	700	10	-	7,710
Investments	2,000	-	-	1,000 (2)	1,000
Total assets	20,650	3,860	265	1,550	23,225
Current bank debt	2,000	1,000	50	-	3,050
Trade payables	4,500	1,200	5	-	5,705
Intercompany payables	20	400	130	550 (1)	-

continued

Table 13.1 continued

	A	B	C	Eliminations	Consolidated
Total current liab	6,520	2,500	185	550	8,655
Term debt	5,000	440	-	-	5,440
Net worth	9,130	920	80	1,000 (2)	9,130
Total liabs & NW	20,650	3,860	265	1,550	23,225
Ratios					
Current	1.79	1.26	1.38		1.68
TL/NW	1.26	3.20	2.31		1.54
TBF/NW	0.77	1.57	0.63		0.93

Notes to Table 13.1:
(1) Assumes no other intercompany transactions. If there were other subsidiaries not included in the partial consolidation, the analyst would need to take a view as to how much related to them. This amount would not be eliminated.
(2) Assumes investment in subsidiaries carried at book value, excess represents other types of investment.

Comment to Table 13.1:
The subsidiaries are significantly less liquid and more highly leveraged than the parent, although not more so than is reasonable for the sales company. Because they are fairly small and because some of their higher liabilities represent intercompany items, only a part of their heavier leverage shows up in the consolidated figures. However, as an exercise, work out what would be the effect if the parent insisted on immediate payment of intercompany receivables, and used the collections to reduce its own short-term debt. Assume the payments by the subsidiaries were financed with additional bank debt.

Further work out the impact if the parent unloads inventory on the subsidiaries and calls them sales, for which immediate payment is made. Decrease Company A's inventory and bank debt by 1000 each; increase Company B's by 750 each and Company C's by 250 each; then rework all four sets of ratios.

Table 13.2 Sample rough consolidation of profit and loss statement

	A	B	C	Eliminations	Consolidated
Sales	22,000	6,200	500	2,200(1)	26,700
Gross profit	7,000	2,100	100	700	8,500
G S & A	5,000	1,500	50	-	6,500
Royalties etc. rec	500	-	-	250(2)	250
Operating profit	2,500	600	50	950(3)	2,200
Dividends rec	250	-	-	250(4)	-
Interest	500	100	10	-	610
Royalties etc. paid	-	200	50	250(2)	-
Net before tax	2,250	300	(10)	-	1,590
Net after tax	1,100	150	(5)	450(5)	795
Div. paid	-	200	50	250(4)	-

Notes to Table 13.2:

(1) Assumes that intercompany receivables turn over at approximately the same speed as trade receivables.

(2) Since only 250 of royalties are paid by the subsidiaries the balance of those received must come from another source and are not eliminated.

(3) The sum of previous items.

(4) Dividends received from subsidiaries eliminated.

(5) Assumes tax rate on 950 profit eliminated of just under 50%.

Comment to Table 13.2:

Of course, these figures will never be completely accurate, but they give an idea of the direction, and the order of magnitude, of the misstatement of profits in the parent. In this example, profits are overstated significantly as a result of royalties and dividends which are extortionate.

Where there are known to be other, perhaps larger subsidiaries for which no information is available, the treatment of these two is at least a pointer to the type of policy the parent is likely to follow. A bank lending to the subsidiary will wish to judge the extent to which the parent is supporting or undermining it. Although in many cases the bank will have a guarantee or some lesser form of support, it should always at least be aware of the strength or otherwise of its direct borrower since in liquidation this is where it will look first for repayment. With weak support, or none, it is even more important to assess local factors relating to the subsidiary; the extent to which it is dependent on the parent for finance, technical support, products, export-marketing assistance or whatever; and the extent to which that support can be relied on or the danger that the parent will instead loot the subsidiary.

There will always be cases where it is impossible to obtain any meaningful figures on the major non-consolidated subsidiaries. Then the bank must look at the non-consolidated figures of the parent particularly closely. With a pure holding company, showing only investments in subsidiaries, there is really little further that the bank can do and the figures are almost worthless. However, if it shows intercompany loans receivable or payable, it may provide a very tentative pointer along the lines discussed below. Where the parent is both an operating company and a holding company there may be some inferences that can be drawn from its figures alone; however, they can be no more than inferences, to be treated with appropriate caution.

A substantial intercompany receivables and/or intercompany advances figure suggests that the parent is financing at least part of the subsidiaries' needs on its own balance sheet. This makes it less likely that the parent is concealing financial weakness by putting it into the subsidiaries. The inference is stronger if the intercompany receivables/advances are large in relation to what is known of the size of the subsidiaries. The reverse inference should be drawn from a large intercompany payable figure; the subsidiaries are probably borrowing in overseas markets in order to provide finance for the parent as well as for their own needs, thus removing debt from the parent balance sheet and understating leverage. (Of course, if the amount and direction of intercompany sales is concealed, it may be difficult to judge what are normal trade terms and what is window dressing; but even an obscure pointer is better than none.) These inferences can be supported or offset if anything is known about the original capital contribution made by the parent.

In the same way, the profit and loss may show sizeable items for royalties, licensing fees, management fees or some such heading; unless there is reason to believe a real service is provided, this suggests that the subsidiaries' profits are perhaps being used to conceal poor profitability in the parent operations. Even without details it will often be possible to discover whether such items are a significant source of revenue. A pattern in the payment of dividends by subsidiaries may suggest that the parent is requisitioning an amount that suits its needs rather than one which it is reasonable for the subsidiaries to pay. Again, the opposite inference can be drawn when there are no such payments, although with less confidence in view of the possibility of transfer pricing.

This assessment of leverage will have more value where most or all subsidiaries are known to be pure sales companies. Where some are manufacturing companies, intercompany receivables and payables will only cover a part of the leverage of the subsidiaries. Even here substantial longer-term intercompany receivables or advances may suggest that the parent is financing part of the subsidiary's fixed assets itself, thus reducing the chances of concealed leverage. The reported value of the investment in subsidiaries may help; if it is known to be carried at cost and to represent funds actually put into the subsidiary, this gives again some indication of the size of the subsidiary's capital; however, without information about the size of the subsidiary's sales, profitability and dividend policy, only the most general comfort can be drawn even from a large investment.

In fact the whole approach, lacking information on the subsidiaries, should really be a way of finding out what questions to ask management rather than expecting to find answers. At best it gives some indication of the policy of the parent towards the subsidiaries, but policy is most likely to change when the parent wishes to conceal problems from the bank.

Thus lack of consolidated figures, particularly where subsidiaries account for a large part of a company's manufacturing operations, can make analysis very difficult. The possibility that the company has not prepared consolidated figures and does not have a clear view as to the overall position merely adds to the worry. Where unconsolidated figures provided cover a minority of the business and where problems in the subsidiaries are suspected, the lack of consolidation may itself justify refusing to lend. Even in less extreme cases the bank may lend on a shorter term or require security or other restrictive conditions because of the risk related to the uncertainty.

Lack of consolidating figures

Even consolidated figures, desirable though they are as a general rule, can conceal as well as reveal. They do not show how well or badly parts of the business are doing or their overall impact on the company. Where the company's performance and balance sheet are weakening, fully consolidated figures may not distinguish between a general weakening and a more dramatic decline in one or a few parts being offset by a continuing sound performance in the remainder. It is best, therefore, to obtain consolidating as well as consolidated statements; these show the positions of the subsidiaries and the various eliminations and adjustments made to reach the consolidated position. Some companies have literally hundreds of subsidiaries and full consolidating figures would be impractical and not much use to the bank; in such a case ask for a consolidating statement of the major subsidiaries only.

The greatest difficulty in the absence of consolidating figures arises when a company is in two or more lines of business with different characteristics. For instance a company may have one division which is mainly a trading operation with the characteristics of that type of operation; another division might be a medium to heavy manufacturing company (perhaps processing some of the products which the company ultimately trades but with no other particularly close relationship to the trading business). Its slower moving receivables and inventory, sizeable fixed asset base, long-term debt, higher equity and lower leverage would be very different to the trading operation. So would its P & L with higher fixed costs and higher margins on sales but comparable or lower returns on assets because of the lower sales volume in relation to them.

A balance sheet and profit and loss statement which consolidates these two operations in effect averages two entirely different and even opposing sets of figures; for instance, the receivable turnover will neither be appropriate to a trading company nor to a manufacturing company but in some indeterminate position between them. No outsider can judge whether a modest deterioration represents a change in receivables arising from one or both aspects of the business or simply a change in their relative importance. There is no sound basis for judging whether the company is adequately capitalised for the mix of businesses that it is doing. Some more detailed information on specific items (such as for instance a breakdown of inventory between raw materials, work in process and finished goods which might give some indication as to changes in relative importance) might help a little; failing that there is very little that the banker can do to distinguish between the various factors causing a change in the figures, except insist on consolidating figures.

Nevertheless to use this specific weakness is no argument against the need for obtaining consolidated figures. Even though occasionally they may conceal part of what the banker needs to know, in most cases they will reveal more than non-consolidated figures. And while they may make the reasons for a deterioration harder to assess, they will not conceal its existence. Once detected, the bank has a better reason to insist on information, whatever the form of the figures received in the first place.

Hidden reserves

Hidden reserves and the possibility that they may be being dissolved to hide a deterioration in operations are a serious problem. By definition they mean that any outsider using the figures cannot know how close they are to reality.

The extent of hidden reserves varies from country to country. Under Anglo-Saxon accounting (with a few exceptions such as banks in some countries) hidden reserves are not permitted. In some other countries they are permitted only for one or two specific assets such as inventory. If the banker knows enough about the local accounting to know where hidden reserves may be taken this at least limits the damage they do. But in other countries companies have wide freedom to take hidden reserves as they like; in these countries published figures may have little meaning and banks will try to obtain the figures management itself uses. However, even where a company uses hidden reserves sparingly so that the figures are in fact reasonably realistic, the bank may not feel able to rely on this and may not trust the figures as a basis for lending.

Many companies and even a few bankers argue that hidden reserves affect conservative accounting, since their existence causes an understatement rather than an overstatement of assets and balance sheet. Unfortunately it is not as simple as that. In the first place, understatement of assets creates problems of its own which will be discussed later in the chapter. In the second place, hidden reserves can only be created by also understating the net worth of the company and this in turn can only be done by understating the earnings. The earnings understatement may take place in just one year or over a number of years but it means that the bank has no clear idea as to the true progression of earnings. And although it may be argued, and may even be true to a limited extent, that understated figures are less damaging than overstated figures, the fact remains that either are inaccurate. The bank is interested in obtaining the most accurate picture of the underlying reality that it can, not in accepting the company's assurance that any distortion is favourable.

But the most important argument against hidden reserves is that their main purpose is to be available for dissolution in poor years, thus hiding the extent or even existence of the deterioration. However much this may be presented as smoothing an erratic earnings trend or avoiding panic on temporary downturns, the fundamental fear is that managements use hidden reserves to give themselves a quiet life when things go wrong. In some cases management may correct the fault which the dissolution is hiding, but in too many cases managements are fooled by their own propaganda; they believe that because they have dissolved some portion of hidden reserves and therefore reported a profit, the situation is as reported rather than as they should know it to be. And if management fools itself it will often fool the banks as well because banks rely heavily on the integrity of management in interpreting the information. (The argument is not that any management which uses hidden reserves automatically lacks integrity; it is that the existence of hidden reserves, and the ability to manipulate the figures, has a tendency to undermine integrity by lowering the accepted standards. Even managements starting out with good intentions can end up believing that they have a right and even a duty to conceal the truth from their banks.)

Moreover, the argument throughout this book is that analysts should study trends and the reasons underlying them, as a means to assessing the future. The use of hidden reserves may mean that a table reporting the trend would be shown as in the first line of Table 13.3 below, while the true figures should be as in the second line.

Table 13.3 Presentation of true and reported figures

Pretax Profit ($000)	Year	1	2	3	4	5
Reported		12	12	12	12	12
True		6	20	16	11	7

The fact that both lines correctly show that profit in year 1 was about the same as in year 5 is far less important than the fact that the position in the first line is wrong in both years and the trend is very different.

Thus, although hidden reserves are a readily accepted feature of business life in many countries, banks should not accept them where they can possibly avoid it. Where, under present conditions, it cannot be avoided they should campaign actively to change those conditions. One way for banks in many countries to do this would be to abandon the use of hidden reserves themselves; the comments made about customers apply equally to the banks.

Tax accounting

Tax-based accounting is one fruitful source of hidden reserves but can also exist in their absence. In some countries the authorities require that the accounts issued to the public be the same as those used for tax purposes. The accounts will then be prepared specifically to produce the lowest taxable income, and to incorporate any adjustments which are permitted for tax purposes. In contrast, where published accounts are expected to show the true figures these are then adjusted openly to meet any distortions which arise from tax concessions. Thus, for instance, deferred taxation may show on the balance sheet when taxes on income are delayed by things like investment allowances; this may distort the balance sheet, but at least the distortion is clearly labelled and can be readily understood.

The intermediate situation is where tax distortions are not fully disclosed but the bank has a general idea of the items affected by them and sometimes of their size. For instance, some Scandinavian countries allow certain reserves against inventory and other items at certain stages of the business cycle, which can be released at other stages. Provided the reserving and the releasing meet the government requirements they are tax deductible and confer a specific benefit on the company which makes compliance well worth while. Moreover these reserves are included in net worth and thus their size and impact on earnings can be broadly assessed even though it may not always be possible to distinguish exactly how much has been reserved against which eventuality. While less than ideal, this type of distortion is manageable although it requires knowledge of the rules of the particular country concerned.

In the worst type of tax-based accounting the company starts by deciding how much pre-tax profits it wants to show (which usually reflects the amount it expects to pay in dividends); it then constructs a profit and loss account upwards from that level with perhaps the only reliable figure in the entire statement being the sales figure. (Even here for an exporter the analyst will need to know something about the billing and currency conversion practices.) The analyst can at least hope that the relationship of the various levels of profit and cost to each other are consistent even if the figures themselves are falsified, and can check this against his knowledge of the industry; too often there is not even this degree of realism and the profit and loss statement is hardly worth analysing. If the adjustments are consistently carried through to the balance sheet this will make it in turn nearly worthless; if on the other hand the balance sheet is reasonably accurate the normal relationships to the P & L will not hold.

In the extreme case the bank really cannot rely on the published figures at all; it must therefore attempt to obtain from the company management figures which show a more realistic picture, or sufficient information about the nature of the adjustments to allow it to construct figures which, even if they are not completely accurate, give a general indication of the position. Clearly, however, this latter exercise is very unsatisfactory; even management figures mean relying wholly on the company for accuracy without any input from outside auditors.

Lack of audited figures

The lack of audited figures generally in many European countries is a drawback, even where there is no question of deliberately misleading figures. If a major failure in financial controls or even fraud goes unnoticed, it can mean that management does not recognise the existence of a serious problem. Of course managements fail to recognise serious problems even with audited figures, but there is still a better chance that the auditors, the bankers or other independent analysts can recognise a danger and can bring pressure on the company's management to identify and correct it.

Unaudited and unreliable figures cause serious damage in many countries where the disclosure and accounting standards are lax. Governments which permit this run the risk of a less efficient industry than is possible; lack of disclosure means less pressure from outside parties on complacent or otherwise inadequate managements. Governments which insist that accounts be prepared primarily for tax purposes actually compel false accounting and create a major impediment to greater financial efficiency and honesty. Admittedly, even in the worst cases of tax-based accounting there are a few pointers which can be used as a general indication of a company's progress. One item on the balance sheet, borrowed money, is almost as likely to be reliable as sales; although some forms of borrowed money may be included in trade payables or discrepancies may arise if foreign currency borrowings are carried at the original exchange rate. The value of borrowing to sales, and interest to sales, as a pointer was discussed in Chapter 8. It is greatest in cases where the reliability of other figures is suspect. Three figures then, the absolute level of borrowing, borrowings as a percentage of sales and actual or imputed interest as a percentage of sales, can give some indication of change. A steady increase in borrowing is less dangerous if it is financing a profitable growth in sales; but if the growth is truly profitable, reinvestment of the profits will restrict the necessity for further borrowing. Some growth in borrowing need not be excessive, but if borrowing consistently grows faster than sales this suggests that profits are inadequate, that the capital base was initially inadequate for the rate of growth or that the cash generated is not being reinvested to maintain a sound base. Growing borrowings accompanied by high dividends, royalties or other intercompany payments are thoroughly undesirable.

The extent to which borrowing can grow and the stage at which it starts to become dangerous depends on a number of factors which will be particularly hard to judge in the absence of other information. These relate partly back to the discussion in Part Three about the impact which various types of business have on a company's financial structure.

Knowledge of the industry may enable the analyst to estimate the cost of fixed and other assets the company is likely to require; he can then estimate how much equity is required or, alternatively, what is the maximum debt that is safe, given reasonable profitability, and compare this with the actual debt. If this is excessive or increasing, this is a warning sign; if it appears to be stable or declining, it gives a little comfort. Similarly, knowledge of the industry may enable him to estimate reasonable fixed and variable costs, profit margins and so on; this will help to refine the estimate of the acceptable level of debt.

At best, the estimates which can be made in this way are very approximate; almost by definition, the lack of information which makes such estimates necessary also makes their accuracy suspect. To lend on the basis of these estimates alone must always be unsatisfactory. However, where there are other good reasons for lending this can at least provide some basis for asking intelligent questions; where a bank is already lending, it can provide some sort of a check, however fallible, on the company's progress.

The estimation can be taken a little further, in the light of known interest rates in the country or currencies (if these are known) of the borrower, after allowing for fixed rate borrowing. An estimate of interest as a percentage of sales can be compared with the operating profit which the analyst believes is reasonable for the particular type of company. If this suggests a substantial and improving, or even stable coverage, there is at least some ground for believing that the company is generating sufficient operating profit to service its debt and other needs. If the reverse is true, if interest moves from, say, 25% of imputed operating profit one year to 35-40% the next and if this year's level of borrowing and interest rates suggests it may be 65-70% next year, then the bank really needs to ask questions. Remember, too, that since such a move probably results from a weakening of profits, true operating profit may be less than imputed and coverage even weaker than the figures suggest.

It is not easy to assess the appropriate level of borrowings to sales precisely even where the bulk of the information is reliable and harder when it is not. The above approach can only use approximate orders of magnitude; precision is not possible. The most important thing is always the trend; if borrowings and interest are rising fairly rapidly in relation to sales then, even if they started from an acceptably low level, this is a warning sign; starting from a high level it can be a bankruptcy warning. If borrowing is rising rapidly, the average throughout the year may be lower than at year end so that interest paid may be lower than the annual rate on the closing borrowings. It may be worth taking the year end borrowing, applying a current rate of interest, and calculating what operating margin would be necessary to provide 2 or 3 times interest cover. If this margin appears to be unattainable, the company is probably heading for trouble. If interest rates are currently low, consider what impact each 1% increase would have on the required level of operating margin.

False valuation of assets and earnings

Overvaluation or undervaluation of assets and earnings can occur even where accounting and disclosure standards are high. The most common form results from the use of historic cost accounting in an inflationary environment. Fixed assets are usually undervalued by the largest amount, although inventory is often considerably undervalued as well. For many years US bankers resisted any revaluation of fixed assets and, when working overseas, regarded companies which revalued as being suspect even where the local accounting system allowed or in some cases required it. The conservative approach was thought to be to use the lower of cost or market value, even if cost was a tiny fraction of market.

It is, however, arguable that the historic cost approach, without revaluation, seriously distorts both the balance sheet and profit and loss statement and is not at all conservative. There is a difference between choosing the lowest value within a range where there is doubt as to the correct value; and, on the other hand, deliberately stating a value for an asset which bears no relation to its true value or to the cost of replacing it.

To understate the value of an asset understates net worth and overstates leverage; it is therefore conservative in the limited sense that it makes the balance sheet seem weaker than it really is. However, it also causes depreciation to be understated and thus overstates earnings. This in turn further misstates most types of return by applying overstated earnings to understated assets or net worth. Furthermore, although cash flow will not change before allowing for tax, the overstatement of profits may mean higher taxes and therefore lower net profit and cash flow. The net result is not just that profits are overstated in absolute terms; the need for profits and cash flow to replace assets as they wear out is also understated and therefore the relative overstatement of profitability is even greater than the absolute overstatement. Put another way, a company may need to spend £1 million to replace its existing fixed assets over the next ten years; if it carries them on its balance sheet at only £100,000 it may provide depreciation of £10,000 per annum and report a net profit of £10,000, giving cash flow of £20,000. In relation to fixed assets of £100,000 it appears to be doing well, whereas in fact it is heading for disaster since the true figures should be fixed assets £1 million, depreciation £100,000, net loss £80,000. Although cash flow is £20,000 on either presentation, the latter shows correctly that it is wholly inadequate to finance the replacement of fixed assets.

There are many cases of companies under-depreciating their assets in this way while paying large dividends. The non-financial directors were deceived by their own figures into believing the company was substantially more profitable than it really was. Thus the danger is not just that the company, whether deliberately or otherwise, deceives its bank; an even greater danger is that management deceives itself and takes decisions based on misleading figures; the less accurate the figures are the greater the likelihood of disaster.

Although the mechanics may be different, the same basic principle applies to the valuation of other assets such as inventory and receivables. Assuming the sales remain accurately stated, undervaluation of inventory and receivables will give the impression of faster turnover and therefore more efficient financial controls than is in fact the case. At the time the value of the assets is reduced, this will in some way reduce the earnings and in subsequent years the earnings will be overstated because inventory valued at x but which cost 2x will be sold at a price of 2½x giving a profit margin of 1½x instead of ½x.

The same, of course, is true in reverse and perhaps rather more seriously when the assets are overvalued. Although fixed assets can be overvalued as a result of poor accounting, it is more likely to be done deliberately; with current assets this is not necessarily the case but the danger to the company is much greater. When current assets turn into less cash than expected, the impact of the adjustment from the overvaluation to the true value will be sharp.

Bankers are clear that there is no such thing as a completely accurate and reliable valuation of all assets. True value depends very much on the use to which assets are put and in particular whether the company using them is a going concern or not. Finished electronic instruments may have a genuine market value as long as the company making them is in business and is expected to be able to provide a continuing maintenance and repair service. If the company goes out of business their value is likely to drop dramatically. And as discussed in earlier chapters much the same is true about various types of fixed assets. Nevertheless companies can provide an approximately accurate value of assets on the assumption that they will continue to be used in a viable business and that they will have to be replaced fairly regularly; so it follows that, if the company is not earning enough to replace them, then in a sense the valuation is wrong. Thus an important element in trying to recognise whether a company's assets are overvalued, undervalued or about right is the level of profit being earned on them (if that can be told through all the other accounting vagaries).

It is not, of course, always easy to tell whether and if so by how much assets have been under- or overvalued. Sometimes the only way the analyst can tell is when a new valuation is provided which is radically different from the previous one. There is a tendency when that happens to treat the change in reported value as if it were real and to say that overnight leverage improved, return declined or whatever. In fact, of course, the change in value normally takes place over a number of years and it is the underlying change in each year rather than the recognition in one large amount which is important. It is probably not possible to go back and adjust the previous year's figures and, if possible, hardly worth the effort. The analyst should, however, recognise that what he is now seeing is a truer version of the previous picture and not a change in the underlying situation.

Recognising the essential

Recognising which information is of vital importance to the analysis, and which merely useful, is important even when both types of information are fully available. It is doubly important with inadequate information since the question is now not merely "what is the judgement about this company?" but rather "do I have enough information to make any judgement on this credit proposal?" To answer the question the analyst needs first of all to be sure that he has made the maximum possible use of the information available. Again this is true at all times but doubly true when the information is inadequate. Then he needs to consider whether his lack of information or uncertainty is one of degree or of kind. Is he satisfied that the company is profitable although not clear how profitable? Does he really not know whether it is profitable at all? Or is he afraid it is actually losing quite substantial amounts? Is he satisfied that each of the various types of asset is of good quality even though he feels that the figures may misstate certain items? Or does he really not know very much about the quality of the assets? Or worse still, does he not know enough about the nature of the assets, let alone their quality, to start to draw some of the inferences discussed in earlier chapters? In each case, the more positive the answer, the greater the chance that the bank can justify lending.

In brief, the aim is to be able to say "Yes, there are some points we're not sure about, but we can make a reasonable guess at the answers. Even if we're wrong, it is unlikely to be disastrous." The position to avoid is: "There are several key points about which we have no idea; an unfavourable answer on one or more could easily make the company non-creditworthy, but we cannot guess how likely such an answer is."

The other aspect to consider is the nature of the facility. If, for instance, the banker is looking at a short-term loan for a specific purpose with a source of repayment clearly indicated, he may be able to be more relaxed about lack of information on other aspects of the business. Or he may be looking at a short-term line of credit for which he knows other banks are also making highly competitive bids so that if he becomes uneasy he can expect to be repaid from this source. The company may, many companies do, tell him that they will discuss their figures in more detail when he has shown that he is serious about their company by making credit available.

In all these cases he should still have a certain basic minimum of information but can afford less detail than where he is being asked to make a seven- or ten-year loan. In particular, although it is always desirable to be able to assess the future of a company, this becomes steadily more essential the longer the life of the loan. It may be acceptable to take an information risk on a short-term loan or a facility which can be withdrawn at relatively short notice if the bank finds that it is not getting additional information or that it is unhappy with the trend shown. On the other hand, with a seven-year loan the bank must either have forecasts or the basis on which to make its own forecasts. Without them it cannot design covenants; if it does not believe in covenants, or cannot obtain them from the borrower, it will not be able to judge whether the borrower is strong enough to justify relaxing covenants or doing without them altogether.

Similarly if the facility is being provided to finance a major capital expenditure or a particular project, then the bank will wish to know something about the project itself and how it fits in with the rest of the company. However, only if the impact of the project's failure on the company's ability to repay the loan is significant will the bank need to make a detailed assessment of the project.

Finally, while all credit assessment is a matter of judgement not science, recognising when a bank has enough information, or alternatively when the missing information is crucial, is one of the key attributes for a lending banker. There can be no hard and fast rules but a main warning is the existence of apparent discrepancies or contradictions in the information the bank has from various sources. A banker who ignores these contradictions or assumes that discrepancies are more apparent than real without checking lacks one essential ingredient of a lending banker, curiosity. A good banker always wants to know why things are the way they are and how the relationships work; not just as an intellectual exercise to satisfy his superiors but as a real desire, almost a pain, to know. Conversely, the banker who when asked to explain a discrepancy says "Oh I didn't check, I didn't think it was important" is missing that essential ingredient even if, in the particular case, he is proved right and the discrepancy was not important.

14 Focus on Risk

A lending banker takes carefully judged risks for an appropriate reward. But he can only judge a risk which he has first identified. It is therefore essential to identify areas of weakness which could put a company at risk or developments to which it is vulnerable; then monitor the company to focus on any particular risk as soon as it begins to become an active threat rather than merely a potential one.

This focus on risk must be specific. It is easy to say that a company would be at risk if its sales declined sharply or if it made losses. This is a truism for any company but it tells nothing about the factors which might cause either of these events, the likelihood that they may occur, how far they can go before they become serious or the defences available to the company against them.

It is not possible to list all the risks that might arise, but this chapter will give some illustrations of the main areas and types of risk, and of protection, for which the analyst should be alert. However, as throughout the book, the aim is to provide an aid to constructive thought, not a checklist; in real life, only thought and understanding of the borrower enable the analyst to assess the risk correctly.

Risks inherent in the nature of the business

Inherent risks can be divided into those which are fairly certain to occur, even if the timing and severity is unpredictable, and those which are merely possibilities. The first arise mainly from the cyclical nature of many businesses, perhaps in some cases reinforced by a high level of capital intensity. In such a situation a volume decline is almost inevitable at some stage; the question is whether it will continue to or below breakeven level and if so how long it will be before volume, and profits, recover. There is the subsidiary risk that when the economy recovers the company will have to increase its borrowing to build up inventory before its profits show any benefit, and the banks may then be unwilling to lend.

The best defence against this type of risk is a strong balance sheet with good liquidity and high equity so that the impact of even an extreme recession is bearable. The second type of defence is strong margins in favourable conditions, so that a major reduction can still leave the company in profit, combined with tight control of costs to limit the reduction in margins as far as possible. And the third and related defence is tight control of net working investment to make possible as large a downward adjustment in borrowing as the nature of the business allows as soon as recession threatens. Control of NWI, and borrowing related to it, is particularly important for a company with a long production cycle; where NWI is likely to be large in the best of times, even a minor loss of control can mean a significant increase in borrowing when it hurts most. A modest improvement can be proportionately valuable and will both reduce borrowing and boost the bank's confidence that the company will use an increase in borrowing in an upturn well. Other types of defence may include breadth of market or the ability to divert sales into alternative markets to limit the impact of a normal recession (although it may be less effective against a serious recession such as that of the early 1980s). And there may be particular defences which relate to some lines of business.

A company may also be (inherently or otherwise) at risk because of the natures of its customers. The weakness is inherent when the customer industry is itself highly cyclical and contains mainly financially weak companies, with a continuing danger that several of them will fail in a cyclical downturn. Or the borrower may, through faulty credit controls, weak marketing or other reasons sell to a disproportionate number of the weaker companies which use his product. Either way, such a risk can have a double effect on the supplier. His sales drop off sharply at the same time as he has to write off a significant proportion of receivables.

A possible, but not certain, risk arises when a company sells to a small number of very strong customers; these may be able to squeeze the supplier's margins or may decide to buy from only one source where before they bought from several, or even to make the product themselves. A company is seriously at risk if it concentrates its sales so that loss of business from just one or two major customers can dramatically reduce volume and profits; the financial protection requires high margins, low fixed costs and a strong balance sheet, although these give a limited time to replace the lost volume. The best defence is to diversify sales to a wider range of customers; failing that, the company must control quality and other key features (cost, delivery, after-sales service, R & D or whatever the customer is looking for) better than the competition or than the customer could do for himself. In some cases rare specialised knowledge may provide a defence; in others the volume used by each customer may be too small to justify them starting their own manufacture. The trouble with this last argument is that it tends to limit growth prospects. These defences are, however, very hard for the bank to judge and dependence on a few customers is a serious risk.

The risk of overpowerful suppliers or heavy dependence on a product such as oil, the price of which can rise dramatically for reasons unrelated to the company's business, is equally serious; the banker must assess not only the degree of concentration but the chances that the risk will become a reality.

Fast-changing technology (or obsolescence) can be a risk, either if competitors produce a better product or if the product ceases to be needed; technology can also dramatically change manufacturing methods.

These are only a few of the more common risks. Whatever the particular nature of the business there will be some risks associated with it, but in some cases they will be more likely to occur than others; the company can foresee some risks and defend itself against them more easily than others; some companies are vulnerable to a single adverse development while others will have a spread of risks and will probably only be in serious trouble if several go against them at the same time. But whatever the risk it is important that the banker understand its nature, its probability, the damage it can do and the extent to which the company has (or can have if management is alert) effective defences if it threatens to become a reality.

Above all, a banker who identifies a risk which is both

out of the company's control and likely to be devastating if it occurs, should not too easily assume that it will not occur. This is perhaps particularly the case if the risk results from potential government action, or withdrawal of existing protection or subsidy. The advent of a political leader who does not believe in subsidies or intervention can too easily upset preconceptions of what is politically possible.

Balance sheet risk

A strong balance sheet is particularly needed and a weak one therefore increases risk in two different types of situation. The first is one of rapid growth where an inadequate balance sheet may lead to overtrading. Here the risk is of loss of liquidity as the profits on the expanding business are outweighed by the costs of financing it; more importantly the sheer volume which needs to be financed outruns the cash generated so seriously that the company cannot pay its bills. When an expanding and (at least apparently) profitable business reaches the stage where its suppliers are reluctant to supply it or it cannot pay its wages, this is a sign of extreme overtrading. The answer is an injection of capital well before the company reaches this stage although it is also advisable to check that growth really is profitable. Lack of financial controls may indicate a deeper weakness in controlling, or even identifying, costs.

At the other end of the spectrum a weak balance sheet may mean that a company cannot ride out even a minor temporary downturn in sales and profitability. As a result, what should be a hiccough in the company's progress becomes a crisis and possibly a disaster. And the two risks can be combined. When a company with high fixed costs tries to obtain volume at any price to avoid the second danger, it may run into the first.

The risk from balance sheet weakness can arise either from illiquidity or from excessive leverage (or from the opposite point of view under-capitalisation) or a combination of both. As with any other type of weakness, illiquidity always carries some risk but more for some companies than for others. For instance, a company with an inherently high net working investment has a high need for liquidity and little ability to reduce that need quickly; if it is also growing fast (or about to enter a period of fast growth) this adds to the risk of illiquidity. Companies with low net working investment, low liquidity requirements and greater ability to adjust quickly are less in danger from apparent illiquidity, unless growing rapidly.

A company with low margins and modest depreciation generates less cash flow from a given increase in sales than one with high margins or depreciation. In some cases, this will be offset by a faster inventory and receivable turnover and lower additional need for NWI, so requiring less extra liquidity for a given increase in sales. Where low margins are combined with slow turnovers, rapid (or any) growth will use liquidity rapidly and therefore increase the risks arising from initial illiquidity.

Inadequate capital is often a source of illiquidity. In addition, where capital is replaced by borrowing to finance fixed assets or slow-moving current assets, the interest is a fixed cost which becomes a major drain on liquidity in a downturn. It also reduces the profits of a company which is trying to grow quickly, thus reducing ability to generate new capital from earnings and compounding the problem. Again, it is more serious if margins before interest are low than if they are high. The danger can be reduced if debt is largely low cost or if the capital is supplemented by liability reserves, pension reserves etc. which carry no immediate interest cost or repayment requirement. It is aggravated if the debt is high cost or if it is floating rate and there is the prospect of a sharp increase just when the company can least afford it.

All liabilities carry some risk that the company will need to pay them and their mere existence may make lenders consider the company too heavily leveraged and reluctant to increase or even maintain their lending. But any level of leverage can be more or less dangerous depending on its structure and the assets it is financing. Pension reserves, for instance, carry no interest and often only limited payment requirements. Short-term debt used to finance truly liquid assets is less risky than when used for medium-term purposes. In the former case, the assets can be quickly reduced which will in turn reduce both leverage and interest cost. Medium-term assets, by definition, are harder to turn into cash quickly, and carry more fixed costs, both of which increase the risk of borrowing in a way which could, for any reason, cease to be available. Even medium-term borrowings can be dangerous if the borrower does not space the amortisation properly so that a high concentration becomes repayable in a short period. Here again, high earnings and cash flow are a partial defence by providing a direct source of repayment; they also make it more likely that maturing debt can be refinanced. However, the value of this defence depends partly on the availability of sources of refinance. These in turn depend partly on the breadth of the financial markets in which the company is operating, and even the broadest markets have periods of tight money when availability is lower (and cost higher) than normal.

These, and other items discussed in Chapter 5, affect the degree of risk involved in a particular capital structure. The risk must be assessed by relating the structure to the company's business, the profitability, the level and stability of interest rates in the market to which the borrower has access, and their sophistication. It must also be considered against management's competence and attitude. A company with an over-leveraged balance sheet is at risk if a slowdown in sales is not matched by a reduction in production and thus causes a big upturn in inventory; this increases debt and interest costs at exactly the time the company can least afford them. This affect will snowball unless the company is able to reduce production rapidly. The ability to do so quickly without heavy losses depends partly on management's alertness and skill, partly on the nature of the company; the recognition of the need and skilful action to meet (or avoid) it is a question of good management. The necessary action may have emotional overtones, however; if management is committed to growth it may be reluctant to admit an error; a family management may refuse to face the need to lay off long-serving employees or be frightened of a union; or may feel that it is the bank's job to see such an old customer through a bad patch.

Risks to profitability

The greatest risk is of losses or inadequate profits. But even adequate profits are subject to risks of various sorts, some of which could cause a sufficient decline to endanger the company's viability.

For instance, earlier chapters discussed the impact of high fixed costs on income. A company which is working at a level only slightly above breakeven level may currently be quite profitable but a small decline in sales or a small increase in fixed costs, perhaps through bad management, perhaps due to factors outside management's control, can have a dramatic effect on profits. Good management will thus always be considering ways to reduce fixed costs, so that a decline in demand can be absorbed more easily, and perhaps offset by a reduction in price which keeps volume up and allows some, even if smaller, profits. Management failure to control fixed costs in good times can prove to be a major risk in bad times.

A company with a high level of variable costs, on the other hand, is more vulnerable to a change in them than to a change in volume; if it already has a low operating margin, even a small rise in raw material or fuel costs, for example, may cause losses. The degree of risk to profits will depend partly on the ability to raise prices. In some products this is almost automatic because all suppliers are dependent on the same factor. In others, competition with alternative products may make it impossible to raise prices without losing market share; or demand may be price sensitive, so the company may merely maintain its share in a declining market. And the higher the cost, the greater the risk from inefficient usage of the raw material or fuel.

Where operating profit is a small percentage of sales (whether due to fixed, variable or combined costs) other costs must be an even smaller percentage if profits are to be more than marginal. Thus if operating profit is 10% of sales, a decline in the gross margin from 60 to 55% of sales, with no offsetting changes elsewhere, halves the operating margin; if interest, in turn, is 4% of sales (with no non-operating income), interest cover declines from a moderate 2.5 times to 1.25, and the pre-tax profit margin from 6 to 1%. This leaves no room for an increase in interest rates or a further reduction in operating margin. Thus a company with low operating margin and interest cover is more at risk from a modest change in almost any cost than one with high margins. It sounds obvious, but is often overlooked.

An adverse exchange rate move poses a risk to profits and balance sheet strength which can be dramatic for some companies. It can arise through various combinations of importing or exporting in foreign currency and mismatching of foreign currency borrowing against assets. The risk on long-term investments may be of an accounting rather than a cash loss; but the burden of borrowings really changes in terms of the local balance sheet and interest is a direct cash payment which can be much higher than anticipated as a result of currency moves. The value or cost of receivables or payables also change in a way which directly affects cash needs. Moreover, while it may be possible to avoid heavy loss on existing assets or liabilities by taking out forward cover, the underlying cost of raw materials or the competitiveness of export prices can be adversely affected long into the future.

Any type of cost which is a high proportion of sales carries the risk of a sharp increase reducing profits. In most cases there is an inherent risk, and there are various things management can do which may reduce the risk, or which may increase it; an increase in risk can come either through sloppy management or through a conscious decision to take the risk in order to improve profits now.

For instance, a high labour content makes a company more than usually vulnerable to a general inflation of wages but at least competition (in the same country) is also affected; a management failure to control wage costs or maintain a competitive level of productivity is unique to it. Similar comments apply to, for instance, the market price of raw material and management's ability to control waste or otherwise reduce the amount of the expensive material used. Similarly with marketing costs, R & D, interest rates and other major cost items, including the volume of exports and therefore vulnerability to exchange risk.

The analyst must identify costs where a relatively small percentage change will have a major impact on margins; then assess the risk of such a change and the effectiveness of the company's likely response. Be particularly careful not to dismiss a danger because it is outside management's control or because, while critical, it has never happened yet and would require a major change in the government's (or unions' or banks') attitude. Such changes have become increasingly common in the late 1970s and early 1980s.

Risks of management

There are several types of management risk. One arises from an inadequacy which in good times is less important and therefore often not apparent. For instance, a company with poor controls over receivables and inventory may appear to be sound while demand is high and its customers are healthy and need its product; a downturn can cause receivables to slow down, a number of customers to fail, and inventory to jump sharply. A company which uses raw materials with volatile prices may then find that its high inventories reflect prices higher than are now available in the market, so that it is sitting on large losses, quite apart from the extra interest.

A gradual decline in the relative quality of the product, or a apparently minor reduction in efficiency of manufacture (and thus increase in cost) may not be readily apparent while demand is strong; if it shows at all it may be in what appears a marginally slower rate of sales growth, or slightly lower margins, than the competition. However, if demand starts to grow more slowly, or even to decline, the impact may be much greater on the less attractive product or the company with higher costs. Many companies which appear to deteriorate suddenly are in fact merely showing the impact of a decline in demand on one or more weaknesses which have developed unnoticed over a long time.

This is one area where industry comparisons may be useful. It is difficult for a bank to assess the effectiveness of a company's costs and financial controls, product development, manufacturing quality, marketing and brand loyalty in isolation. However, if a company, while apparently healthy, is doing less well than its competitors there is often a good reason. It may not be obviously a reflection on management; but indirectly it usually is. (And the more minor it seems to be, the more important the curiosity referred to in the last chapter.) The industry comparison may help to pinpoint the area in which the company is weakening, and the bank can then discuss the reasons with management. In some cases, management will be aware of the problem and able to show the bank why it is only temporary; in others, the bank may actually improve its customer's creditworthiness by drawing attention to a weakness while management still has time to correct it; or the bank may come away from the discussion with a less favourable impression of management than previously, in which case it should adjust its assessment of the overall credit.

The larger and more diversified the company, the more questionable the validity of industry comparisons and the harder to identify a specific weakness rather than a general failure to keep up with the competition. Similarly, the less detailed the information available on the company and its competitors, the less useful are industry comparisons. Nevertheless, while no panacea, they are a tool which should be kept available.

The second type of management risk (apart from visibly bad management which is not so much a risk as a pressing danger) can arise from a dominating individual, from a preponderance of one or a narrow range of disciplines in a management team, or from the failure of a successful management to develop to cope with the results of its success.

A one-man management creates problems if the man dies or leaves the company with nobody to replace him. This risk is obvious and can be partially guarded against by assessing his health, his devotion to the company (which he may well own) and sometimes by insuring his life. In addition, if the company is healthy it may be readily saleable, or it may be an attractive opportunity for a capable outsider.

The more subtle risk arises when the one man stays too long and refuses to develop any depth of management support. He may become old and too set in his ways to make necessary changes; worse still he may become plain senile so that instead of merely failing to adapt he actually mismanages the company beyond the point of no return. Finally, while remaining competent to run a small company on a personal basis, he may fail to recognise when the company outgrows his ability and requires professional management techniques which he neither has nor is interested in developing.

There are equal dangers where a management team is too narrowly confined to one discipline. A company run entirely by engineers may produce an excellent product and even market it well, but lack personnel or financial management. Here again it is partly a question of growth. A small company with an unusual product may have profit margins which enable it to ride through the other weaknesses for a while. As it grows, this becomes harder to do; its success may attract competition which can match its product or offer better service, a wider range or other advantages.

But even large companies are sometimes managed almost entirely by engineers who place great weight on the quality of the product; they may ignore the question of whether the quality is needed by the customer, whether it is being produced economically or just elegantly and whether its market is changing; financial controls often barely exist and cost or risk are treated as irrelevant compared with the pleasure of producing a perfect product, even if the delay means that someone else dominates the market with something less perfect (but more practical).

Perhaps the greatest risk in these situations is that they usually arise in companies which have been successful, often for a long time. It is hard for a bank to recognise when conservatism deteriorates into obscurantism, a productive concern with quality into unrealistic perfectionism and so on. It can be even harder to tell a successful owner of a business (and perhaps valued personal customer) that he is no longer capable of running his own company; or the chairman of a famous company that it will fail in two years if it does not get a competent finance director (or, worse still, a new chairman).

The danger of a single discipline is not confined to engineers. A company which is run wholly or mainly by accountants can have different but equally serious weaknesses. Over-attention to financial controls may cause neglect of R & D, marketing and other functions. Too much aversion to risk may cause sound business opportunities to be lost. Similar examples arise if the company is run by marketing men, personnel experts etc.

The point of this is not that engineers or accountants or marketing men are in themselves bad; it is that none of them are good enough on their own. Companies need managements which can balance imagination with discipline, quality against costs; the need to satisfy the customer against the cost of meeting whimsical needs; the benefits of long production runs against too rigid a production schedule and so on. The larger a company becomes, and the worse the economic conditions, the greater the risk of a major failure in any area.

Thus the greatest risk is not that of rank bad management. This is of course a risk but is likely to be obvious fairly quickly. The danger is either of weaknesses which develop slowly, or which are offset by strengths in other areas, so that the company appears well managed until there is a change in conditions with which it is not equipped to cope. The change may be internal (the death or deterioration of a dominant chairman or, more subtly, the loss of inspiration of a technical or managerial driving force); it may be external (a slump, newly effective competition, an unforeseen change in demand for the product, or a change in relative cost of different raw materials or production methods). And banks probably lose as much money in cases where they see the danger but treat it as theoretical only as they do by failing to recognise it at all.

Management's attitudes can create risk. The previous comments mentioned some aspects in passing, but the risk needs to be spelt out more clearly.

Some managements are reluctant to raise new equity however badly it is needed, because to do so would dilute management - or more often family - control. Others are reluctant to reduce or cancel the dividend for family reasons or to protect their own positions. Family managements, or managers who identify closely with a particular part of the business, may be reluctant to sell it or close it down because to do so would be "against the company's tradition". Often they are equally unwilling to take other action to offset the failure and make the company viable. For instance, it might be possible to justify a refusal to close a plant and lay off several hundred people if the company embarked on an imaginative new advertising programme to raise volume. But this would require a change in agency and a new approach. The end result of failure to close the plant now, or recognise the need for a dynamic alternative, is that it is closed down later, at much greater cost, in a way that threatens the survival of healthier parts of the business. Even where outright closure of a plant is not involved, paternal reluctance to cut staff now often means much larger cuts later.

Inflexible attitudes on "giving a total service" or meeting various types of traditional standards can be risky when the standards are no longer appropriate; so can disdainful attitudes to proper cost control. These are only a few of the specific examples. The point is that any rigid attitude relating to family interest or any interest other than that of the company is dangerous; so is the clinging to any tradition or standard which, however valuable it may have been once, is no longer valid.

The risk of competition

As with many other risks, competition can be either a present danger or a potential future one. The present danger must be taken seriously but the bank can usually assess it reasonably accurately and decide whether it poses a threat. Where competition is more potential than actual, the bank may have to assess the company's ability to manage a change which appears unlikely in the short run but if it happened could substantially undermine the company's present business. Usually this risk from competition will be related to at least one of the other types of risk discussed.

The obvious risk arises when there are already a number of competitors producing the same or closely similar products and competing for the same customers. Here the bank must assess the risk of a relative change in product or marketing strength, whether greater financial strength may enable competitors to cut prices and if so how likely they are to do it. In particular cases, protection may arise from patents, from market reputation, from cost-effective manufacturing, from a better distribution network, an installed customer base and so on. The risk of a company losing ground, either because it weakens, or because the competition improves, must be carefully considered; so must the likely signs that it is beginning to happen.

Many industries show rapid growth in their initial stages and attract companies which install extra capacity. When the growth levels out or even declines (sometimes temporarily, sometimes permanently), the resulting excess capacity means that there are more companies in the industry than can survive. There are also some highly profitable companies making specialised products for which total demand was for a time fairly small, so that even though profits were good the volume did not justify new entrants. As demand grows some companies which previously bought the product may find it worthwhile to produce it themselves; very often they install more capacity than they need themselves so that the borrower not only loses a customer but gains a competitor. This is particularly dangerous where there is a combination of high profit margins and low capital requirements so that companies can enter the industry cheaply.

Other industries have a high proportion of small companies with fully depreciated machinery which, perhaps through bad management, are selling at a price which does not cover their replacement costs. Often they are family owned and as long as the family makes a decent living they do not worry too much about the level of profits and the future of the business. There are many other examples of industries where the existing competitive situation is already tough and can rapidly get tougher. Among the most worrying are those where the competition comes from overseas, from a country which either has a specific advantage or which subsidises exports.

But there are other industries where the threat of competition is future rather than present. These include many mass-production industries with labour costs accounting for a high proportion of the total; as the less industrialised countries develop their skills, their lower wage costs become a crucial element in their competitive ability. Many companies which have conceded the lower end of the market fail to recognise the danger that the low cost producers will improve their quality and gradually move up-market and overcome the advantages even of high-quality products and famous brand names. Well-known cases such as motor cycles, television, radio and hi-fi testify to the risks of this type of competition and banks must be fully cognisant that this may apply to specific companies to which they are lending.

But low wage companies are not the only foreign threat. Companies which have what looks like a secure niche in their domestic market may find foreign multi-nationals attacking it. The invader may be successful because of more sophisticated marketing; greater volume of production which reduces costs; or the ability to finance a loss leader. If the secure domestic position rests wholly or partly on protection there are four possible threats: a change in domestic policy to open up the market and save costs; an international treaty; a change in currency rates that offsets the protection; or the invader setting up operations in the home country.

One-product companies or companies which sell specialised products to a narrow range of customers may in the short run appear well protected from competition by their special skills and perhaps a market too small, or too difficult to enter, to attract competition. Nevertheless, they still face the inherent risk of a new product or a new process providing better quality or lower manufacturing costs, greater reliability, less pollution or other side-effects or some other advantage.

Companies which produce either raw materials or components which are incorporated into other companies' products may find that the market either disappears or is drastically reduced for reasons which have nothing to do with their product. The same point in a slightly different form applies to companies which, while they sell to a wide range of end users, are dependent on a particular raw material or group of raw materials. Steel has been challenged by aluminium, which has been challenged by plastics, which are being challenged by more modern products in many uses. The manufacturers of each product have gone through a stage where the number of end uses expanded and are now in various states of contraction. All these are cases where the risk is actual and visible; is your customer in the industry where the risk is potential now, but will be real in the next recession?

Similarly, companies which rely on a particular production process may find it superseded by a process which is less energy intensive, causes less pollution, gives more consistent quality or uses cheaper materials. If both processes are capital intensive, a company which has invested heavily in the old process, and fails to generate the expected cash flow from it, may be unable to afford to install the new process.

Competition can also be given a chance by management which rests too complacently on its laurels; it may find that new and better products are introduced and that although it could have matched them its failure to do so has lost market share and allowed a competitor to establish a strong position.

And, of course, if any of these competitive risks face a company which either has a weak balance sheet or already inadequate profits, the need to apply substantial financial resources to meet the competition may simply be beyond it.

Miscellaneous risks

In addition to the generally recognisable risks outlined

above, many companies face risks which are peculiar either to themselves or to a fairly narrow range of companies and which are difficult to describe in general terms. The rise of product liability suits in the United States and the danger that this will spread to other countries is one example. The risk that a drug will turn out to have unacceptable side-effects and will either have to be withdrawn (which can give rise to product liability suits as well) or never be introduced can endanger a company which has spent heavily on research. Other types of technological product carry similar risks of failure, whether outright or because a rival comes to market with a similar or better product. Law suits for patent infringement can cripple a company but are very difficult for the bank to foresee. And bad labour relations, particularly in a country with a difficult social and governmental climate, can face a company with alternative risks. Either it takes strong action and risks a crippling strike; or its productivity is undermined as well, perhaps, as its quality and reliability.

Conclusion

This chapter has mentioned only a few risks and has not dealt with the possibility that two or more will combine to multiply the danger. Most of the risks should be evident from various aspects of the analysis; to some extent, therefore, the chapter consciously repeats other chapters. However, it is very easy to get too involved in the techniques of analysis; with apparently strong companies it is particularly dangerous to recognise the strengths and pay too little attention to the risks against which the strengths provide protection. It is a very useful exercise, before concluding the analysis, to ask: "If this company is in serious trouble during the life of my loan, what is most likely to cause the trouble? And what else, however unlikely it may seem now, has the power to do so?"

An analysis which cannot answer these questions, with reasons why the risks are still acceptable, is not complete.

Part V
Presentation

15 Form and Structure[1]

The general aims

Two approaches. Two basic approaches can be taken in presenting a credit proposal, depending on how each bank sees its primary function. The first requires the presenter to make the decision himself; the presentation's function is then to explain why he believes it is right, with adequate discussion of strengths and weaknesses, risks and protections. The proposal then asks the reader to ratify the decision which the account officer, in American terminology, has already made.

The alternative is to present the facts and say, implicitly or explicitly, to the reader "here you are, you're a good judge of a credit, you tell me what to do". The function then is to provide material for the reader to analyse. As is so often the case most banks use neither approach in its purest form but mix the two. However, this book prefers the first approach and the comments which follow relate to it. In practice, many of them are appropriate to either approach but some of the more detailed points make most sense when related to the first.

Why a written proposal?

There is a tendency, which is not confined to younger and less experienced bankers, to believe that only the quality of the decision counts, while the way in which it is presented or even the need to make a formal presentation is of secondary importance, perhaps even "cosmetic" or "administrative". This view is wrong.

The content and presentation of the memorandum are important for a number of reasons. The first is to help the

(1) Reference is made to the examples found at the end of the chapter.

reader to make a good decision with the minimum use of his time. Since he will usually be more senior, sometimes a great deal more so, than the writer, the memorandum should aim to reduce the time needed to read it even if it takes longer to write. Secondly, while some readers may be familiar with the credit of the borrower, allowing the memorandum to concentrate on the particular transaction, this should not be taken for granted. Apart from anything else the decision-maker, for whom it is originally expected, may be unavailable and somebody who is less familiar with the borrower may read it.

Moreover, helping the reader to make a sound decision quickly, which may be possible even without a memorandum if the senior knows the credit already, is the primary but not the sole purpose. The presenter also needs to demonstrate his own understanding of the credit and in particular of the risks and weaknesses. If he does not a decision-maker who is not familiar with the borrower cannot be sure that the whole picture is presented, nor what of consequence is left out. More importantly, even if he knows the borrower well, the decision-maker will not monitor its progress during the life of the facility. Banks allocate this task differently, but the writer of a credit proposal memorandum is more likely to have to monitor the borrower than the decision-maker. A writer who has not properly understood the credit and cannot recognise the risks and weaknesses is unlikely to identify them when they start to change from potential to real, and this failure increases the risk of loss.

Doubts about the ability to monitor may be a factor in the decision as to whether to lend, but will only become crucial in the difficult decisions. However, while the majority of decisions are clear-cut, there are certainly some slightly more risky than usual credits which are only acceptable if the bank is satisfied that it can monitor the credit closely; the ability of the writer of the memo to do this then becomes a key factor in the decision. While most banks will argue that they never turn down a good loan because of a poor presentation, they may impose more restrictive conditions than they otherwise would and lose the business as a result. Moreover, a good memorandum demonstrates the writer's ability to his superiors and this may be a significant factor in their assessment of his overall ability and therefore in his career prospects.

As well as a basis for the original decision, the memorandum is a basis for review by the bank's auditors and by any internal loan audit or inspection functions. The exact nature of the review varies between banks but most do it in some way. Even if the process does not cover every loan initially, it will certainly cover any loan that gets into trouble and everybody concerned will need a clear understanding of the basis on which the loan was made.

The memorandum also acts to some extent as an audit trail, both in the literal sense of providing the auditors with evidence that the loan was properly approved and in the more general sense of providing a point of reference. If there is a subsequent dispute either within the bank or between the bank and the customer, there will be a source of information which will tell the banker clearly the basis on which he or his predecessor made the loan. More generally, indeed, the increasing mobility of bankers makes it likely that the banker responsible will change, perhaps several times, over the life of a medium-term facility; it is therefore important that the new banker should understand the reasoning which persuaded his predecessor to recommend the loan and the weaknesses which were foreseen.

The need for a clear and well-thought-out presentation helps to ensure, as well as demonstrate, that the writer understands the credit. A banker who has not thought through and clearly understood his credit will not be able to write about it clearly and concisely. The discipline of writing it down and the realisation that what comes out is not very clear may assist the banker to recognise those points which he has not fully understood and to focus on specific areas where his thinking is contradictory or unclear. There is nothing like looking at your own written work and deciding it really does not hang together to make you think again about whether you have fully understood the subject. Furthermore, even where overall understanding is sound, a presentation which contains apparent contradictions or inconsistencies may enable the analyst to recognise these and to check whether they are important. He can then explain why they are not or, if by any chance they are, he can modify his conclusions as a result.

But these are passive benefits in the sense that they arise when the analyst needs little or no help in understanding the credit, only in presenting it. The greater benefit comes when he uses a sound presentation as an aid to clear thinking about the fundamentals of the credit. A logical form of presentation, which requires the analyst to focus on the key issues, the risks and the relationships between the points, can help to ensure a sound intellectual framework for thinking about credit. It can thus significantly help in understanding it and making sure nothing has been overlooked.

The second part of this chapter suggests a framework which is structured enough to make organised thinking easier, but flexible enough to adapt to the wide variety of different types of company. These make the use of a standard format for all presentations impossible, unless they are simply a form-filling exercise with little or no thought required as to the meaning of the contents.

Analysis and presentation differ. There are some general comments which apply whether or not the outline format is used. One concerns the need to distinguish between presentation of a proposal and analysis of a credit. Different banks handle the two aspects in different ways and it is easiest to make the distinction between presentation and analysis where they are written by different people. For instance, some banks have a separate financial or credit analysis department which acts as a support to the banking division and provides written analyses of credits. These analyses are not credit proposals and the analysts have no lending authority and take no decisions. They are simply one input, nearly always important and often primary, which the banker uses in coming to his conclusion and presenting it. In other banks the analysis and proposal may be done by the same person. In others, there is a mixture. But when the banker both analyses and presents the credit it is arguable that he should write two separate memos; if this is impractical he must at least clearly distinguish between the two aspects in the one memo he writes.

The purposes of an analysis and a presentation are different. An analysis is a dispassionate review of all the facts and of the implications which can be drawn from them designed to help to reach conclusions; by definition it should start with no preconceived positions and is not intended to support any particular answer. A presentation can only start when the analysis is complete and has been used to enable the writer to say "I have decided that". The presentation must be balanced and include all important weaknesses and risks, but nevertheless the purpose of a presentation is to advocate a position; that of an analysis precludes having a position. Mixing the two in the same memorandum may make the writer appear to be twisting the analysis to support his conclusion; this undermines the credibility of both the analysis and the conclusion. The writer must therefore both be clear in his own mind, and make clear, which part is which.

Relevance, brevity, clarity. A memorandum which confines itself to relevant points is more likely to be brief and clear than one which includes a mass of detail without considering its relevance to the major points which are being made in the memorandum, or without linking the various details together in a way which shows their relevance. There can be quite a delicate balancing act between the need to state conclusions briefly and the need to be specific and to support opinions with factual evidence. This requires a well-thought-out structure, the purpose of each part of which is clear. Only then can the writer express views and draw conclusions coherently and support them with only that factual information which is necessary. Without such a structure and clear aim the difficulty of deciding which facts are relevant becomes overwhelming. The result is likely to be a mass of detail which obscures the key points rather than supports them; or a series of vague assertions without proper support which therefore fail to carry credibility (Example 1).

The banker must, then, focus on those aspects of the credit which are crucial to the decision, whether they support his view, contradict it or qualify it. Too often people reach a position without a clear idea of how or why they reached it; the requirement to state the key points and support them may help to overcome this failing. Many memoranda fail in the early stages to find a focus and therefore wander around without any real idea of where they are going. They are often long and they may well show signs of great effort, but they do not answer the vital questions about what the bank is trying to do, what the risks are it takes in doing it, why these risks are acceptable and what the reward is the bank receives for taking them.

Many memoranda mishandle references to other material, whether a brokerage report, a previous memorandum by the same writer, a review by the financial analysis department, an annual report, a spread sheet or any other information. Most writers tend to go to one of two extremes in referring to such material. They either say something like "my memorandum of June 1st describes the key aspects of the company's business" but give no indication of what those aspects are; or they quote large extracts from the reference material. The first approach leaves the reader with no information as to what the reference material contains unless he reads it, when he may find that only a small part is relevant to the decision. On the other hand, mere repetition gives no choice as to whether to read it or not; nor does it show whether the writer thought about the situation in the light of the specific proposal.

A better approach is to mention briefly the main conclusions or highlights of the reference material and, if appropriate, any changes since it was written; if not attached, the material should be clearly identified (Example 2). This has the advantage that it reminds the reader of the key points, which may be sufficient if he has read the material or knows enough about the company so that he only needs pointing in the right direction. At the same time, a reader who needs more knows where to find it and can choose whether to read it immediately or only after reading the rest of the memorandum. It may be easier to absorb the main points in one reading and then go back and check the details rather than break off in the middle.

Later sections return to the question of choice more specifically. Since most credit proposals are read by several people with differing knowledge of the borrower and other relevant information, it is best to give the reader a choice as to how much detail he actually needs to read.

<u>Interim conclusions</u>. The purpose of a credit proposal memorandum is to present a decision in a way that makes it easy for an experienced reader to absorb the arguments and reach the right decision quickly.

This requires the writer:

(a) To understand the key factors of the credit.

(b) To develop and follow a logical structure so that the parts of the memorandum relate to each other and to the whole.

(c) To present, in each section, both the conclusions, reasons, relationships and the facts which support, illustrate or qualify them. Unsupported views are as frustrating as facts which illustrate nothing.

The specific approach

The form of credit presentation. There is no standard form used by all banks for making credit proposals, nor should there be. Some banks may have forms, others have a flexible format and others not even that. No format fits every case and many take away the writer's ability to express his own views and choose his own priorities. To encourage bankers to express views and to focus on priorities and at the same time to insist on a precise order and headings is contradictory. This chapter therefore does not lay down a precise format; rather it suggests an outline which can be used by banks which have no conflicting requirements; it also establishes some principles and discusses in more detail ways of making a presentation easier to read and easier to write, whatever the format.

The first thing to decide is whether the memorandum should be broken down into sections with headings or whether it should read more like an essay. There is no hard and fast answer, but headings can be useful if they accurately delineate the subject of each section of the memorandum.

However, a required list of headings may not mean the same thing to everybody, and gives no certainty that the writer will even wish to write about those subjects. Thus it is better to recognise that headings are useful only if they come naturally to the writer. Their use in the rest of this chapter is intended as a general indication of approach, not a rigid format nor a checklist which must be used in a particular order.

Indeed, the order in which the various sections should appear is very much a matter of judgement in each case and of the style of each banker. However, it is desirable for the Decision and the Rationale sections to be presented first since they affect the structure and detailed aspects of the rest of the memorandum.

The decision/proposal/recommendation. It is always best to spell out immediately the nature of the proposal being considered and the key elements which affect the decision. This may not be in the best literary style; some bankers certainly argue that the scene should be set first and the company described and analysed before the nature of the decision and recommendation are revealed. However, a credit proposal memorandum is a decision document, not a literary masterpiece. To assess the analysis of the company and the arguments for and against making the loan, the reader needs to know what type of risk is involved. He needs, for instance, to know whether the loan is a seven-year one to be paid from cash flow, or a seasonal overdraft to be paid from liquidation of assets, before he can assess whether the analysis covers the right material.

It also helps the writer to focus immediately on the nature of the decision and the key aspects of it which he is going to justify in the rest of the memorandum.

There are two ways in which to present the outline of a decision. One is under a series of headings down the left-hand side with details opposite them. For instance:

BORROWER:	XYZ Company plc
GUARANTOR:	XYZ Company Inc
AMOUNT:	$50 million
MATURITY:	1991

and so on through the interest rate, commitment fee, amortisation pattern and perhaps the principal covenants. At first glance this appears clear but in practice it can be surprisingly difficult to absorb and wastes paper, typing time and reading time. A complex deal can take three-quarters of a page to describe in this way, and if the memorandum covers several different facilities for the same borrower this method can take two pages or more. By the time the reader has reached the end of the second page, and perhaps the fourth facility, he has quite forgotten what was the beginning and moreover has no idea what the facilities total.

The alternative approach is to describe the decision under review in a few sentences.

"Proposal. To lend XYZ Company Ltd. $50 million unsecured

for seven years with amortisation beginning at the end of the third year, under the guarantee of its parent XYZ Company Inc. Revolving for the first two years, fixed thereafter, spread ½% over three- or six-month LIBOR for the first two years, rising to ⅝%, commitment fee ⅜% on the unused."

This is both shorter and clearer than the first method, although it can be a little harder to use where the proposal covers a number of different facilities. But the points which are keys to the decision can be summarised in a sentence or two; full detail can be shown in an appendix if necessary. Often, moreover, the writer attaches a credit authorisation form for signature which then provides input to the bank's computer. This may well be a satisfactory way of providing the details.

The description might then read something like "To approve a 5 year £5 million unsecured term loan, at a margin of ½% over the cost of money, with amortization beginning at the end of the third year and covenants to be negotiated.

"And to renew short-term working capital facilities, totalling the equivalent of $15 million, to subsidiaries in France, Germany and Italy under the guarantee of the parent and at the local prime rates.

"Also to review and confirm the company's continuing compliance with the conditions of our 7 year $10 million loan agreement already in place."

In every case, whether or not all of the facilities available to the company are being reviewed, the bank's total exposure is always relevant to the decision. Particularly when dealing with facilities in several different currencies the reader may not be able to calculate it easily, from a listing of £x million, FFy million, DMz million and so on; it should therefore be stated in one short sentence. Some cases may also require a breakdown between short-term and medium-term, or between guaranteed and unguaranteed facilities or some other basis.

<u>Rationale/reason for the recommendation/summary and conclusion</u>. Once the nature of the decision has been clearly identified, the next point is to set out briefly the main factors or issues about the credit which are key to the decision. These should emphatically include all adverse

factors or risks which have been identified and despite which the decision is made, or against which it is believed there is reasonable protection.

The purpose of such a section (under whatever name) is three-fold. First to enable the reader to assess quickly and easily whether the subsequent discussion supports the key points adequately or whether he wishes to disagree or requires more detailed explanation, or feels that some points have been missed. Secondly to give the reader a choice. If he knows the credit sufficiently or if it is clear cut, he may be satisfied that the writer has understood the key points correctly and may be able to make the decision without reading the rest of the memorandum. Indeed, in straightforward decisions the Rationale section, perhaps slightly expanded, may be enough on its own. Thirdly, to compel the writer to establish at the beginning the key points which he wishes to address, making it more likely (although nothing can make it certain) that he will in fact address them; this in turn makes it surer that the various sections will relate sensibly to each other so that the memorandum shows the connection between the points as well as their individual importance.

A frequent weakness in presentations is failure to think through clearly the points to be addressed and how they relate to each other. Memoranda often read as a disjointed set of facts, with no obvious connection to each other or to the decision requested. A good Rationale can be helpful in overcoming this weakness.

A Rationale gives the outline only of the case, and will thus normally have more opinion and conclusion and less factual support than the memorandum as a whole. Nevertheless some factual support is required, not so much to provide proof of the argument, but to indicate the general nature of the factual base. Without that support a Rationale is often vague. With too much detail it ceases to be an outline. Brevity should not be confused with vagueness.

For instance, a rationale which begins "I recommend the proposal because of the company's strong balance sheet" and then moves on to the next point does not say what aspect of the balance sheet is strong nor give any indication as to what "strong" means and why, in this situation.

A slightly more specific version which reads ". . . because of the good liquidity and satisfactory leverage" still leaves very little idea as to how the writer assesses liquidity or leverage. However, ". . . because of the good liquidity (current ratio 1.8) and satisfactory leverage (TBF/NW 0.7)" specifies what is good liquidity and satisfactory leverage. Provided the reader can assume other indicators point in the same direction, he has an outline of the basis for the argument.

Of course, some aspects cannot be briefly supported as easily as with a leverage or liquidity ratio. They may be subjective, as is a view of management, but even here the writer should be able to give some basis for the judgement. Thus "our favourable view of management" on its own is better than ignoring the subject altogether, but only just. "Our confidence in financial management, with which we have worked closely for several years, and our favourable general impressions of other senior management" gives some idea that we know financial management well but our view of the rest of the management is less firmly based. Similarly, a phrase such as "satisfactory distribution" has some value but is less specific than "network of distribution outlets in key cities".

The physical layout of the Rationale is less important but it can be helpful to present a series of individual points rather than rounded paragraphs, although either can be effective. For instance:

I recommend approval of the proposal in view of:

- sound leverage (total borrowed funds to net worth 0.5) and good liquidity (current ratio 1.8).
- Consistent profitability and high cash flow (ROA average 12% for the last five years, cash flow average 18% of total liabilities).
- Market leadership (40% of home market, 15% worldwide) and strong brand names.
- High technical knowledge and capital intensity which deter new entrants.
- Favourable experience with the financial management and the high reputation of the technical management.

which more than outweigh

- The reliance on oil as a primary raw material for 40%

of products.
- The weakness of the construction industry which accounts for 30% of sales.
- Our doubts about the succession to the present rather elderly management.

In addition:

- Our relationship with this company has earned us an average of £200,000 p.a. in the last several years.
- The purpose of this loan is for an acquisition in the United States which will give us an opportunity for further business there.
- The margin of ¾% fully reflects the limited credit risk.

This presents a fairly clear outline of what the writer thinks are the key strengths and weaknesses. He has not attempted to substantiate his points fully at this stage, but has shown the nature of the support he expects to demonstrate later. The Rationale, or some parts of it, might need to be somewhat longer if there were conflicting pointers. For instance:

- Leverage is satisfactory, with low borrowings (TBF/NW 0.4) offsetting the rather high TL/NW of 1.5, which mainly reflects deferred tax and pension provisions.
- Overall improvement in liquidity, with a strong current ratio (2.0) and moderate receivable turnover (90 days) balancing a rather slow inventory turnover (190 days).

Except in those cases (which almost by definition have to be fairly straightforward) where the Rationale is the main presentation, it should always be fairly short, a maximum of two pages for a complex credit and normally no more than a page.

Business and background. While the Decision and Rationale should nearly always be the first two sections (or paragraphs if the essay approach is used) of a memorandum, there is no particular order which is appropriate in all cases for the remainder. Very often a brief discussion about the nature of the business, background information on plant location, the types of product, the basis of competition in the industry and so on fit in next. A Business and Background section can be an alternative to several longer sections on, for instance, operations, management, technology and so on but should not be an excuse for avoiding a more detailed presentation of these aspects when appropriate. Where a detailed presentation of one or more such subjects is required it is normally better in a separate section.

With this proviso the prime purpose of a Background section is to inform the reader of features of the company which affect risk, financial structure, profitability or other features in a way which explains rather than simply lists facts.

For instance, to have five factories in the United Kingdom may be a plus, a minus or neutral, depending on the nature of the business and of the factories. At one extreme the company may be running small, old and inefficient plants, and need to invest heavily in one or two modern replacements. At the other, five well-located plants close to the market, where no competitor has more than two or three, may be a major advantage. Therefore to say "the company has factories in Glasgow, Newcastle, Manchester, Birmingham and Southampton" is not very helpful. This is just one example of the importance of expressing a view or a conclusion to be supported by facts, rather than facts on their own.

For example, the section might include any of the following comments: "The company's five modern well-located factories enable it to deliver cheaply almost everywhere in the country, unlike its leading competitors." Or alternatively "The company's small, old and inefficient plants make it very difficult to match the competition on cost and make heavy investment in new facilities an urgent priority." Or "Senior management includes highly qualified people in each of the main disciplines. The Finance Director has been well known to us for years and we have a high regard for him, as we do for the Managing Director whom we also know fairly well. We have had frequent contacts with middle management and believe there is considerable depth." Or alternatively "Mr X, the founder of the business, has always run it as a one-man band and it is now becoming too large for him to handle; however, he refuses to bring in qualified support in the finance, marketing and technical areas, which we feel is badly needed." Or "The competition consists mainly of small companies with a less extensive product range and less ability to fund R & D." Or alternatively "The competition includes a number of companies which have a wider product range and are more able to fund heavy R & D expenses than our customer." Or "The company's main products are included in much larger products; their cost is a small proportion of the total costs of these products but they are crucial to their reliability. Thus quality, reliability, prompt delivery are all more important in generating sales than price." Or alternatively "The product is highly price sensitive; to meet price competition requires a large volume of sales but also extremely tight cost controls on manufacturing." Each of these comments provides useful background which will affect the reader's understanding of the risks or advantages the company faces. It will thus make it a little clearer what sort of financial and other strength is required and enable him to judge better from the rest of the memorandum whether it is available.

The type of comment to avoid is "The company's brand names are . . ." and then a list of eight or ten names which says nothing about their significance. It may, however, be useful to mention one or two brand names in support of a statement such as "the company's strong brand names (Persil and Hoover) give it market leadership; market shares range from 30% to 50%".

The above examples have all been brief. Clearly in some cases, particularly if the credit proposal memorandum is not supported by any form of analytical or descriptive memorandum, more detail will be needed. Nevertheless, too detailed a section can begin to lose form, particularly if it covers several different features. Where detailed treatment of one aspect is needed, it may fit better in a separate section. For instance, if the factors affecting the location of operations are different for each product line and justify detailed discussion, this could be put into a section headed perhaps "Operating Locations". Similarly, recent management changes may justify discussion under a separate heading. Other possible although less frequent headings could include "Competition", "Sources of Supply", "Customer Industries", "Labour Relations".

The Business and Background section therefore deals with

those categories which do not warrant a separate section in the particular case, but where a summary is nevertheless helpful to understanding the rest of the material.

Financial condition. The first decision is whether to present Financial Condition as a simple heading or break it into categories such as "Balance Sheet"; "Operations" or "Profitability"; and "Cash Flow".

A split into two or occasionally three sections has some attractions. It may make it easier to focus on each aspect and to avoid confusion between the different parts of financial condition. Where detailed discussion is required a split can prevent the section becoming too unwieldy.

Nevertheless the danger of thinking and writing about the sections as if they were unconnected mostly outweighs the advantages of splitting. Too many bankers find it difficult to make the connections and recognise the close interrelationships between the balance sheet strength, the profit and loss statement and cash flow to run any risk of making it even harder. Using one heading cannot guarantee that this mistake will be avoided but it removes one excuse for making it.

In presenting financial condition (and this comment really applies to the whole of the presentation but is most important and is most often breached in the section on financial condition) each paragraph should state the conclusions, interpretations or questions which are drawn from the facts, before the facts themselves. Many writers either give unsupported opinions without giving any basis, even in subjective terms; or they give only facts with no indication of their significance. Sometimes it is not even clear whether they regard the points as favourable or unfavourable.

Typical examples are: "the company's balance sheet shows a strong financial condition with good leverage and liquidity. Profitability is also good as are cash flow and interest coverage." Or "total liabilities to net worth increased from 1.7 in 1980 to 2.2 in 1981. Current ratio also increased from 1.4 to 1.5 and cash flow decreased from 15% of total liabilities to 10%."

The first simply repeats at slightly greater length the similarly imprecise statements already criticised under Rationale. It overlooks the need for the reader to judge whether the writer's assessment is correct. The second example goes to the opposite extreme giving no indication as to whether the writer considers the facts to be favourable, unfavourable or a mixture of both. Nor does it make any attempt to pull the various aspects together into a balanced appraisal.

Neither of these examples, in addition, pay attention to the trend. Banks analyse the past finances of a company to develop a basis for judging the likely future performance; one off snap shots, whether vague or specific, fail to do this. Three or preferably five years' figures are required not just as a ritual, but to discover whether there are any trends, the reasons for them if so, and to assess how far those reasons will continue to apply in the future. Where analysis shows a changing trend or conflicting patterns, the reasons for the change or conflict help to decide their likely impact on the future. They cannot be guessed from the vague generalities in the first example nor does the concentration on what has happened in the most recent year in the second suggest much vision of the future.

Substance and presentation become inextricably mixed at this stage. A banker who is allowed to write either of the above examples does not demonstrate that he has thought the problem through, assessed the trends and come to his own conclusion, nor does he allow the reader to make an independent assessment. This does not prove that he has not used the trends to think about the future in coming to his conclusion, but it certainly raises a question.

A weakness which sometimes contributes to the last two is that of jumbling too many figures in with a written text. A memorandum which is trying to describe a fluctuating pattern of receivable and inventory turnover will be difficult to understand if it reads something like: "In 1977 receivable turnover was 90 days but improved sharply to 75 days in 1978 and 72 days in 1979. However after that it deteriorated to 80 days in 1980 and 95 days in 1981 before recovering slightly to 90 days in 1982. Inventory turnover also fluctuated sharply from 120 days in 1977 to 110 days in 1978 and 100 days in 1979 before deteriorating in 1980 and 1981 to 110 and 130 days respectively and recovering somewhat in 1982 to 115 days." (The example would be just as confusing if instead of discussing the development of two items over five years, it discussed five or six over two years.)

Apart from being very difficult to read it again says nothing about the writer's views as to the significance of the movements. It does not preclude a subsequent comment, but in practice writers are often so involved in getting it all down that they forget to consider implications and consequences. Alternatively, recognising the difficulty of reading all this (or else being just lazy) they simply say what has happened in the most recent year.

This problem can often be solved by the intelligent use of tables (see next section).

As well as presenting trends in a coherent fashion, the memorandum must present and balance the relationship between various aspects of the balance sheet, profit and loss and nature of the company's business. A Business and Background section, or a section describing some particular aspect of the business, may be incorporated by reference. Otherwise, the need to discuss it in the Financial Condition section may make that section more complicated and harder to read than it otherwise needs to be. For instance, if it is supported by the sort of table discussed in the next section, the following is clear as far as it goes: "Liquidity is sound overall. The stable though slow receivable turnover reflects the impact of government and government guaranteed sales; the steady improvement in current ratio and inventory turnover, due to better controls and the increasingly strong cash flow make it acceptable." However, if this is the first mention of government sales, the reader may need a further explanation, which would lengthen the section and perhaps divert attention away from the discussion of the financial condition. If the nature of sales to the government has been described in the Business and Background section, however, the reference is clear.

Other examples of ways in which various aspects can be linked could be (again the text assumes a table which will give factual support and illustration): "The apparently high leverage is partly due to the level of liability reserves and pension funds. More importantly, however, it results from financing the major capital expansion programme, the first benefits of which show in the 1981 improvement in earnings and cash flow coverage. Further improvement is forecast in the next two years, as well as much lower capital expenditure. This, combined with continued tight control of NWI, will allow a substantial reduction in debt by 1985 reducing the leverage to an acceptable level, particularly in view of the flexibility of the assets." (Again, this assumes a knowledge of the nature of the capital expenditure and the fixed assets which is justified if they are covered elsewhere in the memorandum. If it is not, the need for an explanation may make the paragraph clumsy.)

Use of tables. A good solution in many cases to several problems is the intelligent use of tables, which have several major advantages. First, they set out factual information clearly and briefly and allow the text to concentrate on conclusions and interpretation; secondly, they must cover a number of years (five is the preferred number) so that they almost automatically make the writer look at the trend; thirdly, the clarity of a well-designed table makes it harder for the banker to stick to preconceptions which the facts do not support.

Of course like anything else tables can be misused. One misuse is simply to insert as a table an extract from fuller information provided in an appendix or spreadsheet; if this is then taken to represent the whole financial analysis, tables can actually be counter-productive. Another way is to select only those items for inclusion in the table which support the point the banker is trying to make and to exclude or ignore items which do not. (This point is of significance in more than just tables; it can represent a deliberate attempt to deceive but more often represents a failure by the banker to think through his preconceptions and to check them against the facts or recognise that some of the facts conflict with them.) Thus, if the banker uses a single line in the table to describe a concept such as liquidity or leverage, the reader must be sure that it is consistent with all other aspects of the concept.

Another misuse which is quite common in tables is simply to repeat in words the information contained in a table without adding any comment to it or even in many cases any new information.

Some of the above points are best illustrated with examples.

Some examples of tables. "Financial condition has strengthened steadily over the last several years to a satisfactory level, with strong cash flow allowing steady improvement in leverage and liquidity; this has been supported by sound and gradually improving control of net working investment and the reinvestment of a substantial proportion of strong earnings.

	1977	1978	1979	1980	1981
TL/NW	1.5	1.2	1.1	0.8	0.7
Current ratio	1.25	1.40	1.50	1.55	1.65
OCF/TL	18	18	19	21	22
Rec T/O (days)	80	77	76	74	71
ROA	20	21	21	23	24
Div % NAT	35	34	36	37	33"

On its own, the opening paragraph is clear but not very specific. The table provides the detail without reducing the clarity. Note that it includes only one ratio each on leverage, liquidity and net working investment; since there are other ratios which measure facets of each of these concepts this implies that they give a similar picture. If there is any significant difference of trend between, say, TBF/NW and TL/NW, or between receivable and inventory turnover, then modify both the comment and the table, perhaps as follows:

"Overall financial condition is now sound as the result of continuing reinvestment of growing earnings and cash flow. A modest deterioration in TBF/NW and NWI results from borrowing to take advantage of attractive discounts on trade payables. Tighter control of receivables has more than offset the slight slowdown in inventory (due to the opening of several new distribution depots to allow prompt delivery).

	1977	1978	1979	1980	1981
TL/NW	1.5	1.4	1.2	1.1	0.9
TBF/NW	0.4	0.4	0.5	0.5	0.6
Current ratio	1.25	1.40	1.50	1.55	1.65
Rec T/O (days)	90	85	80	75	73
Inv T/O (days)	90	91	92	94	95
Payable T/O (days)	45	43	30	25	20
ROA	10	11	11	13	14
Div % NAT	35	34	36	37	33"

On a superficial view, a banker might easily be tempted to make the first comment about the second company. If he prepares the table with due care, however, this will draw the contrasting movements to his attention; in checking the reasons he will learn more about the credit of his company. This is truer, the greater the contrast; in this example, the reasons for the discrepancies are favourable or neutral. Where the contrast points to a deteriorating situation, the resulting investigation can be vital to the decision. For instance:

	1977	1978	1979	1980	1981
TL/NW	4.1	4.0	4.2	4.1	4.0

on its own suggests a stable, if high, leverage. But:

	1977	1978	1979	1980	1981
TL/NW	4.1	4.0	4.2	4.1	4.0
TBF/NW	0.8	1.0	1.5	2.0	2.9

suggests that the stability is illusory. There are a number of possible explanations, some more adverse than others, but it is clear that the bank needs to know which is correct.

A typical weak comment such as "1981 leverage as measured by TL/NW was 0.8 in 1980; current ratio was 1.65 against 1.55 and ROA was 14 against 13" is harder to make, because more obviously inadequate, if it is followed by a table covering five years.

Finally, using the facts in the first example, it would be possible to write them all, giving the details in the text rather than a table. However, it would be hard even then to avoid a jumble of figures and comments which sacrificed a great deal of clarity. With the only slightly more complicated facts of the second example, it would be a nightmare, and with really complicated facts it becomes impossible; something has to give, which is why bankers sometimes write:

"Leverage measured by total liabilities to net worth improved from 1.5 in 1977 to 1.1 in 1979 but then deteriorated to 1.7 in 1981. Liquidity as measured by the current ratio deteriorated sharply from 1.7 in 1977 to 1.1 in 1980 and recovered slightly to 1.3 in 1981, but receivable turnover, after improving from 90 days in 1977 to 85 in 1979, worsened sharply in 1980 and 120 in 1981."

Apart from being difficult to read, this gives no indication of the writer's views or interpretations of the facts. A following paragraph may of course do so, although many memoranda do not. Even if they do, the result is both longer and more obscure than if the ratios are set out in a table.

The intelligent use of tables thus makes a memorandum shorter and clearer. It also helps the writer to check that all the facts, not just some of them, point in the direction the memorandum suggests. Sometimes it shows up contradictions or divergences not previously noticed; investigation of the reasons behind these can improve understanding of the credit.

To qualify as intelligent the tables must:

(a) support and illustrate conclusions and interpretations in the text;
(b) be complete; this does not mean including every possible item; rather, nothing should be left out which would contradict, or modify, the conclusion drawn from what is included;
(c) be consistent with what is said in the text; and
(d) be selected only after consideration of all the possible ratios which might be relevant to the point, not just the first one looked at.

Other types of headings. As indicated earlier there are a number of other headings that can be used but which will not be appropriate in every case. In many cases such a heading will cover a factor which is either more important or more complicated in this case than in most. For instance, it is not always necessary to have a heading describing the operations of the company; often that can be done briefly under Business and Background, but sometimes their nature is so complicated and carries such important implications that it justifies separate treatment. This is particularly likely with a multi-divisional company, where it may be necessary to describe each division's operations and their impact on the overall structure, profits and cash flow, before trying to assess the balance of the consolidated figures.

Often there is not much to be said about management and a few sentences under the Business and Background heading suffices; sometimes a complicated or changing management justifies a separate heading. Similarly with R & D, technology, competition, marketing and distribution, labour relations and other subjects. It is a matter of judgement in each case whether to use such headings and in what order. However, when one or more of them are used there must be a specific reason; secondly, the text must be relevant to the nature of the heading; and thirdly, both the use of the heading and the particular subject matter must fit logically in the overall structure of the memorandum and relate back to the Rationale. They can either expand on some of the points made in it or at least be clearly relevant to its theme and conclusion.

Repeat or partial presentations. The chapter has so far mainly discussed the requirements of a full presentation. There are many cases, however, where a shorter presentation may be better suited to everybody's needs. While there may be others, the three most common are:

(i) Where a full review was done recently, and the need for a presentation arises from a request for additional credit.
(ii) Where a full review was done a year or more ago, and the only change is that the bank has more recent figures; these, however, are very much as expected when the earlier review was written.
(iii) The credit is strong or well known and/or the amount so small that the decision does not warrant a full review.

In all three cases, the banker must show that he has thought about the credit, but does not need the full-length review of all the features. The approach will be different in each case, but the principles - showing thought in relation to the current proposal without excessive repetition or unnecessary detail - remain the same. For instance:

Date 15th July

(i) Proposal: To increase our current unsecured overdraft facility from £10 million to £20 million, and thus total exposure from $50 million to $67 million all short-term. Terms and conditions remain unchanged.

Rationale: My memorandum of 1st June recommended establishing the £10 m overdraft and renewing the existing facilities. The strong credit was shown to rest on solid sales growth (average 3% real p.a.); sound profitability (NAT margin 5%, ROE 12.5%); liquid and well capitalised balance sheet (CR 1.8, TFB/NW 0.4); strong interest and cash flow coverage (interest cover 4.8 times, OCF/TBF 57%). Despite the risks of more intensive competition and recession in customer industries accounting for 20% of sales, we expect similar performance in the next few years.
The purpose of the overdraft was to handle half the company's sterling operations. In the last six weeks we have seen profitable volume, with occasional credit balances, and the company now wishes to close its account with another bank and put the whole volume through us.
Nothing has happened to alter our conclusion in the June 1st memorandum that this is a strong credit; we believe it remains valid for the larger amount.

(ii) Proposal: To renew the following short-term facilities . . . totalling $40 million direct to the company or to subsidiaries under its full guarantee.

Rationale: Last year's full review of this specialist chemical company showed that it had strong product niches, good R & D, modern and well-maintained fixed assets. Its broad spread of customer industries, the strong market position of most of its major products, and their low-volume, high-technology content gives its strong defensive qualities against both recession and competition. Financial management is strong and well known to us; we also know the managing director well and believe the company has both breadth and depth of management. None of these features has

changed significantly since then.
The review also showed a liquid balance sheet, with a sound capital structure and consistently good profitability; interest and cash flow cover were satisfactory and improving. As the following table shows, the year ended December 31st 198- showed a continuation of the favourable trend, with only minor modifications and no surprises. We understand that semi-annual figures, due out next month, will show a further modest improvement.
On the basis of the company's continued progress from a strong base, we recommend renewal of the facilities for a further year.

(Note: In addition to the table, the memorandum should say something about the relationship, its profitability to the bank, and how these facilities help, but these are not necessary for the main point of the example.)

(iii) Proposal: To lend $5 million to XYZ Ltd. under the full guarantee of its parent Imperial Deutsche General Corp (IDG).

Rationale: This loan is requested by IDG to enable its subsidiary to meet local legal requirements. IDG is the largest automotive/petrochemical company in the world, with a net worth of $20 billion, average profits of $5 billion p.a. and no debt. Approval is recommended.

(Note: The first two examples involve large amounts of money to sound credits which the bank knows well. In addition to showing that the banker has thought about each proposal, they follow the principle of choice. They say enough about the company and its credit to remind a reader who already has some familiarity with the name about its strengths; they also point him to where to look for more detail if he needs it. Probably the writer should attach the earlier memoranda in both cases. However, both credits are strong, with little or no change since the last memorandum. Weaker credits, or even still strong credits where there had been adverse developments, would require a fuller approach.)

Outlook. A good closing heading is often Outlook, although other sections may deal with the future enough to make a separate heading unnecessary. Nevertheless it is often a good idea to use it as a way to pull the reader's and writer's thoughts together about where the company is going, and the implications. If a specific forecast has been prepared, or better still a Base Case and Worst Case forecast, this may be the place to discuss them. Even without forecasts, the review should say something about the likely demand for the company's products in the next year or two; the impact of this on profits; if the balance sheet is weak, the prospects for strengthening it or the risk of a further weakening; any known new product or other developments which might improve market position; and, perhaps most importantly, any threat from competition.

Summary and conclusion

Overall then this book is about the need for thoughtful analysis of the financial figures and business features of companies before banks lend to them and as long as the loan continues. The argument in favour of a written presentation and of some effort in getting its form satisfactory are: first, that a good written presentation helps to reach a faster and better decision; secondly, that a written presentation actually helps the writer to put his thoughts in order and make sure that he has understood the credit and check that he has not missed any major points; thirdly, it demonstrates that the banker will be capable of monitoring the credit and any specific weaknesses effectively; fourthly, it acts as an audit trail; and fifthly, it provides information to other people who may be either temporarily or permanently taking over responsibility for the relationship.

Even the best presentations can vary in length from as little as half a page to as much as perhaps eight to ten pages so the amount of detailed thinking in each case varies. To suggest that every item discussed in this book should be laboriously thought through in every credit would be absurd. Rather, the book tries to indicate, with a fair amount of detail, the approach which a sensible banker will take to analyse credit and to the decision as to whether or not to lend, and on what terms. Those who already have a thorough understanding of corporate credit go through this process rapidly and often largely unconsciously. But a banker who is either new to the business, or who has been trained in a more static approach, may find a thorough reading of this book, and perhaps references to it during his work, improve the quality of the analysis and of the broader understanding of credit.

That at least is the book's aim.

Example 1

(a) "The credit is acceptable because of the sound financial condition." (On its own, vague, with no indication of how the conclusion was reached; moreover, whether financial condition is sound in each case is a matter of opinion, not fact.)

(b) "Total liabilities to net worth increased from 0.5 to 0.6. Cash flow to total liabilities declined from 15% to 12%." (Is this good or bad?)

(c) "Despite a modest deterioration, financial condition remained sound; TL/NW of 0.6 in 1981 (0.5 1980) is acceptable in view of the still satisfactory OCF/TL ratio of 12% (15%)." (Not very profound, but opinion is clear, "modest deterioration . . . remained sound", and so are the facts (or some of them) on which it is based.)

Example 2

(a) "A recent credit department review dicusses the financial condition." (How recent, where do I get hold of it, what does it - and you - think about financial condition?)

(b) "My memorandum of May 5th (attached) concluded that XYZ was a strong credit with a sound balance sheet (TBF/NW 0.5, CA/CL 2.0), sound earnings (NAT of $20 m, margin of 10%), good returns (ROE 15%) and coverage ratios (OCF/TL 18%, interest cover 4.5)." (Tells why the conclusion was "strong credit" with some contributory conclusions and brief facts. Enough for many decisions if the reader knows the name; if not "my memorandum of May 5th" gives more.)

Index